THE NEW MIDDLE AGES

BONNIE WHEELER, *Series Editor*

The New Middle Ages is a series dedicated to transdisciplinary studies of medieval cultures, with particular emphasis on recuperating women's history and on feminist and gender analyses. This peer-reviewed series includes both scholarly monographs and essay collections.

PUBLISHED BY PALGRAVE

Erotic Discourse and Early English Religious Writing
by Lara Farina

Odd Bodies and Visible Ends in Medieval Literature
by Sachi Shimomura

On Farting: Language and Laughter in the Middle Ages
by Valerie Allen

Allegory and Sexual Ethics in the High Middle Ages
by Noah D. Guynn

ALLEGORY AND SEXUAL ETHICS IN THE HIGH MIDDLE AGES

Noah D. Guynn

ALLEGORY AND SEXUAL ETHICS IN THE HIGH MIDDLE AGES
© Noah D. Guynn, 2007.

First published in 2007 by
PALGRAVE MACMILLAN™
175 Fifth Avenue, New York, N.Y. 10010 and
Houndmills, Basingstoke, Hampshire, England RG21 6XS
Companies and representatives throughout the world.

PALGRAVE MACMILLAN is the global academic imprint of the Palgrave Macmillan division of St. Martin's Press, LLC and of Palgrave Macmillan Ltd. Macmillan® is a registered trademark in the United States, United Kingdom and other countries. Palgrave is a registered trademark in the European Union and other countries.

ISBN-13: 978–1–4039–7147–0
ISBN-10: 1–4039–7147–1

Library of Congress Cataloging-in-Publication Data

Guynn, Noah D.
    Allegory and sexual ethics in the High Middle Ages / Noah D. Guynn.
       p. cm.—(New Middle Ages)
    Includes bibliographical references and index.
    ISBN 1–4039–7147–1 (alk. paper)
       1. Enéas (Romance) 2. Alanus, de Insulis, d. 1202. De planctu naturae,
    3. Jean, de Meun, d. 1305? Roman de la Rose. 4. Allegory. 5. Sexual
    ethics in literature. I. Title. II. Series: New Middle Ages
    (Palgrave Macmillan (Firm))

PQ1459.E353G98 2006
841'.1—dc22   2006046048

A catalogue record for this book is available from the British Library.

Design by Newgen Imaging Systems (P) Ltd., Chennai, India.

First edition: March 2007

10 9 8 7 6 5 4 3 2 1

Printed in the United States of America.

For Hugh

CONTENTS

ACKNOWLEDGMENTS

Though *Allegory and Sexual Ethics in the High Middle Ages* represents almost entirely new work, the original blueprint for the project was a PhD dissertation directed by Lynne Huffer and Daniel Poirion at Yale University. Sadly, Professor Poirion did not live to see the dissertation completed, nor was he able to guide me in the arduous process of reconceiving and refining my argument for the book. Nevertheless, the present work bears many traces of his influence, and I would be remiss in not acknowledging the contributions he made to my intellectual development. I also owe a considerable debt of gratitude to Professor Huffer, who supervised the dissertation through its completion, and to David F. Hult, who generously agreed to serve as a reader for the dissertation and has been an unfailing source of erudition, guidance, and friendship ever since.

Other scholars who have made direct or indirect contributions to this project include Emily Albu, Joan Cadden, Carolyn Dinshaw, Margie Ferguson, Simon Gaunt, Ralph Hexter, Maria Manoliu, Peggy McCracken, Nancy Freeman Regalado, Debarati Sanyal, Benjamin Semple, Julia Simon, Gordon Teskey, and Georges Van Den Abbeele. My work was immeasurably improved by their sensitive interventions and timely offers of support.

I am indebted as well to William Burgwinkle, who peer-reviewed the manuscript for the press, and to Bonnie Wheeler, Series Editor of The New Middle Ages. Sharron Wood, a gifted editor and steadfast friend, read the manuscript in its final stages and ensured its stylistic and logical coherence. The UC Davis Humanities Institute, under the stewardship of Professor Van Den Abbeele, provided a fellowship to support my research. The College of Letters and Science and the Provost at UC Davis defrayed some of the costs associated with publication, including copyright permissions.

I am grateful for permission to reprint material from the following books: *Eneas: A Twelfth-Century French Romance*. Trans. John A. Yunck. By permission of the publisher. © 1974 by Columbia University Press, New York, New York.

Guillaume de Lorris and Jean de Meun, *The Romance of the Rose*. Trans. Charles Dahlberg. By permission of the publisher. © 1971 by Princeton University Press, Princeton, New Jersey.

The Medieval Academy of America has generously allowed me to reuse material from my essay, "Authorship and Allegorical/Sexual Violence in Jean de Meun's *Roman de la rose*," which appeared in *Speculum* 79/3 (2004): 628–59.

The cover image is from Guillaume de Déguileville, *Pèlerinage de vie humaine* (Cod. Pal. Lat. 1969) and is used with permission from the Universitätsbibliothek Heidelberg.

INTRODUCTION

The enemy is right inside you, the cause of your erring is there, inside, I say, shut up in ourselves alone.

Ambrose, *Hexaemeron*, 1.8.31

Over the past twenty-five years or so, medievalists have increasingly turned their attention to the history of sexuality, asking questions about the ways in which the premodern West represented, organized, and legislated sexual acts and desires. The work of Michel Foucault has spurred particularly vigorous debate on how medieval sexualities should be conceived, with many scholars arguing that modern clinical, psychological, and sexological categories are simply inadequate for interpreting the premodern past. If we are to avoid anachronism, we must struggle to grasp the specific discursive, cultural, material, and ideological forces that give shape and meaning to the body and its drives in specific historical moments. As Foucault observes, sexuality is not "a kind of natural given which power tries to hold in check," as it has sometimes been conceived; nor is it "an obscure domain which knowledge tries gradually to uncover." It is instead

> the name that can be given to a historical construct: not a furtive reality that is difficult to grasp, but a great surface network in which the stimulation of bodies, the intensification of pleasures, the incitement to discourse, the formation of special knowledges, the strengthening of controls and resistances, are linked to one another, in accordance with a few major strategies of knowledge and power.[1]

Building on Foucault's historical claims, scholars of premodernity and early modernity such as David Halperin and Louis Montrose have argued that a distinction must be drawn between *sex*, meaning biological and somatic realities that stand outside history and culture, and *sexuality*, meaning ideological appropriations of sex that are subject to both synchronic and diachronic variation.[2] Although sexuality has often been conceptualized in modernity as a static, determinate set of real conditions and essential natures, Montrose and Halperin argue that it is instead a cultural fiction that is above all arbitrary, contingent, and variable. In investigating the sexual cultures of the past, we are able to perceive that sexuality, like all Foucauldian "discursive regimes," is a capillary system of relations in which there are no fixed structures or positive terms, and in which language, desire, knowledge, and power are intricately and inextricably linked.

One of the crucial roles for the historian of sexuality in a post-Foucauldian world is therefore to theorize how the body and desire have been marshaled in the past in order to accomplish ideological goals—how, for instance, modes of representing the body are linked to modes of social organization and political domination, or how the norms of sexual morality are used to naturalize existing political hierarchies and hegemonics. To take a classic example from modernity (one that fascinated Foucault), there is an unmistakable continuity between psychoanalytic symptomatology and the laws of bourgeois alliance, between the diagnosis of psychopathology and the social, economic, and political configuration of Western capitalism. Psychoanalysis is bound up with a whole constellation of ideological manipulations and mystifications that are inseparable from the historical and cultural matrix in which they arose. Indeed, one might argue that psychoanalysis has often acquired validity as a scientific episteme precisely by suppressing awareness that all forms of knowledge, including its own, are subject to diachronic and synchronic variation and are shaped or instituted by ideology.

Turning to the literary traditions of the High Middle Ages, I will argue that a similar kind of continuity can be found in the relationship between allegorical figuration and incorporated, institutional power; between sexual ethics and the formation of social and political elites; between the ontological, deontological, legal, rhetorical, and cultural codes that govern sexual desire and expression and the strategic construction and symbolic or actual elimination of threats to the ruling classes. In this book, I propose to read codifications of sexual morality and immorality in a number of highly normative and broadly influential allegorical texts: the *Roman d'Eneas*, Alan of Lille's *De planctu Naturae*, and Jean de Meun's continuation of the *Roman de la rose*. My overarching goal will be to demonstrate, first, that allegory and ethics, even if they claim to transcend particulars and discern essences, are inevitably inflected by the material, lived reality of social and political struggle; and second, that in the secular and ecclesiastical literatures of the High Middle Ages, rhetorical figuration, sexual desire, and political control are always coefficient terms. Adapting theoretical models from Foucault as well as major exponents of Marxian ideology critique, I argue that medieval allegorists typically deploy their tropes and narratives in such a way as to empower restricted classes of readers and to exclude, circumscribe, or appropriate readings that might threaten the privileges of those classes.

This is not to say that medieval allegories are mere propaganda or that their meaning is utterly consistent and predictable. Quite to the contrary, medieval allegory habitually draws the reader's attention to the discursive construction of reality (including the body and desire), to the play of meanings in discourse, and to the ambivalence of cultural artifacts generally. I agree wholeheartedly with Sheila Delany that allegory reflects and sustains the "economic foundation" of medieval society, and indeed that it is "admirably suited to the needs of any ruling class which feels itself threatened by change."[3] Yet I would contest Delany's concomitant claim that the value of allegory as an ideological tool is its realist conception of analogical order and the rigidity of its "abstract *a priori* scheme."[4] She is mistaken, I believe, in arguing that "the allegorical character can display no free will, no irrational or inexplicable ambivalence," or that "the allegorical persona is perfectly predictable, functioning within a narrative frame which is also perfectly predictable."[5] While it may be the case that allegory permits "the powerful to justify the present social structure as eternal, inevitable and immutable by analogy to cosmic structure,"[6] this is only part of the story.

As we shall see in this book, allegorists in the twelfth and thirteenth centuries also tended to understand *all* structure (including the cosmos itself) as verbal and textual—and therefore liable to interpretive difference and change. There is, in other words, a permanent tension in medieval allegory between an overarching, formalized, and essentialist textual design and a more fluid, variable, or protean conception of textual meaning. This tension is particularly striking where sexual desire is concerned: allegorists conceive of desire both as an object of representation (one that can be reified and contained through figuration and personification) and as a consequence of representation (an unpredictable effect of reading that actually undermines strategies of reification and containment). On one hand, medieval allegory seeks to limit the possibilities of sexual desire and expression and to enforce compliance with a moral, intellectual, and cosmic structure that is itself typically the projection of a dominant ideology. On the other hand, allegory consistently locates deviant, subversive, and apparently irresistible desires within signs themselves. In the process, it internalizes ambivalence and transgression within figurations of law and order and suggests that the forces it seeks to counter are simultaneously alien and familiar, inassimilable and proximate.

The principal question I will ask in this book is how ideology critique can make sense of this fundamental and irreconcilable antinomy without privileging one tendency over the other, as critics in the past have tended to do. How can we grasp the relationship between medieval allegorical poetry and "a few major strategies of knowledge and power" without flattening or reducing the complexity, inconsistency, and ambivalence of the allegorical mode? In seeking answers to these questions, I will begin with the assumption that any approach to medieval allegory must strive to understand the ways in which semiotic ambivalence authorizes the production and enforcement of normative codes but also, conversely, the ways in which those codes are themselves dynamic practices that generate meaning through slippage and play. As Peter Haidu has incisively argued, the "scene of ideology" in medieval literature is "not the hierarchized logocentrism of doctrinal theology or clerical ideologies of stabilization, but discourse as active critique and intervention, whose very existence acknowledges multiple value-systems."[7] Following a similar logic (though finding instability in clerical discourses and ideologies as well), I will claim that medieval allegory typically exploits the instability of discursive meaning in order to generate anxieties about the *actual* instability of regimes of power and of the cultural and ideological fictions that support them. These anxieties in turn are used to sanction greater oversight and control within existing hierarchies. If a deviant, intolerable form of otherness is internalized within figurations of intellectual and moral truth or social and political power, that otherness in turn motivates moral vigilance and a drive to extirpate threats to established forms of sovereignty.

I fundamentally concur, then, with Delany's materialist argument about the relationship between literature and economics, culture and power. To be sure, her argument offers a welcome corrective to apolitical readings of allegory—those that take its claims to pure, essential, or universal meaning seriously. And yet I believe Delany misconstrues the dynamics of both allegory and ideology when she asserts that medieval allegorical texts exert force simply by constructing analogies between archetypal fictions and political hegemonies. While this claim is not entirely without merit, it overlooks another, equally valid reading: that medieval allegory generates meaning and stabilizes ideological order by emphasizing the unmasterable play of differences in signs and the instability of all systems of political domination. As scholars like John Fiske have argued, ideology is itself never truly static or unified but is always internally contested.[8] It would be a mistake, then, to understand allegory simply as a fictional instantiation or projection of a rigid social arrangement. On the contrary, medieval allegorists often use interpretive difference and internal contestation to motivate and galvanize a disciplinary, ideological agenda. Put simply, allegory does not only depict the dominant order as an immutable, essential structure of being; it also plays on the instability and unpredictability of its own meaning in order to authorize more aggressive and more violent forms of social and political control.

Now, for readers well versed in modern historical materialism and moral skepticism, it will perhaps not be terribly surprising to learn that ethics and domination go hand in hand in the premodern world. Friedrich Nietzsche famously asserts that moral judgment and revelation are little more than a collective make-believe concealing the struggle for control within a stratified social and political order: "The judgment 'good' did *not* originate with those to whom 'goodness' was shown! Rather it was 'the good' themselves, that is to say, the noble, powerful, high-stationed and high-minded, who felt and established themselves and their actions as good, that is, of the first rank, in contradistinction to all the low, low-minded, common and plebeian."[9] In other words, the privileges of the powerful are transformed into moral virtues, and eventually into evidence of spiritual elevation: "A concept denoting political superiority always resolves itself into a concept denoting superiority of soul."[10] When it comes to post-structuralism or Marxism, feminism or psychoanalysis, critical theory has consistently emphasized the validity of Nietzsche's critique, arguing that concepts of moral necessity are elaborated within materially and historically determined frameworks and typically serve to naturalize the power of a ruling class. As Geoffrey Galt Harpham observes,

> Virtually all the leading voices of the Theoretical Era. . .organized their critiques of humanism as exposés of ethics, revelations of the transgressive, rebellious, or subversive energies that ethics had effectively masked and suppressed. . . . For all of [these thinkers], the truth of ethics was announced by Nietzsche: "a mere fabrication for purposes of gulling: at best, an artistic fiction; at worst, an outrageous imposture."[11]

Given this rich, longstanding tradition, an analysis of medieval ethics as an ideological fiction designed to strengthen hegemonies and bridle dissent may seem a bit superfluous.

The uniqueness of my argument, however, lies less in the observation that ethics does ideological work than in my approach to the operations of ideology itself and its various appropriations of rhetoric. In the medieval period, the link between goodness and power, between moralizing tropes and political control, is not at all as mechanical as Nietzsche suggests. Indeed, the texts I consider in this book seek simultaneously to strengthen and undermine their own moral authority. On one hand, these texts deploy a variety of essentializing tropes, especially personification, in order to signify the timelessness and universality of a set of moral, cultural, and political values aligned with a ruling ideology. Theorizing that an immaterial, intellectual, or transcendental truth is somehow embedded within signs, they manipulate rhetorical tropes and narratives in order to signify the legitimate rule of a dominant class, be it secular (the feudal nobility, the dynastic monarchy, or emergent nation-states) or ecclesiastical (the clergy, the papacy, or the so-called monarchic Church). On the other hand, these same texts work to destabilize figurative meaning and to disarticulate the major signifiers of institutional authority. Pointing to tears in the fabric of their own fictions, they allude to the failure of a discursive model of power that can only signify or act through verbal repetition and therefore must be susceptible to interpretation, contestation, and change. And yet by subverting coherent or absolute meaning, these texts generate anxiety about the stability of a particular ideological regime and in turn sanction, and stimulate desire for, greater disciplinary rigor within prevailing structures of power. If words are not capable of bridging the gap between meaning and being, if there can be no true identity or continuity between rhetorical figures and transcendental truths, then power is unsettled by the very process of signification. In order to reestablish equilibrium, ideology cannot simply naturalize forms of domination through discursive productions of truth; it must also find ways to exert its power through rhetorical or physical violence—either the fictional depiction of violent acts of subjection, exclusion, or elimination, or alternatively, actual violent acts imbued with symbolic meaning. I am not proposing that rhetoric and ideology are simply coextensive, but rather that the apparent destabilization of discursive meaning and contestation of ideological fictions can serve as a highly insidious ruse of power. In short, my argument is that the subversion of ideology from within ideology can lead to even more subtle and coercive forms of domination.

A vital step in this argument is to recognize (as many modernists still have not) that medieval intellectuals do not naively believe in the transparency of verbal signifiers to sublime essences. Few would have accepted the validity of cratylism, which repudiates the arbitrary nature of the linguistic sign in favor of a natural correspondence between words and things, or ultrarealism, which emphasizes the continuity between meaning and being. On the contrary, sign theorists from Augustine to Dante were profoundly aware of the unbridgeable gap between discourse and reality, and found models for understanding discursive difference in Scripture itself. Thus if Adam's naming of the animals (Gen. 2.10–11) evinces a primordial identification between signifier and referent, the destruction of the Tower of Babel (Gen. 11.1–9) marks a devolution away from proper, unified, and sanctified meaning toward a *confusio linguarum*.[12] Once the people of Babel are scattered and their languages multiplied, the dream of a pure language is lost, and the world can no longer be interpreted without a guide or key. Through Christ's Incarnation as the Word, Babel is redeemed, but language remains symbolic and enigmatic rather than transparent. Augustine (and many thinkers who follow in his footsteps) argues that humans can achieve partial enlightenment, including knowledge of God, through the interpretation of signs, especially the sacred eloquence of Scripture. That enlightenment is, however, necessarily mediated "per speculum in aenigmate" [through a glass darkly]—and will remain so until the end of history, when humanity will glimpse the truth "facie ad faciem" [face to face].[13] Language prepares us for this moment of revelation and fulfillment; but before the arrival of the Parousia, language can only show us opaque symbols that emblematize but at the same time conceal ineffable truths.

This is not to say that medieval writers do not hypostasize certain privileged signifiers or locate timeless truths beneath an outer shell of verbal artifice. Medieval theories of rhetoric and poetics often subsume an unmasterable discursive difference to the more limited differences of essences. Moreover, medieval intellectuals frequently argue for the mystical value of certain sacramental signs and are in this sense typically logocentric. Yet there is almost always some degree of awareness, whether latent or fully articulated, that discursive, tropological meaning is internally and irremediably split, that signifiers are always "other" with respect to an essential, unvarying, and ineffable signified. Indeed, the notion of "other speaking" [alieniloquium] is fundamental to classical and medieval definitions of allegory, including those of Cicero, Donatus, Augustine, Isidore of Seville, and Hugh of St. Victor.[14] According to Gordon Teskey, allegory has always implied "an oscillating movement" between a negative, chaotic otherness (the uncontrollable proliferation of alternate meanings) and a positive, transcendent otherness (unchanging essences and truths that lie beyond the world of accidents and that are exempt from fluctuations of meaning). Neither tendency can prevail over the other for long, since allegory always "means something other than what it says and says something other than it means."[15] If there is a permanent conflict between these tendencies, allegory works simultaneously to disguise it and to expose it to view.

My argument in this book is that in the Middle Ages, positive and negative conceptions of "other speaking" are *both* co-opted by ruling ideologies and are *both* used to consolidate power within a dominant group or class.[16] The ideological usefulness of transcendental models of meaning is fairly obvious. Ecclesiastical authors profess that Scripture, if properly interpreted, will eventually disclose sacred truths. The medieval Church sought to preserve its monopoly on the path to salvation by thwarting attempts to translate sacred texts into the vernacular or to allow laypeople the right to interpret or disseminate holy truths. Theologians insisted that the language of Scripture was mystically perfect, but that one could only participate in its sublime truths through official, orthodox modes of exegesis or through some form of clerical mediation. Examples of this ideological fiction abound, especially in the period following the Gregorian reform movement. Christian sects such as the Cathars and Waldensians, which encouraged followers to read the sacred texts in their own languages and to ignore Church teachings they found irrelevant, were brutally subdued as the Church sought to standardize the practice of the faith and to centralize its own power. The intellectual clergy vigorously defended the Church's exclusive right to determine the nature of scriptural meaning and Catholic orthodoxy and to root out heretical beliefs. Allegory and allegoresis were crucial tools for accomplishing these goals.

Vernacular authors, themselves often clerics, also used transcendental strategies of representation to normalize the rights and privileges of a particular class of readers. As Erich Auerbach famously argues, medieval romance is a utopian genre in the sense that it "gives those who submit to its dictates the feeling that they belong to a community of the elect, a circle of solidarity. . .set apart from the common herd."[17] In responding to their interpellation by romance texts, aristocratic audiences are rewarded with the illusion that the world of the court transcends "all earthly contingencies"[18] and achieves, with textual closure, a state of pure social cohesion. Many critics since Auerbach have argued that indeed closure in romance often involves the bracketing of subversive elements within the romance narrative and the production of a seemingly unbreakable moral and political consensus.[19] In the process, romance teaches vital lessons about social conformity and class solidarity in an age that witnessed the rise of incorporated, monarchic nation-states. Delany is at least partially correct when she argues that allegory (and analogical thought generally) was a particularly "important ideological weapon in the arsenal of the feudal class," in that it could be used to deny expression to groups competing with that ruling class.[20]

And yet it is also the case that many secular and ecclesiastical authors foreground the contingencies intrinsic to medieval reading practices and often work assiduously to undermine normative signifiers and totemic figures of power. Thus if Scripture encompasses multiple meanings, it is also open to interpretation—perilously so if it is used to justify anomalous or heretical views. I would venture to speculate that when ecclesiastical authors draw attention to this predicament, more often than not, it is to demonstrate the need for defending Catholic dogma against schismatics. Indeed, schismatics are often thought to be threatening precisely because they read the same texts and use the same techniques of persuasion as Catholics do, and are therefore difficult to distinguish from "true believers." The power of orthodoxy depends not simply on seamless continuity between religious language and ultimate truths, but also on the perilous contingency of Scripture and the terrifying proximity of heterodoxy and orthodoxy, both of which amount to strategies of interpretation.

A similar argument can be made about vernacular genres like romance, in which social cohesion and textual closure are nearly always unsettled by some form of epistemological, moral, or political uncertainty. Romance poses challenges to the unity of the courtly world so that it may eventually exclude dissent and forge solidarity through censorship and moralization. Yet it also suggests that the multiple voices and subject-positions intrinsic to courtly narratives can never coalesce into pure unanimity but will remain permanently in conflict. The dominant ideological fiction thus appears no longer to dominate, authority is unsettled by textual interpretation, and romance uses dialectic to destabilize a rhetorical and ideological system that otherwise appears immovable. As a result, the ideology of the text remains elusive or hidden—and is therefore all the more difficult to contest. More to the point, if the dominant ideology fails to silence or contain dissent, then that failure suggests an urgent, recurring need to rearticulate and ratify the law. As Haidu maintains, the aristocratic courts "were not manufacturers of monosemantic ideologies. They—and the texts written for them—staged encounters between differentiated and conflicting codes and interests. The results were often hybrid or contradictory, and ineluctably ideological."[21] If ideology, as a discursive, rhetorical, and fictional practice, is inherently tenuous, then it must require constant reinforcement and repetition.

Again, these opposed strategies are not mutually exclusive but often coexist in a single text, author, or allegorical figure. Strategies of closure are never entirely conclusive, especially in a culture of *mouvance*; and the fictions of righteous power, moral harmony, and social cohesion do not actually manage to preclude contingency or suppress dissent. Of course the opposite is also true: if medieval authors acknowledge that difference unsettles structure, they may also seek to shape difference through formal means, conflating it with threats to solidarity (perversion, error, sin) and distancing it from authoritative codes (morality, orthodoxy, law). Thus even texts that are fascinated with the disarticulation of norms, including their own intellectual or moral authority, may seek to deflect difference onto a socially alienated "other" and, to the extent that they can, to exempt certain privileged signifiers, tropes, or narratives from disruption. Often they do so simply by masking the reality that a particular group or class controls the means for interpreting and disseminating the written word. An implicit social hierarchy therefore precedes and predetermines the text's fascination with the slipperiness of its own meaning.

The allegory of nature affords an illuminating example of these contradictory but closely intertwined strategies. Lady Nature, whose very name connotes essence, element, or law, signifies the underlying principle or spirit of the physical creation, a generative principle emanating from God, or a power that lies somewhere between the sublunary order of existence and the celestial order of essences.[22] According to Jon Whitman, Nature is not simply a deification of the elemental universe but rather an outcropping of scriptural typologies: "Even the earliest traditions of systematic biblical interpretation suggested the possibility of turning the exegesis of Scripture into the allegory of nature. The belief that God authored not one book, but two—the Bible and the world—implied that the elucidation of the one complemented the understanding of the other."[23] By the twelfth century, Nature had in many respects become a sacramental symbol: a text through which humanity could reach beyond the material world to acquire knowledge of an immaterial and ineffable otherworld. Though she is necessarily discursive (since the universe itself is created by the sublime utterance of the divine Word), nevertheless she appears to resist the play of differences in signs, whether diachronic or synchronic.

And yet it is undeniable that in lending voice, poetry, and gender to the ineffable, precultural, and universal, the personification of nature also reveals its status as a contingent linguistic and rhetorical construct. As is always the case with allegory, Lady Nature betrays the difference between signifier and signified, language and essence through *alieniloquium*, the act of speaking the truth "otherwise." In point of fact, medieval allegorists do not simply depict Nature as the essence of the natural; they also reveal her to be a rhetorical *fabula* that can only ever approximate or substitute for that essence. As Whitman explains, allegory must continually strive to mediate between "two conflicting demands—the divergence between the apparent and actual meanings, and yet the correspondence between them. . . .The more allegory exploits the divergence between corresponding levels of meaning, the less tenable the correspondence becomes. Alternatively, the more it closes ranks and emphasizes the correspondence, the less oblique, and thus the less allegorical, the divergence becomes."[24] He concludes that allegory is almost always "at odds with itself, tending to undermine itself by the very process that sustains it."[25] This is all the more true of the allegory of nature, which purports to embody the metaphysical and moral order of creation as it was authored by God but is also rather clearly a discursive construct authored by man.

If the allegory of nature is always "at odds with itself," how does it manage to exert force in the world? If it calls into question the very authority or truth it seeks to signify, how can it be used to persuade or discipline? Before we attempt to answer these questions, it is essential to note that the inconsistencies and tensions internal to the fiction of Lady Nature almost always lead to the anointing of a privileged class of readers. The point is not simply that Nature is denatured by rhetorical artifice or that meaning and being are fundamentally disjoined in allegory. It is also that artifice and disjunction are used to accomplish specific ideological goals: first, to exclude the common reader, who lacks the training necessary to distinguish between superficial falsehood and underlying truth; and second, to grant true (or at least *truer*) knowledge only to an elite class of readers whose superior wisdom has supposedly prepared them to glimpse higher realities. As the paradoxical figuration of an ineffable truth, Lady Nature can never disclose her essential meaning to anyone. That knowledge remains unknowable and untransmissible and can only be signified through metaphorical transfer. And yet as a personification, Nature is endowed with agency and voice and can "choose" whom she is willing to admit further into her confidence and whom she will simply exclude. Even though she represents a universal order of being to which all of humanity presumably belongs, Nature discloses higher meaning only to those who have been admitted to her circle, who are charged with receiving her wisdom and administering her law. Though as a fictional invention she lacks true agency or authenticity, still she mirrors the ideological world that has produced her. More to the point, she constructs (or is constructed by) a model of textual meaning in which only those readers whom she addresses—and who understand her language, which is of course really their own—can claim to have access to her truth.

Macrobius's early-fifth-century *Commentary on the Dream of Scipio* is, in this and other respects, a crucial reference. Evoking the Epicurean critique of "Plato's sacred scroll and majestic discourse on Nature," Macrobius meditates on the appropriateness of "fabulous narrative" to the philosophical pursuit of truth.[26] He asserts that Lady Nature, like the Eleusinian goddesses, will never reveal her naked truths to men without the mediation of an allegorical narrative or veil. Because "a frank, open exposition of herself is distasteful to Nature" and offends her womanly propriety, she has instead "withheld an understanding of herself from the uncouth senses of men by enveloping herself in variegated garments" and having "her secrets handled by more prudent individuals through fabulous narratives."[27] Like the other "spirits having dominion in the lower and upper air" (Plato's archetypes), Nature offers a figuration of truths that are otherwise unrepresentable: "A decent and dignified conception of holy truths, with respectable events and characters, is presented beneath a modest veil of allegory."[28] Even if the archetype of nature is presumed to exist beyond the phenomenal world, Nature's disclosures must always remain within the imperfect realm of verbal representation. Thus her garments are modest and variegated rather than revealing and transparent. Moreover, the order of representation suggests a regression of figures rather than an unveiling of truth: Nature is *already* a personification before she decides to withhold the truth hidden beneath her allegorical veil. Though Macrobius understands nature as an essential being that is prior to, or immanent within, the personification of nature, that essence is strikingly absent here. It would seem that the allegory of nature works to vitiate its own claim to disclose "holy truths."

And yet while Macrobius questions the notion that allegory could ever find the power to transcend an imperfect system of signs or to discover unequivocal moral truths, he also clearly understands allegory as a tool for controlling the production of meaning and naturalizing social hierarchies. He writes that Lady Nature veils her "sacred rites" in "mysterious representations so that she may not have to show herself even to initiates. Only *eminent men of superior intelligence* gain a revelation of her truths; the others must satisfy their desire for worship with a ritual drama which prevents her secrets from becoming common."[29] By her very status as an allegory, Nature establishes a process of exclusion such that respected, educated men alone have access to her mysterious truth—or at least perceive that truth from a privileged vantage point. The vulgar, unrefined reader must seek the truth of Nature through the mediation of rituals administered to them by those who are "chosen" by Nature—or rather those who adopt her voice in order that she may in turn legitimate their power. If Lady Nature implicitly undermines her own transcendental claims, self-subversion eventually becomes a source of strength by evoking fears that the truth will be contaminated if it is confided to the uninitiated and impure.

In the hands of medieval allegorists, this exclusionary logic frequently lapses into violence—indeed, violence that is institutionally sanctioned and that often takes the form of official pronouncements.[30] At the very end of Alan of Lille's *De planctu Naturae*, Lady Nature's priestly consort Genius pronounces an anathema excommunicating unnatural sinners from the order of nature.[31] Alan's poet-narrator describes this anathema as an *exterminium*, meaning "banishment" (in Classical Latin) but especially "ruin, devastation, destruction" (in Vulgar and Medieval Latin). It seems reasonable to presume that this destruction is meant both literally (physical annihilation) and metaphorically (spiritual alienation), and that the anathema effects the exclusion of sinners from their own natural bodies. Indeed, Alan would have been familiar with this word from Jerome's Vulgate Bible, in which it is used exclusively in the literal sense of physical devastation (see 1 Mac. 7.7; Wis. 18; Jdt. 4.12; 2 Esd. 10.10; Sir. 39.36). Jean de Meun's Genius (borrowed from the *De planctu*) considerably amplifies the sense of physical and corporeal punishment. He declares that unnatural sinners (those who refuse to procreate or who "pervert what is written when they come to read it") should not only suffer social ostracism and disgrace but also mutilation and battery:

> May they, in addition to the excommunication that sends them all to damnation, suffer, before their death, the loss of their purse and testicles, the signs that they are male. . . .May they have their bones broken without their ever being mended! May all those who want to follow them live in great shame!

May their dirty, horrible sin be sorrowful and painful to them; may it cause them to be beaten with sticks everywhere, so that one sees them as they are.[32]

It is a matter of some dispute whether Jean intends Genius's sermon as a parody of the clergy's penitential rhetoric, or whether, on the contrary, he intends it to be taken seriously. Either way, it seems clear that Jean, as a reader of the allegorical tradition that precedes him, understands clearly the relationship between the allegorical depiction of nature and a violent mutilation of natural bodies.

Indeed, a major element of my argument in this book is that if medieval allegory draws attention to the ambivalence and indeterminacy of textual meaning, there is usually a compensatory strategy, often involving the violent displacement of anxiety onto a marginalized, scapegoated "other." The anxious awareness that the "reality" of the dominant ideology might not be incontestable but is instead a cultural fiction subject to interpretation is projected outward in the form of physical destruction. Often, as with Genius's anathema, the violence is merely symbolic or latent. Yet it can also be quite literal, including brutal acts of mutilation and killing that seem to be motivated as much by the failure of allegory to capture the truth or stabilize ideology as by narrative expectations or generic conventions.

There is at this point a fairly significant body of criticism examining the relationship between allegory and violence, meaning both fictional and ideological manipulation and physical coercion and destruction. Jody Enders has argued that in certain medieval ritual practices, violent rhetoric begets actual, physical violence. She theorizes that rhetoric does not simply ask that audiences surrender to the civilizing power of oratory, as both Cicero and Alcuin propose. It also authorizes a form of concealed violence that "needs not only souls and minds but bodies."[33] Enders offers the example of English Maytime festivities, in which small boys were beaten for the purposes of delineating and commemorating "the spatial circumspection of the polis."[34] My own example (which I will discuss toward the end of chapter 1) is the symbolic purging of dissent through public execution of sodomites in the Late Middle Ages, typically by burning. These executions clearly serve a rhetorical purpose as well as a legal one: the flames, which in scriptural typologies symbolize revealed law and divine wrath, virtually eradicate the body of the sodomite, reducing to near nothingness both the sinner and the sin. The auto-da-fé and the stake thus signify the power of the dominant ideology to invent and then eliminate threats to its intactness. The ritual of public execution obviates a crisis of legitimacy for ecclesiastical or secular forms of sovereignty by deflecting difference and dissent onto a marginalized "other" and then ritually and violently excluding that "other" from the community. Clearly, this kind of rhetorical and corporal punishment fulfills, as Enders puts it, "the need for actual bodies as the recipients of rhetorical lessons."[35] It buttresses the persuasive, coercive force of rhetoric against its own internal difference by imprinting ideologies on the body of the "other" or by demonstrating that ideology is capable of annihilating bodily existence altogether.

Teskey, in his masterful book *Allegory and Violence*, makes a similar kind of argument, theorizing that allegory stages ideological struggles that motivate or anticipate violent results. He argues that allegory's attempts to capture intellectual truths or to raise earthly experience to the level of pure abstraction inevitably fail. As allegory attempts to mitigate this failure, it lapses into conceptual forms of violence such as the Neoplatonic *raptio*, or "seizing": the imprinting of feminine matter by masculine form, a form of subjugation that is necessary to understand the nature of reality itself. This metaphysical act of capture is often literalized in allegorical texts, taking the form of the most pernicious of sexual mythologies: "the fantasy of the suppressed smile of the woman who only appears to resist what is happening to her."[36] Yet Teskey believes there is an even more characteristic move in allegory: violence is "concealed so that the female will appear to embody, with her whole body, the meaning that is imprinted on her. When this occurs we have personification."[37] For Teskey, personification involves the violent subordination of a body (often, though not always, female) to an abstract conceptual order that is at its origin ideological. However, he believes that "allegory is more than the literary representation of. . .ideological order. As the basis of the social practice of interpretation, allegory actively sustains that order."[38] Teskey cites Angus Fletcher, who writes, "Allegories are the natural mirrors of ideology."[39] He then refines this argument considerably: "Allegories do not just reflect ideological structures; they engage us in the practice of ritual interpretation by which those structures are reproduced in bodies and reexpressed through the voice. As a substitute for genuine political speaking, allegory elicits the ritual repetition of an ideologically significant world."[40] The violent force of allegory thus becomes quite clear. Pace Delany, allegory does not merely seek to transcend the uncertainty of language and the sublunary world through essentialism, abstraction, and mystification. Nor does it legitimate ideological structures simply by analogizing them to "eternal, inevitable, and immutable" categories. Allegory also, and at the same time, engages the reader in interpretive contingencies that are directly linked to ideological strategies for social and political control. As Teskey writes, allegory, speaking the truth "otherwise," simultaneously exhibits and conceals "the fundamental disorder out of which the illusion of order is raised."[41] The disarticulation of allegory's "grand metaphorics of paternity" motivates even more aggressive attempts to "capture the substantiality of beings and raise it to the conceptual plane," to negate "the integrity of the other, of the living," and to exert a "power to seize and to tear."[42] In other words, allegorical violence is not simply the imposition of essential, archetypal ideas on accidental social and political realities; it is also a discursive, iterative ritual that uses the contingency of its own meaning to accomplish ideological goals.

In the ensuing four chapters, I will interpret allegorical codifications of sexual ethics as ideological fictions that work to preserve the power of specific classes and institutions through twin strategies of articulation and disarticulation. In chapter 1, I offer a historical and theoretical analysis of the relationship between allegory, ethics, and sexual desire in the intellectual, cultural, and ideological worlds of Late Antiquity and the Middle Ages. I am especially interested to note the violent, eliminationist dimensions of a "privative" account of evil that requires that moral evil "be" nothing at all: a privation of goodness and being that is limitlessly vulnerable to the disciplinary force of a dominant ideology and ruling class. In chapter 2, I examine one of the earliest Old French romances, *Eneas*, an Anglo-Norman rewriting, or *translatio*, of Virgil's *Aeneid* in which the epic journey from Troy to Rome is reconceived as a narrative of state formation and an allegory of familial, racial, and national identity. The potential or actual failure of the rhetoric of incorporation is consistently linked in this text to physical violence, including the piercing and dismemberment of deviant bodies. In chapter 3, I turn to Alan of Lille's *De planctu Naturae*, in which allegorical representations of physical and moral order are consistently disrupted by perverse desires and meanings that are not alien to allegory but are instead internal to it. Alan's poem suggests that the extirpation of deviance from the community of faith is a necessary moral goal but one that cannot be achieved without contaminating ethics itself. Finally in chapter 4, I offer a reading of Jean de Meun's signature in the *Roman de la rose* as an allegory of authorship and male discursive and sexual power. Whereas many scholars have interpreted the allegorical love quest and subsequent plucking of the rose as a liberation from courtly asceticism and stylistic indirection, I argue that it works to authorize a particular class of readers (namely, the elite male clergy) and to relegate women to the status of mute, nameless, and inert victims of sexual and rhetorical violence. In each of these chapters, I will be concerned to demonstrate that in the High Middle Ages, sexual ethics is a cultural and ideological fiction that works to sustain institutional power and to legitimate violent forms of subordination, though often through strikingly contradictory means.

CHAPTER 1

RHETORIC, EVIL, AND PRIVATION: FROM AUGUSTINE TO THE "PERSECUTING SOCIETY"

Li mauvés ne sunt pas home.
[The wicked are not men.]

—Reson in Jean de Meun, *Le roman de la rose*, line 6292

If, indeed, the well-being of the whole body demands the amputation of a limb, say in the case where one limb is gangrenous and threatens to infect the others, the treatment to be commended is amputation. Now every individual is as it were a part of the whole. Therefore if any man is dangerous to the community and is subverting it by some sin, the treatment to be commended is his execution in order to preserve the common good.

—Thomas Aquinas, *Summa Theologiae*, 2–2.64.2

As is well known, the twelfth century marks the advent of a new "symbolist mentality" in the Christian West, spearheaded in large part by the Platonists of the School of Chartres and the Abbey of St. Victor.[1] Inspired by the Latin *auctores* and a partial knowledge of Plato's *Timaeus*, the Chartrians were instrumental in reviving interest in the rational study of visible phenomena and the rhetorical, mythographical, and poetic implications of a Timaean cosmology. According to authors like Bernard Sylvester, Alan of Lille, and John of Hanville, scientific observation and allegorical poetry provide readers with experiential and intuitional knowledge about the divine ordering of the universe and in so doing allow the mind to ascend from divine immanence toward divine transcendence, from the natural toward the supernatural. Figuration, especially of nature or the cosmos, serves the purposes of wisdom and understanding by providing access to the inner reality of things as well as the sublime reality of essences. For their part, the Victorine scholars largely eschewed secular poetry and accorded only a limited value to a *theologia mundana*. They preferred instead an intuitionist, anagogical, and mystical approach to biblical exegesis and cosmic sacramentalism. The Victorines were nevertheless fascinated with the process whereby sacred symbols and observable nature could take on conceptual and ethical significance in response to divine illumination. Hugh of St. Victor writes, "By contemplating what God has made, we realize what we ourselves ought to do. Every nature tells of God; every nature teaches man; every nature reproduces its essential form, and nothing in the universe is infecund."[2] Hugh discovered symbolic codes in Scripture and the visible world and described these as mystical gateways leading from the *opus conditionis* (the created universe) to the *opus restaurationis* (the universe restored to divine grace). Not only do symbols provide evidence of God's mark on nature, but they also draw the mind toward celestial perfection, allowing the spirit to achieve supernatural insight. This communion teaches man about moral conduct, natural and divine law, and the inner meaning of justice, wisdom, and faith.

The influence of this new symbolism, whether rationalist or mystical in orientation, can be felt throughout the various strains of intellectual life in the High Middle Ages, including both sacred and secular traditions. As Marie-Dominique Chenu observes, "In the whole range of its culture, the medieval period was an era of the symbol as much as, indeed more than, an era of dialectic."[3] The "world vision" of the twelfth century, he argues, comprehended "two levels, with the second level lying beneath the surface and becoming accessible through transposition, via imagery, onto the first."[4] Though there were a number of conservative reactions against rhetoric and the liberal arts generally, Chenu finds evidence of the basic techniques of allegory in "the total behavior of Christian society."[5] Winthrop Wetherbee largely agrees and notes that the symbolist mentality extends well beyond Christian typologies to encompass courtly traditions as well: "The major vernacular poets possessed the same grounding in classical poetry and rhetoric as their contemporaries writing in Latin" and worked to adapt "the materials of school-poetry to the uses of *courtoisie* and romance."[6] It is true that "the courtly poetry of the later twelfth century is social rather than philosophical," and that "its primary emphasis is on concrete emotional situations and *avanture*, rather than the abstract dialogues and tableaux of Chartrian allegory and mythographical lyric."[7] Still, it could be argued that secular and ecclesiastical authors alike perceive rhetoric as the structuring principle of an earthly reality and allegory as the master trope of imaginative literature. In his classic study of medieval aesthetics, Edgar de Bruyne proposes just that: since God has inscribed "the figure of supernatural and mysterious realities on the structure of historical and physical facts," it is possible to see "at least a seed of allegorical signification" in the literal and historical narratives of the period.[8] Thus whether symbolization is linked to *courtoisie* or *clergie, amor* or *caritas,* it is clear that in speaking of things, events, or states of being, medieval writers have a tendency to allegorize nature and history, to construct a vision of the sublunary world as a set of *signa veritatis* that ultimately refer to the celestial realm of essences.

Rather than assuming that medieval thinkers construe the symbolic order as a purely substitutive, vertical mode of representation, we should first take into account the innate ambivalence of their rhetorical and cosmological models. According to Alan of Lille, "Every creature in the world is, for us, like a book and a picture and a mirror as well." Bernard Sylvester specifies that God is the "Supreme Scribe" whose finger has marked down "the text of time, the fated march of events, the disposition made of the ages." Both authors echo Hugh of St. Victor's well-known aphorism: "The entire sense-perceptible world is like a sort of book written by the finger of God."[9] A striking feature of this ubiquitous image is that, in striving to imagine an utterly pure origin beyond space and time, these thinkers arrive instead at an infinite regress of rhetorical figures. Hugh employs a carefully qualified simile to describe the world as "a sort of book" (and therefore a rhetorical disposition) authored by a synecdoche: the finger of God. Thus even as he describes the imprint of the divine Author on the entirety of creation, he reduces God, the ineffable, indivisible origin of all being, to the status of a partitive figure of speech. Of course Hugh clearly intends that his tropes will not be taken literally and is careful (as are the others) to qualify his statements: it is not a book but "a sort of book," a figuration of the unfigurable. As with biblical symbolism, we must move beyond the literal meaning toward a metaphorical concept and then proceed "through the concept to a thing, through the thing to its idea, and through its idea arrive at Truth."[10] Still, the potential for error is intrinsic to the figuration of God's creation of, and authority over, the universe. Hugh's aphorism requires that the reader look beyond its potentially misleading verbal constructions in order to grasp the ineffable mysteries of the faith. Yet there is always a danger that interpretation will go astray and will yield perverse, heretical meanings rather than mystical insights.

Indeed, as I will seek to demonstrate in this chapter, there is a profound ambivalence about the conceptual and moral function of signs that is embedded deep within the symbolist mentality.[11] This ambivalence can be traced at least as far back as the Patristics and is laden with ideological meaning. According to a patristic theology of the word, cognition and faith are necessarily mediated through verbal signs. Words are the privileged vehicle for revelation and one of the means of bridging the gap between a lapsed humanity and an angry, punishing God. And yet whatever else they signify, words inevitably are also a marker of man's fallen state, in that they provide only partial knowledge of the divine mystery and can never be purely referential or representational. The truth that is arrived at *through* language is only a partial perception of an essential truth that lies *beyond* language, and exegesis at some point requires the negation of symbolic codes as vehicles for theological truths. Indeed, if there is no acknowledgment of the limitations of language, signs will yield little more than fraudulent, idolatrous, and heretical meanings. In spite of the privileges they accord to symbols, Victorines and Chartrians share with Augustine the anxiety that a foolish or misguided reader will be seduced by oratory and eloquence and will remain mired in worldly things and deceptive fictions rather than moving toward higher truths.

The legacy of this anxiety is handed down from the cathedral schools of the twelfth century to the urban universities of the thirteenth. It survives even the advent of the new Aristotelianism, which typically replaces symbolism with the empirical science of definitions and categories and prefers dialectic to rhetoric. Like Augustine, Aquinas is profoundly aware of the limitations of human cognition and verbal signs and is careful to articulate the need to transcend natural science and rhetorical images through intuition and faith. The symbols of Scripture are not "a place for our mind to rest in," but rather "a place it can start climbing from, to immaterial things."[12] Following the pseudo-Dionysius, Aquinas believes that Scripture "presents the divine under even the vilest symbols, to minimize the chances of our staying attached to them."[13] Moreover, he agrees with Boethius that to scrutinize "the divine form itself" is not to know "what God is" but to deny "all images."[14] In short, whether they are interested in the empirical observation of the creation, the poetic evocation of mystery, or the pursuit of the mystical significance of the "thing," the medieval symbolists are always conscious of the ultimate incomprehensibility of the divine plan and are profoundly mistrustful of the human intellect and its ability to discern or signify higher truths in signs.

The goals of this chapter will be, first, to examine the roots of the symbolist mentality in Augustinian sign theory, metaphysics, and ethics; second, to consider the place of the body and sexual ethics in this intellectual, literary, and cultural movement; and third, to offer an ideological analysis of the symbolist mentality, its various moral claims, and the impact those claims may have had on historical realities and actual, embodied subjects. I will ask the following kinds of questions: How does the symbolist mentality make sense of the human body as a part of the "book of the world"—that is, as a text endowed with specific moral functions and meanings? Can the truth of the body, including the sexual drives, be captured in signs and elevated to the level of conceptual or mystical realities? What is the relationship between the rhetorical appropriation of the body and the various ideologies attached to representation and persuasion? What is the nature of evil, especially concupiscence? How can evil be conceived by the mind and represented in signs? How does the cultural, literary, and philosophical depiction of evil operate within a historical and material frame? In what ways does it mystify real conditions in order to stabilize a dominant mode of social and political organization?

Ultimately, I will argue that a philosophy, theology, or aesthetics of the symbol does not simply lead to an awareness of human laws as discursive and contingent, but also motivates attempts to distinguish more rigorously truth from falsehood, good from evil, *in bono* readers from *in malo* ones. Intellectual models of evil as a privation of being or an absence of meaning are, moreover, not simply intellectual or conceptual exercises. On the contrary, they are actualized in bodies, especially the reduction of sinful bodies to an irredeemable existence so close to nothingness that it may be killed without committing murder.

Augustine, Aquinas, and the Body

Let me begin my exploration with a discussion of the body and its place in the Christian West. For the Neoplatonists of Late Antiquity (whose impact on the Middle Ages can scarcely be overestimated), the body is simply discarded as the soul is perfected through enlightenment. Matter itself is categorized as defective and feminine as opposed to ideal, masculine form, and is ultimately debased for its irredeemable flaws. Neoplatonic idealism requires the subjection of a material, feminine Other in order to allegorize the concept of man. One might imagine that the same holds true for medieval Christian philosophy, in which the suspicion of the flesh is frequently coupled with misogynistic vitriol. This is, by and large the case, and Augustine, as he so often does, offers powerful models for medieval intellectuals. Augustine incorporates the Neoplatonists' loathing of feminine-coded flesh and idealization of a masculine-coded soul into a monotheistic belief system and an intuitionist ethics: God created man with a conscience so that he might intuit and follow moral law; and love for God draws the soul of man away from material and moral corruption toward holy truths, eventually arriving at mystical communion with the divine. At the same time, Augustine cannot discard the body altogether. For Christians, God is both divine Father and incarnate Son, spirit and flesh. Moreover, the bodily resurrection of Christ, the so-called first resurrection of the holy martyrs (Rev. 20.4–6), and the promise of a general resurrection at the Last Judgment suggest that the state of embodiment cannot be intrinsically shameful or sinful. According to Augustine, the body must be disciplined and purified; but as a divine creation, it cannot be condemned outright. Augustine maintains, therefore, that the soul does not shed the body as it ascends toward God, even if the body's "corruptibility" remains a marker of moral incontinence and a "burden" to the soul as it attempts to rise.[15] He readily (and fatefully) acknowledges that the condition of postlapsarian existence is to "bear in our members, and in our vitiated nature, the striving of the flesh, or, indeed, its victory."[16] Yet if we are able to despise the flesh "in its infirmity" and subject it to the coercion of "the spiritual law," the flesh will eventually "become spiritual. . . .all corruptibility and all reluctance gone."[17]

This spiritualization of the body is accomplished not only through moral restraint, but also through rhetorical reading and writing: the careful interpretation of, and distinction between, literal commandments pertaining to the "truth of the faith" and "transferred expressions," whose ambiguities "require no little care and industry."[18] Having deduced the truth of the faith from judicious readings of sacred texts, the theologian imparts the spiritual law to the faithful through various rhetorical forms: orations, epistles, sermons, expositions of Scripture, and so on. And yet as Augustine makes clear in his *Confessions*, his mistrust of the "striving of the flesh" is matched only by his dread of "the persuasive sweetness" of false eloquence—that of the Manichean bishop Faustus, for instance, or any of the philosophers who "do not know him who is the Way."[19] The consequences of errors in reading could even be fatal: "What the Apostle says pertains to this problem: 'For the letter killeth, but the spirit quickeneth.' In other words, when that which is said figuratively is taken as though it were literal, it is understood carnally."[20] Augustine's citation of Paul suggests not only that Christians must seek the truth in Scripture, discovering figurative meaning where the literal is insufficient, but also that in order to heal the wound of sin, the flesh itself must be viewed as a natural sign or allegory of the divine will: an animal body that can be made immortal only by grace. To read figurative passages literally, without seeking the spirit within signs, is to read carnally without the possibility of illumination, to lapse into material defect and a death without resurrection. Similarly, to read the body as a law unto itself is to debase or enslave the soul through fleshly sins: "There is a miserable servitude of the spirit in this habit of taking signs for things, so that one is not able to raise the eye of the mind above things that are corporal and created to drink in eternal light."[21] Rhetoric is thus simultaneously a gateway to enlightenment and a vehicle for heretical error and fleshly sin.

Paradoxically, the spiritual liberation of the body also seems to involve its subjection to ecclesiastical and public sovereignty. For in order to rise above his corporeal defect, man must be willing to submit to physical servitude; and in order to guide lost souls toward enlightenment, the priesthood must not withdraw from the world but must instead wield secular power. Augustine believes that in order to free the spirit and allow it to ascend toward God, man must renounce all notions of personal sovereignty and must not seek to contest the secular power that rules or enslaves him, unless it happens that "those who rule him. . .compel him to do what is impious and wicked."[22] He proclaims, "By nature. . .in the condition in which God first created man, no man is the slave either of another man or of sin."[23] However, the result of the Fall is that "servitude itself is ordained as a punishment by that law which enjoins the preservation of the order of nature, and forbids its disruption."[24] If Adam and Eve had not violated God's law, "there would be no need for the discipline of servitude as a punishment."[25] Augustine paraphrases Ephesians 6.5, saying, "The apostle therefore admonishes servants to be obedient to their masters, and to serve them loyally and with a good will."[26] Although he sees in human government evidence of corruption and sin, Augustine's theory of a universal, corporeal error also provides religious justification for the cooperation between imperial Rome and a new imperial Church. Not only does he endorse the use of coercion by secular government (especially if it is to suppress heresy), but he also uses political vocabulary to describe the basic tenets of Catholic dogma, most notably the "revolt" of the body against the "rule" of the mind. As punishment for their rebellion against God, Adam and Eve were condemned to suffer the "stirring of their flesh, which had become disobedient to them as a punishment, in requital of their own disobedience to God."[27] Damaged by Original Sin, man requires divine grace in order to expiate the spiritual failings he lives out in his rebellious body, to gain access to the holy truths contained within Scripture, and to avoid the damnation that results from fleshly error and heresy. Grace can only be bestowed through the agency of the Church, which requires strict obedience both to its own rule and to that of imperial Rome. The invention of universal culpability serves not only to regulate rhetoric and the body, but also to stabilize an established ideological order. Evoking the potential for error embodied in all human agents, who can, through their waywardness, introduce defect into the sacred language of Scripture, Augustine suggests the ongoing need for vigilance on the part of a disciplinary clergy.

Nearly a millennium later and after massive historical, political, and cultural shifts, the mistrust of the body and language in elite intellectual milieus remained more or less constant, as did the awareness that the body (as an aspect of a divinely authored creation) and language (as the primary instrument of revelation) must be rigorously disciplined by some form of institutional power. Aquinas's view (derived from Aristotle) that cognition is not impeded but made possible by the corporeal senses, his theory of an analogy of attribution between material being and divine Being, and his critique of the Platonic body/soul duality—all merely complicate the issue of embodiment without in any way allaying Augustine's fears about the "striving of the flesh." Since for Aquinas intellection consists in the perception of sense data rather than the divine illumination of an essential reality beyond physical existence, there is indeed all the more reason for carefully regulating the body and sensory operations. In order to ensure conformity with the literal and figurative "truths" of Scripture (or, rather, prevailing, orthodox readings), Thomistic psychology and naturalism must also guarantee that the reality apprehended *through* the body does not violate moral or revealed law *about* the body. Colish describes this kind of argument as evidence of a "metaphysical bias": "Before he starts to theorize, [Aquinas] knows a great deal more about the universe than his insistent empiricism would immediately lead one to suspect. In the case of the knowledge of nature, he has a large selection of presuppositions about reality which permit him to measure the adequacy of a given intellectual sign to its object."[28] Indeed, as Aquinas writes in the *Summa Theologiae*, "It is clear that natural law is nothing other than the sharing in the Eternal Law by intelligent creatures."[29] He makes plain, moreover, that both natural and eternal law require, above all else, strict obedience to the "custom of the Church" [*consuetudo ecclesiae*],[30] which he believes should prevail over any individual authority (even that of Jerome or Augustine), and the absolute prohibition of fleshly incontinence, especially the sexual vices.

Now, it would be a mistake to see a seamless continuity between Patristic and Scholastic modes of thought, or to assume that these traditions are wholly consistent with themselves. And yet as Colish proposes, it is also clear that "from the patristic period roughly until the end of the thirteenth century. . .western European thinkers produced a number of different yet reciprocal expressions of one basic mental universe."[31] This mental universe, grounded on the "radically ontological emphasis"[32] of monotheism, offers a theory of the sign in which moral and spiritual truths are both translated in and traduced by verbal signifiers. My argument here is that this imbrication of sign theory, epistemology, and ethics, much as it may vary from thinker to thinker or period to period, is motivated by ideology and performs ideological work. Thus in the Middle Ages, and particularly in the wake of the Gregorian Reform (which sought to organize the Church hierarchically and establish clerical control over virtually every area of secular life), the Church exhibited its power by theorizing a causal, sacramental, or analogical link between a sublime, timeless order of being and historically variable systems of religious practice, between the mysterious power of the divinity and the power of the Church to bind and loose. Moreover, by targeting specific moral errors and heretical readings, it implicitly legitimated an orthodox set of norms and practices and further consolidated power within the ruling clerical class, whose function was to ensure conformity of belief and ritual. This is not to say that difference and dissent did not exist internal to this ideological world or that medieval intellectuals were not aware of the contingencies of textual, cultural, and religious meaning. On the contrary, the monarchic Church mobilized cultural anxieties about the uncertainty of human knowledge (and especially moral knowledge) in order to authorize the enforcement of laws and the power of those responsible for interpreting, ratifying, and implementing the law.

Leaving Augustine aside for the moment, let us consider the ideological inflection of Thomistic naturalism. Aquinas does not simply derive sexual morality from the empirical observation of nature or the exegetical treatment of Scripture. On the contrary, his concepts of natural order and eternal law normalize and transcendentalize a specific ideological fiction: the Church's authority to criminalize "unnatural" behaviors and to mete out punishments to offenders. John Boswell critiques Aquinas's sexual ethics, arguing that it is "particularly significant" that

> Thomas's ideas about homosexuality triumphed just at the moment when the church began to enforce orthodoxy more rigorously than ever before and to insist that everyone accept in every detail not just the infallible pronouncements of popes and councils but every statement of orthodox theologians. . . . The effect was to eliminate all opinion in the church which did not accord with accepted theology on every matter.[33]

In Boswell's view, moral responsibility and pastoral care are not the only or even the primary motivations for Aquinas's prohibition of sexual deviance. Instead, proscriptions against certain sexual behaviors (those that were already considered immoral and were prohibited by civil and canon law) serve as a pretext for the ideological construction of an embodied and therefore vulnerable subject—one whose salvation depends upon pastoral care and subjection to the Church's moral, intellectual, and religious authority. As Boswell illustrates, homosexuality here achieved "a new and singular degree of enormity among the types of behavior most feared by the common people and most severely repressed by the church."[34] But implicit in this interdiction is a larger attempt to construe the body as a site of moral weakness, and to insist that the flesh requires constant regulation in order to prevent a lapse into irredeemable error.

Similarly, the faithful, if they are concerned with their personal salvation and social standing, must comply with the moral and spiritual dictates of the Church in matters relating to the exegetical treatment of sacred texts. Recognizing that Scripture contains multiple meanings and could be appropriated for heretical purposes, Aquinas is careful to insist on the utter uniformity of the faith under papal leadership: "There must be one faith for the entire Church; *That you all speak the same thing, and that there be no schisms among you.* This norm could not be followed unless every question arising out of faith were resolved by the one having care over the whole Church. A new version of the creed, then, falls to the sole authority of the Pope, just as do all other matters affecting the whole Church."[35] Christians who knowingly and willfully commit errors of interpretation should, after two admonitions, be separated from the Church, and furthermore be delivered "to the secular court to be removed from this world by death."[36] Plainly, the theological and rhetorical interpretation of Scripture carries with it an implicit ideological content: the authority of the Church to minister to the faithful includes the power to define the truths and symbols of the faith, to ostracize those who resist ecclesiastical rule, and to call upon secular authorities to exterminate sinners and dissidents. Orthodoxy depends upon the invention and subsequent eradication of a supposedly inassimilable heterodoxy, as well as the infinitely renewable threat of a lapse into, or contamination by, moral error.

Rhetoric, Ethics, and Ideology

In essence, what I am arguing here is that the link between rhetoric and ethics in medieval intellectual movements does not suggest an opening to otherness but instead a ruse of power that the ruling class uses to normalize its hegemony. Before taking this argument further, I should acknowledge that it flies in the face of an alternate approach to Augustine and his legacy—what Sarah Spence refers to as the "hermeneutics of charity." Spence describes Augustine's theory of reading as an ongoing process of interpretation in which the open-endedness of textual meaning is valued over claims of definitive truth and in which the coercive power of Ciceronian oratory gives way to altruism and pluralism. Spence proposes that

> while Cicero sees the argument of the speech as the establishment of a structure that encloses the right meaning and exiles the wrong, Augustine sees reading as the motion from one to the other, a motion that recognizes both poles, acknowledges the existence of each, and asserts that the true reading, the charitable reading, is that which will acknowledge the difference between the two, as well as the path from one to the other.[37]

The duty of Christian readers is to understand all texts as fragmentary and incomplete, "to locate the wounds in the text—the spots where the text is not of a piece—and through our reading bandage the text."[38] The point is not to complete or perfect textual meaning by assigning a gloss. For "even as a bandage acknowledges the existence of a wound even as it simulates bonding, so our reading will make use of rifts to come to higher unities."[39] By acknowledging the necessary errors and inconsistencies of rhetorical formulations of divine mysteries, the Christian orator (now a preacher or teacher) embraces the deficiency of verbal signs and the "power of becoming"[40] intrinsic to charitable reading: a longing for the moral, the ineffable, and the divine that remains necessarily suspended and incomplete. According to Spence, the power of becoming requires the rearrangement of traditional oratorical and social hierarchies. Since the preacher cannot possess the truth but can only acknowledge that he is seeking it, he must "persuade laterally, not from on high."[41] In preaching the truth of the gospels, he seeks out "new possibilities for the text" and establishes horizontal, noncoercive relationships with his congregation.[42]

Spence's argument does not limit itself to sacred texts, and in her view the hermeneutics of charity is not "inherently sacred."[43] On the contrary, Augustine's model of the "power of becoming" had a direct impact on later rhetorical traditions in which the goal was to signify "something that is by definition unreachable within the limits and strictures of language, the journey to which is motivated by desire."[44] Indeed, Spence sees troubadour lyric, especially the *canso*, as a translation of sacred *caritas* into profane *amor:* an unfulfilled, frustrated longing for communion with the beloved. However, she also holds that the troubadours ultimately repudiate the Augustinian notion of a nonhierarchical, open-ended rhetorical method and subordinate the theme of erotic unfulfillment to structures of rhetorical mastery: "As poet, the troubadour, be he Guilhem IX or Raimbaut d'Aurenga, is in control—of language, of medium, of audience. He can and does create *ex nihilo* and so controls the truth of his poem. As lover, however, he articulates the position of an Augustinian orator who must wait for his audience to complete the dialogue."[45] Troubadour lyric, which is "emphatically a performed literature," suggests a theatrical distance between the frustrated lover and a poet who "attempts to assert control over both audience and work."[46] The troubadours thus offer a decisive modification of Augustinian hermeneutics, paving the way for Dante's *Divina Commedia*, in which there are clear distinctions between author and work, orator and audience, and in which rhetorical structure is used to subordinate desire to hierarchy.

I find Spence's analysis of troubadour lyric highly persuasive, and I agree that the troubadours provide later secular writers with models for bracketing interpretive contingencies through strategies of closure. Nevertheless, my perspective on the legacy of Augustine, and in particular the ideological inflection of his process-oriented hermeneutics, is quite different from hers. First, I do not believe that Augustinian hermeneutics offers inexhaustible possibilities for the cooperative, collective mediation of textual mysteries. Rather, I see it primarily as a tool for regulating textual meaning and for appropriating and repressing dissent. Second, I would argue that the troubadours' technique of stressing the incompletion of textual meaning while also exploiting formal structures of containment is already at work in Augustine's writings. The hermeneutics of charity is the starting point for an ideological strategy in which the rhetor's humility and self-effacement, along with an awareness of the protean nature of textual meaning, are easily coopted for the purposes of ideological domination: the elimination of rival sects, faiths, and strategies of reading; the formation of a uniform Catholic orthodoxy; and the legitimation of existing social and political hegemonies insofar as they serve the purposes of institutional religion.

As we have seen, Augustine is careful to emphasize that Scripture is infused with the singularity of absolute Truth but is nonetheless capable of multiple meanings—and, indeed, is liable to carnal or deviant misreadings. However, the vulnerability of Scripture in turn strengthens and unifies Catholic orthodoxy, allowing Augustine at various moments in his career to target specific groups he wished to exclude from the power of the Word. For instance, the inherent polyvalence of Scripture allows him to describe Judaism in *On Christian Doctrine* as a misdirected, arrogant, literal misinterpretation of the law: the Jews "took signs of spiritual things for the things themselves, not knowing what they referred to, yet they acted as a matter of course that. . .they were pleasing the One God of All whom they did not see."[47] The errors of "Jewish literalism" (a fantastic contrivance!) are then transformed into the singular, enduring truth of Christian allegoresis: Christians read Hebrew Scripture in the light of the Incarnation, removing the "covering. . .which concealed useful truth"; this is "what happens to those who earnestly and piously, not proudly and wickedly, seek the sense of the Scriptures."[48] The ultimate truth of Scripture is, for Augustine, charity; and he is careful to insist that Christians are obliged to love the Jews and tolerate their beliefs and spiritual practices. As Jeremy Cohen has argued, Augustine, in his mature writings, eventually abandons this preference for the figurative over the literal, and indeed considerably moderates his understanding of carnality, desire, and the experience of the world. In an attempt to moderate Christian belief to the standards of Roman society and to counter the appeal of Pelagian antiasceticism, Augustine comes closer to the doctrines he earlier associated with the Jews. To a certain extent, this new outlook "temper[ed] his attack upon the Jews," or rather pushed it in a different direction.[49] In his mature writings, Augustine offers the fullest development of his Doctrine of Witness, specifically elaborating on Psalm 59.12, "Slay them not, lest at any time they forget your law; scatter them in your might." Augustine reads this passage as according value to Jewish religious observance but principally insofar as Jews bear witness to the completion of the Law in Christ. As Cohen explains, for Augustine,

> The Jews preserve the literal sense, they represent it, and they actually embody it—as book bearers, librarians, living signposts, and desks, who validate a Christological interpretation of the Old Testament. Unlike the "true bride of Christ," the Jew knows not the difference between letter and

spirit. While precisely this blindness obviates his salvation, it simultaneously facilitates his role as witness. From such a perspective, the more important the literal—that is, the original, historical meaning of biblical narrative in the instruction of Christianity, the more valuable the Jewish presence in a properly ordered Christian society.[50]

The reason for brooking Jewish belief is not tolerance or pluralism. Indeed, Cohen believes that even though Augustine comes closer to Jewish positions on exegesis, history, and sexuality and moderates his anti-Jewish polemic, the reason is not that he has any meaningful contact with the Jews. Instead, he develops his Doctrine of Witness principally as a function of the development of his own theological system. The Jews' continued existence as subservient, oppressed nonbelievers affirms the absolute victory and overriding validity of the one true faith. Augustine ultimately has no interest in "missionizing among the Jews. In keeping with the teachings of Paul, their conversion will come in due course; meanwhile, the worth of their service as witness and foil outweighs the disadvantage of their living as infidels among believers."[51] In the meantime, the ideological value of this phantasmal Jew is his embodiment of cultural, religious, and exegetical differences. The anticipation of the degradation of the Jews at the end of history (they will be dispersed and converted, and will suffer humiliation "like dogs")[52] signifies the ultimate truth of Christian revelation.

If overly literal reading is the doctrinal error of the Jews at a moment in his career when the literal was closely associated with the carnal and sinful, it is Eve, as archetypal woman, who is responsible for figurative misreading of a literal commandment. Augustine articulates this view of Eve when he begins to take literal approaches to Scripture seriously. He returns to the Book of Genesis and discovers the roots of Original Sin in Eve's misapprehension of the Word of God:

> Not content with the words of the serpent, [Eve] also gazed on the tree and saw that it *was good for food and a delight to behold*; and since she did not believe that eating it could bring about her death, I think she assumed that God was using figurative language when He said, *If you eat of it, you shall die.* And so she took some of the fruit and ate and gave some also to her husband, who was with her.[53]

On the face of it, Augustine's reading of Eve's misreading is doubly speculative ("I *think* she *assumed*") and therefore emphasizes the incomplete, flawed nature of any individual gloss on Scripture or sacred history. Augustine is, moreover, careful to associate misreading with a woman whose moral fragility seemingly can never be in doubt. However, the susceptibility of sacred language to error also clearly allows Augustine to wrest the Word from the hands of women and restore it to men, and to deflect blame for Original Sin away from Adam and onto Eve.

Many critics have argued in recent years that evidence of Augustine's sexism must be balanced against more moderate, and in some cases even antisexist, statements found elsewhere in his writings. Jean Truax observes that Augustine often defends women's moral, intellectual, and spiritual equality and therefore stands in stark contrast to some of his more severe contemporaries, notably Ambrose and Jerome.[54] For instance, she cites a letter to a wealthy Christian woman, Paulina, in which Augustine, paraphrasing Galatians 3.28, exhorts his interlocutor to "lift up the spirit of your mind, which is renewed in the knowledge of God, according to the image of Him that created him, where Christ dwells in you by faith, where there is no Jew or Greek, bond, free, male or female."[55] Truax also points to positive examples of female spirituality in Augustine's writings to counter the claim that Eve is the archetype of a universal, depraved womanhood. On many occasions Augustine's mother, Monica, assumes the role of teacher to her son; and Mary redeems the sin of Eve, proving that if death came into the world "through a woman," so "through a woman came life."[56]

And yet as Kim Power's recent, and far more comprehensive, assessment of Augustine's attitudes toward women demonstrates, his theology is utterly imbued with a misogyny he inherited from Roman and Judeo-Christian sources. Power begins by citing Eric Osborn's argument about Augustine's *ordo amoris:* charitable love for the other inevitably yields to, and is shaped by, a need to preserve and naturalize social and political hierarchies.[57] She argues that gender hierarchy is particularly important for Augustine, and indeed is emblematic of the postlapsarian state more generally:

> Augustine perceived women as inferior and subservient to men, even before the Fall, but he argued that then this subordination would have been a bond of love, a kind of benevolent despotism where men would lead in love and women would love to obey. Since the Fall, this inherent concord is problematic. Spouses may still serve each other with love, but male domination is mandatory to prevent the increase of corruption and sin. Given his overriding assumptions concerning order, the implication here is that female autonomy, as well as female leadership, has a corrupting effect and would inevitably lead to disorder.[58]

Women like Monica who do take a leadership role in spiritual matters must ultimately be subsumed under the category of *materfamilias:* Monica obeys her husband just as a slave [*ancilla*] obeys a master [*dominus*].[59]

Power's most compelling argument has to do with Augustine's attempts to reconcile Genesis 1.28 (according to which woman is made in the image of God) and 1 Corinthians 11.7 (according to which woman, as the image of *man* rather than God, must be veiled).[60] Augustine manages this reconciliation by arguing two things: first, that women belong to the *imago Dei* insofar as they are human beings [*homo*] but are distinct from it insofar as they are embodied women [*femina* or *mulier*]; and second, that *scientia* (knowledge, or the active mind) is feminine, whereas *sapientia* (wisdom, the part of the mind that can know God and that is, therefore, the very *imago Dei*) is masculine.[61] If the active mind is necessary for "the administration of the corporeal and the temporal" and is ultimately "a product of the Fall," it inevitably leads us back to earthly things.[62] Masculine wisdom, by contrast, allows us to transcend the world and grasp higher truths and eternal things. This is possible only if *sapientia* maintains its sovereign power over *scientia*; if the feminine is not restrained, "the demonic will seize control" and will give rise to "bestial appetites."[63]

Finally, Power argues that these symbolic or analogical gender codes are intimately bound up with actual, biological gender and with the social practice of veiling women. Though Augustine attempts to distinguish between sex and gender or between linguistic convention and conceptual reality, he generally tends to conflate "man and the masculine, and woman and the feminine."[64] This biological determinism has real "historical consequences," according to Power:

> As real women must wear a physical veil because they symbolize concupiscence, it may be taken that the veil serves to render women seemly, and yet remind them and their menfolk that they represent the shameful, sinful carnality which put the barrier between God and humanity in the first place. As they are equally *imago Dei* in their inmost (masculine) being, it is their female bodies which are thus designated.[65]

Some of the "concrete consequences" of this theology are "prescribed explicitly by Augustine": "Firstly, men must dominate and restrain women or further corruption will occur and sin will multiply"; and second, "As women had no integrity of body and spirit, but were divided between spiritual *homo* and physically carnal *femina*, men must learn to love the one and hate the other."[66] Power offers a particularly salient example drawn from Augustine's *On the Sermon on the Mount*. Addressing himself to husbands, he writes, "In one and the same woman to love the creature of God, whom he desires to be renewed; but to hate the corruptible and mortal conjugal connection and sexual intercourse: i.e. to love in her what is characteristic of a human being, to hate what belongs to her as a wife."[67]

Augustine thus not only excludes Jews and women from full participation in intellectual and spiritual life, but he also sets up paradigms whereby this exclusion mirrors and legitimates their subordination within the *ordo amoris*. Augustine's awareness of the fractured nature of all textual meaning, including that of Scripture, does not yield a hermeneutics or ethics of charitable openness. Love binds the Church to itself rather than calling it to embrace its others. Augustine works assiduously to affirm the rights and privileges of a particular class of readers (his own: a male intellectual and ecclesiastical elite) and the validity of a particular orientation and practice of Christian belief (Catholic orthodoxy). When the Jews "misread" the Old Testament as literal or Eve "misreads" a divine commandment as figurative, they do so because the ideological structure that reads them misreading links truth to a hierarchy in which an institutional elite alone is endowed with the right to mediate the divine Word, to interpret and enforce the eternal law.

Augustinian rhetoric is therefore much closer to its Roman counterpart than Spence allows. Though Augustine, unlike Cicero, does not define rhetoric as a branch of political science [*scientia civilis*], nevertheless it is clear that he uses eloquence to empower Catholics to defend the Church against dissidents of various sorts and to empower the clergy to act as arbiters of moral, intellectual, and spiritual truth. Of course, Augustine clearly states that the truth is outside of, and never entirely compatible with, verbal and rhetorical representation. But if he is able to persuade his readers that certain kinds of readings represent inadmissible, calamitous errors, then his own readings of Scripture, and the orthodoxy they eventually construct, may be thought to provide superior insight into truth.

Succinctly put, in order to bolster the authority and orthodoxy of his interpretation of the faith, Augustine invents scapegoats whose moral failures or deficiencies must be mitigated in order to guarantee, at least provisionally, the wholeness and moral rectitude of the community of true believers. The apprehension of an approximate truth through rhetorical reading prompts the invention and elimination of an untruth that is perceived to threaten the reigning ideology. Similarly, the susceptibility and open-endedness of sacred texts serve to legitimate the use of social constraint and overt physical force and are coextensive with a coercive, rather than charitable, ethical system. Augustine offers a model of rhetoric and ethics in which the defect or lack intrinsic to representation can be conflated with a socially constructed, ostracized Other, thereby producing an elite group charged with preserving moral truth and authority by controlling or eliminating immorality and dissent. The emphasis must, however, be on general questions rather than individual cases, abstract universals rather than historically contingent particulars. For the rhetorical text is most effective and persuasive when it conceals its ideological content behind an allegorical veil.

Allegory and Ideology

Turning to the literary traditions of the High Middle Ages, I would argue that the probing self-consciousness and self-reflexivity of medieval allegory could similarly be construed as strategies for dissimulating, and at the same time advancing, underlying ideological agendas. If allegory appears to be about the inexhaustible difference between representation and truth, I would argue that it also plays on the uncertainty of its own meaning in order to authorize a particular kind of reader to distinguish between proper and improper, orthodox and heterodox, interpretations. Allegorical texts bring about ideological cohesion by evoking anxieties related to the semantic and moral ambivalence of signs. Writers from Augustine to Alan of Lille and Jean de Meun relinquish mastery over the system of language and figures they use to express inexpressible truths; but that relinquishment serves to generate other forms of mastery. By unmasking its own internal contradictions or pushing them to the point of near-incoherence, allegory appears to throw its own representational and moral order into crisis. And yet it does so principally so that it may eventually impose order through alternate, typically violent means and empower the ruling classes as agents of discipline.

To elucidate my claim, I will offer two examples from Alan of Lille—not simply because of Alan's tremendous influence on medieval literary traditions, but also because he is so obviously invested in the consolidation of ecclesiastical power. In the prose prologue to his *Anticlaudianus*, Alan of Lille evokes the multiple levels of meaning in traditional allegoresis and suggests that those levels correspond to a hierarchy of intellectual training and insight among his readership: "In this work the sweetness of the literal sense will soothe the ears of boys, the moral instruction will inspire the mind on the road to perfection, the sharper subtlety of the allegory will whet the advanced intellect."[68] Obviously, women are excluded as readers, as are secular readers generally, since they cannot read Latin and therefore cannot acquire the instruction necessary to discover the text's higher meanings. Presumably, boys will eventually become men, and imperfect minds will gradually acquire advanced intellect. Yet Alan wishes also to exclude any reader who might be tempted to derive sensual or prurient meanings from the text: "Let those be denied access to this work who pursue only sense-images and do not reach out for the truth that comes from reason, lest what is holy, being set before dogs be soiled, lest the pearl, trampled under the feet of swine be lost, lest the esoteric be impaired if its grandeur is revealed to the unworthy."[69]

Though it speaks of archetypal concepts in abstract terms (including the very idea of Man), Alan's allegory is hardly universal speech. Precisely because it is liable to misinterpretation or misappropriation, the text must be withheld from readers who are content with sense-images and do not adhere to Alan's own conceptions of reason and truth. In other words, the limitations of language as a medium for disclosing intellectual or moral truths are easily translated into an ideological weapon. Those "sensualists" who misread the text, or who threaten to expose and exploit its ambiguities, are not merely bad readers but dogs and swine, Christ's own metaphors for shameless, unclean, or hostile outsiders. The vulnerability of the allegory is thus mitigated by its method of constructing the reader, of producing an occult meaning discernable only to an elite group of intellectual clergy, and of affirming a hierarchy according to which privileged initiates alone are capable of discerning and disseminating higher wisdom.

Obviously, this passage cannot be read as emphasizing the humility of the Christian rhetor. However, another passage from Alan of Lille, this one from his *De planctu Naturae*, provides a clear example of how the Augustinian gesture of self-abnegation or the internalization of moral and intellectual defect within allegory can be reappropriated for ideological purposes. Appearing to the poet in a dream vision, Lady Nature (who refers to herself as God's own vicar) speaks in "what one might call archetypal words that had been preconceived ideally."[70] She proclaims, "From all eternity the order had gone out from [the heavenly commander] that each and every thing should be inscribed and made known in the book of his Providence."[71] Writing in a language that is already a marker of social distinction, class solidarity, and political power, Alan appropriates the voice of God's own vicar in order to offer a pronouncement on the divine will and foreknowledge. And yet Nature's concerns are not simply theological but moral as well. She demonstrates in her speech to the poet that any aspect of creation that resists its predetermined, natural role or that runs contrary to the Creator's intentions cannot continue to exist but must be destroyed as irredeemable matter:

> For the movement of reason, springing from a heavenly origin, escaping the destruction of things on earth, in its process of thought turns back again to the heavens. On the other hand, the movements of sensuality, going planet-like in opposition to the fixed sky of reason, with twisted course slip down to the destruction of earthly things. The latter, then, draws man's mind down to the destruction arising from vice so that he may fall, the former invites him to come to the source of virtue so that he may rise.[72]

Given that the senses have the power to disrupt the spiritual ascent away from earthly things and to seduce the reader into vice, both body and soul must be subjected to the unified "movement of reason," thus ensuring conformity with God's intentions for the creation. Nature's rhetoric apparently convinces the poet that she can lead him away from vice and destruction toward virtue and salvation. He expresses his conversion, renunciation, and abjection corporeally: "Ad Nature deuolutus uestigia, salutationis uice pedes osculorum multiplici inpressione signaui" [I fell down at Nature's feet and marked them with the imprint of many a kiss to take the place of formal greeting].[73]

Before we accept these kisses as a mark of true conversion, however, we should attend carefully to the language the poet uses to describe his epiphany. Initially, it appears that he has been persuaded by Nature's "archetypal words" and offers a gesture of humility and contrition. He bows down to God's vicar, just as the faithful would kiss the feet of the Pope (the *vicarius Christi*), or as the sinner from Capernaum anointed and kissed the feet of Christ himself (Lk. 7.37–38). Yet the poet's gesture is also rendered in highly ambiguous, self-referential language that yields a distinctly different set of meanings. Indeed, Alan's words rather insistently refer not to natural or transcendental order but to writing itself. *Vestigia* can mean "feet" but is also understood as "foot-mark" or "mark," a vestige of what is no longer present but is known only through signs. Nature might therefore be understood not as an essential being or presence in the text but rather as a marker of an absence. The verb *signo* similarly refers not just to an act of pressing (the lips pressed to the feet) but also to writing or otherwise marking with signs. Finally, *inpressio* means "to imprint" and often denotes an act of inscription, as with a signet or pen. With its elaborate play on words referring to language, textuality, and inscription, this passage suggests that the poet has not discovered higher truth through his dialogue with Lady Nature. On the contrary, he is perversely venerating his *own* discursive creation. Alan's fictional double (the poet-narrator) subordinates himself to Alan's own creation (Nature) and is won over by the power of Alan's own words, which are merely attributed to God's vicar. As we shall see in more detail in chapter 3, the poet-narrator in the *De planctu* is not converted to natural law, but is instead seduced by the results of his own rhetorical labors: an allegory that does not contain that which it signifies but instead marks the vestige of what is no longer present. Alan's allegory is itself unnatural, or, as Alexandre Leupin argues in an essay on the *De planctu*, idolatrous: "Writing for oneself, or writing simply in order to write, is to attribute to the created being what should originate with the Creator. Since this writing begins and ends with sameness, its movement yields to the passion of idolatry."[74] Larry Scanlon argues, however, that the *De planctu* is not simply a "self-conscious text" in which "allegorical signifiers continually expos[e] their artifice, and complicat[e] their claims."[75] The moral and semantic ambiguities of Alan's poem do not in any way mitigate its disciplinary force. On the contrary, it is clear in the passage cited above that Nature serves as a spokesperson for a highly orthodox and deeply punitive moral theology. She does not merely posit the destructiveness of vice, but she also suggests that vice, the plural "movements of sensuality," *must be destroyed* in order to preserve the singular "movement of reason" and the authority of the "heavenly commander." For reason to be essentially reasonable and for God to be both all-powerful and all-good, sensuality and vice must be annihilated. Seeking to shield reason, the creation, and God himself from the effects of, or responsibility for, evil, the poem moves inexorably toward its conclusion: the anathematization of unnatural sinners. This anathema does not simply exclude sin from the order of nature but also calls for the excommunication or annihilation of sinners themselves. Those who have committed crimes *against* nature may be exiled *from* nature, meaning presumably the natural body and being itself.

Privative Evil, Dehumanization, and Violence

Here, Alan's *De planctu* recapitulates one of the most insidious and ideologically effective elements of patristic and medieval orthodoxy, that is, the theory of evil not as the antithesis of good but as a privation of both goodness and being. Scott MacDonald explains that in the Western tradition, from the Greeks through the Middle Ages and well into the modern period, being and goodness have been fundamentally inseparable. Plato claims that "the Form of the Good gives being to all the other Forms"; Aristotle maintains that "the good is spoken of in as many ways as being"; Augustine believes "that everything that exists is good insofar as it exists"; and Albertus Magnus and Thomas Aquinas hold "that the terms 'being' and 'good' are interchangeable (or convertible) and that goodness, like being, transcends the categories."[76] For Plato, an important corollary of this argument is that evil must "be" nothing, an existential lack or nullity. If the world of ideas is utterly real and perfectly good, the world of phenomena is less real, less good, and therefore tends toward evil. Evil in itself is not ontological, however, and has no essence of its own. It is, rather, a deficiency of being and can be known only through things whose existence has been diminished by devolution away from the good. In a decisive move for Christian moral philosophy and theology, Augustine embraced this theory (which he derived from a variety of sources, most notably Plotinus) and used it as the basis for his response to the so-called problem of evil.[77] Writing a generation or two before Augustine, Lactantius frames the problem as follows:

> God either wishes to take away evils and he cannot, or he can and does not wish to, or he neither wishes to nor is able, or he both wishes to and is able. If he wishes to and is not able, he is feeble, which does not fall in with the notion of god. If he is able to and does not wish to, he is envious, which is equally foreign to god. If he neither wishes to nor is able, he is both envious and feeble and therefore not god. If he both wishes to and is able, which alone is fitting to god, whence, therefore, are there evils, and why does he not remove them?[78]

To avoid the conclusion that God is either powerless or, worse, malevolent, Augustine turns to the notion of evil as privation ("evil is nothing but the diminishment of good to the point where nothing at all is left") or indeed as a signifier without a referent ("the non-entity which is called evil").[79] Neither monism (one divine principle responsible for both good and evil) nor dualism (two rival principles, one good and one evil), Augustine's theology defines God as the incorruptible, immutable, utterly singular, and utterly good source of all being. If God's Being *is* Goodness, then God's creation must be good insofar as it exists. Otherwise, God would not have created it or would have used his power to prevent its deviating from the good. If any aspect of the creation can be called "evil," it is so only insofar as its goodness and being have been diminished and insofar as it has moved closer to annihilation (the reduction of being to nothingness).

Now, I am actually less concerned with these basic principles of Augustinian theodicy, which are familiar terrain for most medievalists, than with their ideological implications. By this I mean not simply how an ethical or metaethical theory yields moral and political praxes but how theory is itself a form of praxis—a means for constituting subjectivity as intrinsically frail, and the body as a privileged site of moral vulnerability and rectification. If, as I have argued above, Augustine bolsters the authority of his own vision of Catholic doctrine by inventing scapegoats (heretics, Jews, women), then might the designation of evil as nothingness be used to legitimate the elimination of dissent or the annihilation of dissenters as already tending toward nothingness? To a very great extent this is precisely how Augustine uses privative evil, though his approach is typically ambivalent and involved. He is careful to specify, for instance, that he does not feel entitled to judge whether a thing should or should not exist: "Far be it from me ever to say, 'These things ought not to be'. . . . There is no wholesomeness for those who find fault with anything you [God] have created."[80] Yet he is also clear that the sinner who has forsaken God and goodness has diminished his or her own existence and has "come closer to nothingness."[81]

Does dehumanization in turn work to legitimate violence? Augustine's theory of the just war (and in particular the aspect of that theory that Frederick H. Russell dubs his "doctrine of religious persecution") suggests as much.[82] This theory has often been exaggerated or misunderstood, and it is crucial to grasp Augustine's ambivalence about violence and the evolution of his thinking on legitimate violence over the course of a long, prolific career. As R.A. Markus observes, while Augustine was under the influence of the *libri Platonicorum* and was seeking to break with Manichean ethics and cosmology, he believed in the "rational myth of the state" and the possibility that through the movements of a rational will man would eventually triumph over irrationality, disorder, and evil. At this point in his career, he was willing to acknowledge that "war, in the appropriate circumstances, is part of a well-ordered society's means of conforming to God's universal order and is thus rightly sanctioned by law."[83] In the mid-390s, however, Augustine's thinking evolved considerably, in large part through a rereading of Paul's epistles. He renounced "his earlier confidence in human resources, intellectual and moral" as "delusion" and acknowledged that "salvation is no longer to be thought of as an ordered progression towards a distant goal" but instead as a goal that can only be accomplished by God's grace and in spite of man's innate, "original" powerlessness to resist sin.[84] This realization prompted Augustine to rethink his notions of rational political and legal order:

> Political power has become a means for securing some minimal barriers against the forces of disintegration. In this 'hell on earth' all the institutions of political and judicial authority serve to keep conflict within check, to secure a breathing space. . . .What impresses Augustine is the precariousness of human order, the threat of dissolution and the permanent presence of chaos just beneath the surface, into which the social order could be drawn at any moment, with the failure of human wills to hold the ring against disorder.[85]

If he was horrified at the sinful realities of warfare and human government generally, Augustine insisted that they were the only power that could restrain sin. Markus argues that "no political thinker, not even excepting Hobbes, has ever given a more powerful or more disturbing description of the contradictions inherent in human society" than in this image of the just and wise man who must kill in order to ensure conformity with God's law and within the faith. Augustine continued to hold this view through the remainder of his career. Markus insists that Augustine was not responsible for checking "the pacifist inclinations of early Christian thought; the credit for that—if credit is what is due—must go to others,"[86] namely Eusebius, Athanasius, and Ambrose. "By the time Augustine began to write, his views on the legitimacy of waging war. . .would have been widely accepted among Christians."[87] However,

Augustine crystallized a "fundamental mood of Christian self-identification with a whole social structure, a system of institutions and functions, including that of war."[88]

This is not to say that Augustine merely wished to justify violence of any kind. Robert L. Holmes emphasizes that Augustine was a "personal pacifist" who repudiated the notion that "private individuals may kill even in self-defense."[89] Moreover, as Markus observes,

> The assertion that under certain specifiable circumstances killing in war may be morally justifiable. . .could. . .serve quite opposite ends: either to raise, or to lower, the barriers against violence in a society. . . .It will encourage one set of attitudes in a society in which war is unthinkable as a human activity, and quite different attitudes where it is readily accepted as normal, and sanctioned by the current norms of conduct.[90]

Augustine was horrified by the cruelty, violence, and greed endemic to the *libido dominandi*, the "lust for rule" that so often motivates warfare. He therefore carefully defined the criteria by which the justness of a particular cause could be assessed so as to avoid condoning indiscriminate violence. The just war must be declared by the proper authority, must be fought for a legitimate cause, and must be fought with the intention of righting an intolerable wrong. Augustine insists, moreover, that violence is legitimate only if all alternative forms of remediation have been exhausted. He expressly forbids clerics from engaging in violence themselves. The clergy must serve as moral guides for the laity and in particular for those secular leaders who could legitimately wage war. Finally, Augustine exhorts Christians to avoid trying "to overcome the bad with the bad. . .evil with evil." He taunts those who attack others' wickedness, arguing that they are blind to the wickedness inherent in all humanity: "O you who have said, *Deliver us from evil* [Mat. 6.13], may God deliver you from yourself!" The decision to use coercion against evildoers therefore should not belong to the individual alone but to a governmental body or authority: "I urge you, I beseech you by the Lord and his gentleness, be gentle in your lives, be peaceful in your lives. Peacefully permit the authorities to do what pertains to them, of which they will have to render an account to God and to their superiors."[91] And yet Augustine's ambivalence about individual acts of violence must be read alongside his firm conviction that the Church may (or rather, *must*) call upon secular leaders to wield violence on its behalf if it is threatened by schismatic movements or other antagonistic forces. There is no necessary contradiction, in Augustine's view, between the pacifist teachings of the Gospels or the divine commandment not to kill and military assaults on the enemies of the faith. After the late 390s, he began to argue that nonviolence was appropriate to the Apostolic Age but not to "Christian times," in which, as Markus puts it, "there is prophetic sanction for the use of force on Christ's behalf."[92] Indeed, Augustine vigorously argues that public authorities, on the advice of the Church, may legitimately kill evil-doers if they are motivated by a desire to expunge evil from the world. In these cases, killing should be thought of not as murder but as a benevolent, charitable act that seeks to heal or correct error. Just as a father may punish a child for its own good or a schoolmaster may whip his students to make them learn, so for Augustine physical coercion that is intended to rectify sinful perversion is not a violation of the law but is instead an act of love: "Love, and do what thou wilt."[93]

Holmes observes that this phrase may be read in two different ways, the one consequentialist ("love moves us as it does because that is the direction in which the good lies"), the other nonconsequentialist ("whatever love produces in the way of conduct is thereby constituted good and hence right").[94] The latter reading, that "any acts chosen by love thereby become right,"[95] is in many ways more consistent with Augustine's teachings. In spite of his personal pacifism and careful regulation of the motives and practice of war, Augustine did not stand firmly against the practice of violent coercion. And yet it could be argued that even the consequentialist argument is not incompatible with Augustine's personal commitment to nonviolence. Holmes insists that love for Augustine is "repeatedly associated with notions like 'severity,' 'discipline,' 'correction,' and 'chastisement.' "[96] It is not "preserved by gentleness" and "can inflict terrible suffering"; indeed, "the pain, suffering, and death almost universally taken to be evil become good when inflicted by love."[97] Thus as Russell observes, Augustine does not consider his doctrine of "benevolent severity" to be an exception to Christ's teachings to love one's enemies. On the contrary, Augustine believes it to be "grounded in evangelical precepts":

> Punishment of evil-doers that prevented them from doing further wrong when administered without being moved by revenge or taking pleasure in suffering was an act of love. The precept 'resist not evil' [Matt. 5.39] did not prohibit wars, for the real danger in soldiering was not military service itself but the malice that so often accompanied it, and the command to 'turn the other cheek' [Luke 6.29] referred to the inward disposition of the heart rather than to the outward deed. Patience and benevolence did not always conflict with the inflicting of physical punishment, for when Moses put sinners to death he was motivated not by cruelty but by love. Hatred was to be overcome by a love for one's enemies that did not preclude a benevolent severity. By this distinction between the inward disposition of the heart and outward acts, to be accepted without serious question in the Middle Ages, Augustine claimed to reconcile war and the New Testament.[98]

Augustine uses a nimble exegesis of the Gospels to advance a claim that might otherwise appear logically untenable: "Love for one's neighbor could legitimate his death, and not to resist evil became an attitude compatible with outward belligerence toward him."[99] In short, nonviolence toward evildoers could itself be understood as a form of violence in that it allowed sinners to be overcome by evil and to infect others with their perversion. To prevent contagion, remediate evil, and extirpate heresy Augustine was willing to authorize extreme and even total forms of violence:

> The just war was. . .total and unlimited in its licit use of violence, for it not only avenged the violation of existing legal rights but also avenged the moral order injured by the sins of the guilty party regardless of injuries done to the just party acting as a defender of that order. . . . Any violation of God's laws, and, by easy extension, any violation of Christian doctrine, could be seen as an injustice warranting unlimited violent punishment.[100]

Just warriors "could kill with impunity even those who were morally innocent"—meaning that, by a rather strange twist of logic, the destruction or privation of being (which is, after all, the very definition of evil) is *not* an evil act.[101] Holmes argues that it is "but a short step from this [doctrine of love as violence] to justifying the thinking behind the inquisition."[102] Augustine paves the way for subsequent Christian thinkers "to lament the horrors of war and at the same time actively to support war's perpetuation" and to "run roughshod over the teachings of the Sermon on the Mount."[103] This is by no means the only ideological dimension to Augustinian ethics, nor its only form of logical or conceptual incoherence. As Jonathan Dollimore has argued, the problematic relationship between good and evil in Augustine's theodicy is imbued with ideological significance, and is so powerful that its influence continues to be felt in modernity: "Augustine inaugurates a punitive metaphysic which remains influential today, not only inside Christianity. . .but outside it too: 'secular' politics is also pervaded by this punitive metaphysic."[104] Dollimore observes that if only a good could lapse into evil (since a truly evil thing could not exist), then there is always a "scandalous proximity" between "virtue and transgression," a "tortuous internalization" of the problem of evil within the good that requires a constant process of "displacement and projection."[105] Augustine himself is aware of this problem and writes in his *Enchiridion:*

> Since every being, so far as it is a being, is good, when we say that a faulty being is an evil being, we just seem to say that what is good is evil, and that nothing but what is good can be evil, seeing that every being is good, and that no evil can exist except in a being. Nothing, then, can be evil except something which

is good. And although this, when stated, seems to be a contradiction, yet the strictness of reasoning leaves us no escape from the conclusion.[106]

According to Dollimore, Augustine never fully resolves this contradiction but instead "leaves the relationship between good and evil notoriously problematic, as the endless arguments within the long history of theodicy testify."[107]

Dollimore is concerned less with attempts to resolve the problem of evil, however, than with "the part perversion is made to play in [it]."[108] Indeed, the most ideologically potent move Augustine makes is in replacing the Manichean notion of "evil as independent, coexistent difference" with a notion of "evil as a turning away from good."[109] If "deviation avoids division (psychic, spiritual, and cosmic)," it is "only at the cost of another kind of torment, the worse for being internal to unity itself. In a sense perversion becomes the norm for a fallen human nature, to be ceaselessly policed within both self and other."[110] For Dollimore, Augustine's notion of perversion represents "Christianity's contribution to the violent discriminations which constitute our history."[111] He reasons as follows:

> That evil remains so inextricably bound up with, some would say indistin-
> guishable from, good, renders the theory permanently unstable. But the
> same instability could become a kind of strength. The very proximity of evil
> to good, which makes the distinction between them so precarious, also
> means that one must necessarily and always seek to distinguish the good from
> the evil. As Augustine says, one knows evil only through good. From here it
> is a short step to knowing good by always and vigilantly distinguishing it
> from evil.[112]

Dollimore identifies three consequences of the interdependence of good and evil: "first, evil as parasitic on good and proportionally so (the greater the good the greater the evil); second, in fallen practice, evil is barely distin-guishable from good; third, good is only known through evil."[113] He then argues that "two kinds of relation between the dominant and the subordi-nate may arise" from this "threefold proximity": first, "those proximities will permanently remind the dominant of its actual instability, all forms of domination being unstable to a varying degree, as well as produce a paranoid fear of impending subversion. So there will be both a justified fear as well as an excess of fear"; and second, "that proximity will become the means enabling displacement and projection, while the justified/paranoid fears will be their motivation: proximity becomes a condition of displacement; which in turn marks the same/proximate as radically other."[114] It is easy to glimpse here "the ease with which this metaphysic will be extended from a supposed natural law (and order) to its social counterpart."[115] In a move pivotal for Western ethics, Augustine describes evil not simply as otherness but as an otherness internal to sameness. Evil is therefore inescapable and permanently threatening, an inbred and insurmountable tendency to deviate from the true path. Evil can temporarily be assigned to a scapegoat, whether a proximate or distant Other; but it will inevitably return and will find its place within the good again. In the end, evil is so threatening and requires such powerful forms of prevention and remediation precisely because it originates as, could be mistaken for, and always threatens to undermine, the good.

We can see here how privative evil rejoins just war theory.[116] If, as Dollimore argues, it is "a short step" from knowing "evil only through good" and "knowing good by always and vigilantly distinguishing it from evil," it is an equally short step from distinction to annihilation. Indeed, Russell provides evidence to suggest that medieval readers frequently "bent" Augustine's theory of benevolent severity in order to justify killing more generally:

> Practically any hostile act was justifiable provided it was motivated by love. The good Christian could suffer injury and yet retaliate, could love his enemy and yet kill him, both forgive him and punish him. The evangelical precepts of patience were transformed so that love was no longer an inhibition on warfare. In some cases it even necessitated it. Now the soldier of Christ could fight not only the sin within himself but also that of other men, men whose inward thoughts remained hidden to him.[117]

Following Dollimore and Russell, I would argue that Augustine and many medieval thinkers influenced by him push their ethical and rhetorical systems to the brink of incoherence precisely so that they may generate conformity through violence or the threat of violence. When Augustine endorses the Church's cooperation with empire (including the use of physical or military force in order to ensure conformity within the faith), he does so in full knowledge that the very principle of human government—man's dominion over man—is itself a symptom of sin. Moreover, he understands war as a consequence *of* sin and a remedy *for* sin; therefore, the very acts by which sin is regulated or destroyed are themselves evidence of an internalized, ineradicable evil. From this perspective, sovereign power is made possible precisely by the moral weakness of human nature, and the secular power of the Church depends upon the existence of indomitable sins, moral perversions, and heretical beliefs internal to the community of faith. Augustine invokes Paul in order to elucidate this point:

> For there must also be heresies among you, that they which are approved may be made manifest among you. . . .For many things of importance to the Catholic faith are stirred up by the heat of the heretics' restlessness, and,

because it is necessary to defend them against attack, they are therefore examined all the more diligently, understood all the more clearly, and proclaimed all the more imperatively.[118]

According to Augustine, we cannot understand the truth of the one true faith unless that faith and its sacred texts are in permanent danger of being misread and perverted by the wicked among us.

In the High Middle Ages, a number of intellectual figures built on the legacy of Augustine's ethics, not only internalizing evil within the good but also striving to legitimate aggressive strategies of "displacement and projection." Some of the most potent examples of this tendency are to be found in Thomas Aquinas's *Summa Theologiae*, which provides a systematic approach to theological inquiry and offers models for eliminating dissent within the community of faith. Before citing specific examples, I should first acknowledge that many contemporary critics believe that Aquinas has been unfairly construed as "the guarantor of Catholic orthodoxy" and "reviled as the ideologue of papal tyranny."[119] As Mark Jordan argues, this is especially true of Aquinas's moral theology and sexual ethics, which are considerably more ambivalent and considerably less systematic and dogmatic than is typically imagined. A number of distinguished Catholic thinkers, most notably Jacques Maritain and Yves Simon, have even sought to forge connections between Thomistic moral and political theory and modern conceptions of participatory democracy. Though Aquinas viewed monarchy as the best form of government, it is true that he invokes both Moses and Aristotle to theorize what Paul Sigmund terms a "mixed constitution": one that "combines monarchy with aristocracy (in its etymological sense of the rule of the virtuous) and democracy, involving an element of popular participation."[120] And yet as Sigmund is quick to point out, the category of "the virtuous" in Aquinas's political theory is exclusionary in the extreme. Aquinas had absolutely no notion of "the modern idea of religious freedom"; he describes women as dependent upon and intellectually inferior to men, and sees their primary function as procreation; and he justifies slavery as an "addition" to the natural law "that has been found to be convenient both for the master and the slave."[121] In other words, it is "useful" on social, political, and moral grounds for men of lesser virtue and wisdom to be ruled by the righteous and the wise.[122] On the basis of these statements, Sigmund concludes that "Aquinas's political thought in its original formulation" is "closer to European or Latin American corporatist and integralist conservatism than to modern liberalism."[123]

Just as we ought not to confuse Augustine's process-oriented hermeneutics with pluralism or egalitarianism, we also must not mistake Aquinas's ethics and politics with true participatory democracy. On the contrary, Aquinas, like Augustine, is ultimately concerned with stabilizing and incorporating Church power. For both thinkers, Scripture is intrinsically vulnerable, liable to righteous as well as wicked readings. That vulnerability translates into the exclusive authority of the Church to minister to the faithful, to define the truth and symbols of the faith, to excommunicate those who resist ecclesiastical rule, and to use secular authorities to exterminate dissidents. Also like Augustine, Aquinas seeks conformity between the violent elimination of evil and the message of nonviolence in the Gospels. He acknowledges that Christ's parable of the sower (Mat. 13) teaches that we must not pull up the weeds (evildoers) for fear of taking the wheat (the righteous) along with them. He also acknowledges the objections that killing the wicked prevents them from repenting and that killing a man is intrinsically evil, even if that man is himself evil. At the same time, he vigorously contests the view that it is "a sin to kill the sinner."[124] In support of this claim, he cites Exodus 22.18 ("Wizards thou shalt not suffer to live") and Psalms 101.8 ("In the morning I put to death all the wicked of the land"). He then offers a philosophical argument demonstrating that evil must be extirpated in order to protect the health of the mystical body of the Church, just as a decayed member must be removed from the natural body in order to prevent infection and death. In response to the objection that the weeds ought to be spared in order to preserve the wheat, he counters that this rule applies only if killing the wicked could harm the good. Christ does not teach nonviolence, he explains, but rather nonviolence toward the good. Replying to the second objection, Aquinas asserts that human justice must seek to emulate divine justice. Just as God sometimes kills sinners and sometimes allows them time to repent, humans may do the same. Finally, in response to the objection that killing a man is always evil, he proclaims that the "man who sins deviates from the rational order, and so loses his human dignity in so far as a man is naturally free and an end unto himself. To that extent, then, he lapses into the subjection of the beasts."[125] Therefore, although "to kill a man who retains his natural dignity is intrinsically evil," nonetheless "it may be justifiable to kill a sinner just as it is to kill a beast, for, as Aristotle points out, an evil man is worse than a beast, and more harmful."[126] Aquinas thus draws the implications of the privative theory of evil to a rather terrifying conclusion: evil detracts so thoroughly from being that it deprives humans of their humanity and transforms an embodied soul into an animal. To kill that unmanned man is not to commit murder but is on the contrary to actualize divine justice and to purify the virtuous by eradicating evil among them.

The "Persecuting Society"

To what extent do these thelogical arguments and ideological fictions play themselves out in historical realities? The connection between theory and praxis, intellectual culture and social realities, is a complex one, and I will not suggest any necessary, causal relationships between them. I will argue instead that medieval systems of ethics and sexual ethics should be understood as ideological apparatuses that share many common features with what historians have discovered about medieval forms of social and political coercion. The arguments of John Boswell and R.I. Moore on the "rise of intolerance" and the "formation of a persecuting society" in the High and Late Middle Ages are at this point so familiar that I will not bother to repeat them here.[127] Other histories of marginal groups in this period (including heretics, Muslims, Jews, lepers, witches, and homosexuals) have also sought to demonstrate that demonization is a disciplinary strategy that affects the society as a whole and that stabilizes the dominant ideology in periods of rapid social, cultural, and political change.[128] If Boswell and Moore's studies tend toward a global, essential, and long-durational view (and have been amply critiqued for that fact), there are an increasing number of localized histories that demonstrate how stigmatization operates in specific social and political circumstances. Jacques Chiffoleau has examined the use of the legal terms *nefandum* [unspeakable] and *contra naturam* in the "epidemic" of inquisitorial trials in the fourteenth century.[129] Helmut Puff has built on this research, investigating the typically lethal use of *contra naturam* arguments in trial records and legal manuals from early modern Germany and Switzerland.[130] For the purposes of this discussion, however, the most immediately relevant historical study is Marc Boone's account of the relationship between state formation and the persecution of sodomy in Burgundian Bruges.[131]

Boone argues that there is a clear rhetorical and ideological connection between political centralization and the persecution of homosexuals in late medieval Bruges. The link involves the political and theological concept of majesty: a fiction of sovereignty that refers secular political power to the supreme authority of God over the creation. Philippe Wielant's treatise *Practijke criminel*, which was the standard treatise on criminal law at the time, condemns sodomy as a crime of lese-majesté, a transgression against both the commonwealth and God himself. The polis as a whole was thought to be seriously endangered by this crime, which (according to a denunciation published in 1494) ruled "celeement et en publique" [both in hiding and in public].[132] Indeed, there were widespread fears in late medieval Europe that "famine, pestilence, warfare and other plagues" were punishments meted out by God for evil conduct, just as Sodom and Gomorrah had been destroyed because of their inhabitants' perversions. In Bruges as elsewhere in Europe, the elimination of this danger involved numerous public trials and executions of sodomites, a fairly regular occurrence especially in the mid-fifteenth century. The evidence Boone gathers suggests that Bruges was, along with Venice and Florence, "among Europe's most important centres for the repression of sodomy."[133] Boone attributes the active prosecution of sodomites in Bruges to the Burgundian ideology of state formation. Laws governing sexual morality were implemented for the purposes of suppressing civic independence and consolidating power within a centralized, incorporated government. Given the specific political circumstances of late medieval Bruges, Boone theorizes that the real issue in the sodomy trials was not sexual morality but state formation. The leaders of the Burgundian "theater-state" used models of sexual ethics from Wielant (who probably derived them from Aquinas) in order to lay claim to majesty and sovereignty and to define any abrogation of power as lese-majesté. This crime was punished by death—execution in the name of public welfare, or as Augustine might have put it, in the name of charitable love. Boone believes that the mode of killing is imbued with symbolic meaning: "The sanction imposed for sodomy corresponded to the perceived nature of the crime: death by burning, the fire symbolizing the ultimate attempt to purify heretics."[134] Since fire reduces the body to ashes, virtually eradicating it, nothing remains of the corruption of the sinful flesh other than the memory of an appalling offense and an unmistakable admonition to those who might be tempted to violate civil or canon law.

The body politic remains vulnerable, however, in spite of this symbolic purgation. Boone argues that the repeated executions of sodomites were part of a larger ideological apparatus that linked sexual immorality to political contestation and defined them both as chronic threats. Since the dominant ideology could not achieve true stability, it needed to invent an internal enemy to combat. In the process, it created a model of political subjectivity in which the health of the collective body politic could only be guaranteed through annihilation of individual bodies:

Demonized since the fourteenth century, sodomy had evolved gradually to become the internal enemy to be beaten (more or less like witches). The fact that homosexuals adopted a sexual life not exclusively oriented towards reproduction made them an easy target for those who saw them as a real threat to society. Their behaviour threatened the order given by God and defended by the prince. Repression of sodomy furthermore helped to shape the collective mentality and to strengthen the grip of the ruling elites of both state and city. Others have recently argued that the creations of marginal people in late medieval society proceeded via a process of labeling and scapegoating. Certainly their approach works for Bruges. The promotion of social integration, the canalization of aggression, the enforcing of social discipline, all were served by the repression of sodomites in general.[135]

The violence motivated by this sexual ideology is above all recursive. As the authority of public majesty was contested or in any way unsettled by historical, political, or social change, the violent repression of a scapegoated other would remain the most effective means for imposing obedience and reaffirming sovereignty.

As Chiffoleau maintains, however, we should not think of the repression of marginal groups as an intentional strategy on the part of specific political agents but rather as a particularly active node in a capillary system of power relations. Invoking a Foucauldian model of power, Chiffoleau speculates that the highly publicized inquisitorial trials of sodomites, witches, and other deviants in the fourteenth century worked to internalize and generalize unspeakable guilt and, in so doing, to evoke a "permanent risk" of crimes against public or sacred majesty. In effect, these trials, and especially the *procédure extraordinaire*, which involved techniques of secrecy and torture, installed majesty "at the heart of all subjects," reaching "the most intimate, the most secret zones of a person" in order to secure and stabilize political hierarchies.[136] The obligation to obedience is thus internalized within the civil or spiritual subject, as is the potential to violate public or eternal majesty through moral infractions. If the infraction is deemed serious enough, the subject is deconstituted as a subject and becomes nothing more than a bestial, frail, exposed body to be tortured or killed in the name of love.

★   ★   ★

The trial and execution of sodomites in Bruges offers a compelling example of the relationship between ideology, rhetoric, and violence in the medieval period. In order to legitimate its sovereignty, the late medieval state or the monarchic Church could reduce the existence of individuals to the mere potential for annihilation, what the contemporary Italian philosopher Giorgio Agamben has called "bare life": "the simple fact of living common to all living beings."[137] Agamben points to a distinction in Plato and Aristotle between *zoe*, meaning natural, unqualified, or bare life, and *bios*, a word that "indicated the form or way of living proper to an individual or a group."[138] Bare life is life construed as the potential for extermination, an intrinsically vulnerable, embodied, or biopolitical form of existence. It is "the life of *homo sacer* [sacred man]. . .an obscure figure of archaic Roman law, in which human life is included in the juridical order solely in the form of its exclusion (that is, of its capacity to be killed)."[139] By his very vulnerability to extinction, the *homo sacer* confirms the sovereign authority of the law or the state to exert force and, among other things, to prohibit murder.

Bare life is, however, not merely a political concept or a means for constructing public sovereignty. Rather it lies at the nexus where metaphysics and politics, theory and praxis, merge and become virtually indistinguishable: "Politics. . .appears as the truly fundamental structure of Western metaphysics insofar as it occupies the threshold on which the relation between the living being and the logos is realized. . . .The "politicization" of bare life [is] the metaphysical task *par excellence*."[140] Agamben proposes that metaphysics does not precede and determine political or juridical action. On the contrary, metaphysics is at its base a *political* operation: it constructs and configures being in such a way as to affirm the validity of the law and the legitimacy of an established political order.

Agamben's argument has obvious implications for the metaphysical, ethical, political, and rhetorical practices discussed in this chapter. Having wounded the very majesty of the state, nature, being, or the divinity itself, the evildoer is easily relegated to the status of a corrupt, irredeemable body. Since evil is always embodied in the good, its threat is ineradicable and must be combated through the body itself. Although the theological principle of synderesis ("the pricking of conscience," an innate and inalienable gift from God) and the very fact of physical embodiment and existence suggest that a sinner is never entirely cut off from goodness, in effect this does little to protect him or her from the dehumanizing force of ecclesiastical or secular forms of sovereignty. As Boone and other historians have demonstrated, the late medieval state was willing to execute sodomites in order to consolidate power within the body politic and to silence fears about the actual instability of the polity and its various rhetorical and ideological fictions. Indeed, the body politic mobilizes the perverse body as an indication of its own potential vulnerability and immorality, pointing repeatedly to an unseen enemy within, a cancerous sin that could easily pass unnoticed because in its outward form it is difficult to distinguish from virtue. The need for ever more rigorous social discipline arises from the perception of internal, irremediable differences. The vulnerability of the polity requires a scapegoat, a perverse body that receives a moral and rhetorical lesson on behalf of the corporate manifold. The sinner's body is destroyed by the lesson it receives. It leaves nothing behind but the awareness that rhetoric and ethics, in spite of their susceptibility to difference and error, carry with them a potential and actual lethal force.

This is, in my view, a logical extension of the ideological strategies that inhere in the symbolist mentality generally. Just as allegory is a vehicle both for conversion and perversion, its susceptibility to interpretive differences prepares the ground for the violent, but only temporary, eradication of social differences and dissent. In a period when secular and ecclesiastical institutions were seeking to consolidate their power, intellectuals of various stripes were able to provide justification for new political realities by inventing enemies to combat. The tendency toward political incorporation and consolidation is coupled with the construction of internal but inassimilable threats: threats that must be eliminated in order to guarantee the stability of a particular ideological world. Indeed, sovereignty itself is construed as the authority to define the nature of evil and the legitimate use of force to exclude or annihilate evildoers, thereby signifying a purification of specific models of identity. Thus if Alan internalizes unnatural evil within the allegory of nature itself, or assigns narcissistic perversion to his own fictional double, it is because the contradictions themselves are intolerable and pave the way for a violent imposition of order and a purging of the community through institutional and ideological strategies. As we shall see in the following chapters, medieval allegories often behave in this way. The instability of rhetorical figurations of truth is directly linked to the uncertain morality of embodiment and the quest for institutional and intellectual uniformity. The awareness that the potential for error lies within privileged, transcendental tropes is doubled by the understanding that the body is the very form of the divine creation, at once a source of deviance and sin, and a privileged site of discipline. The enemy within does not impede or disrupt ideology but is instead a ruse of power: a tactic for installing both the law and its frailty within each body and for transforming all bodies into ideological battlefields.

CHAPTER 2

SODOMY, COURTLY LOVE, AND
THE BIRTH OF ROMANCE: *LE ROMAN D'ENEAS*

The title of this chapter should immediately provoke a number of questions. If the word *sodomy* refers to an intolerable violation of natural, human, and divine laws, what could it possibly have to do with courtly love, which, as it is traditionally conceived, maps out a highly refined sexual ethics or even a religion of Eros? Similarly, if the feudal court is the center of social regulation and secular justice, how could sodomy, which is socially marginal and eventually also indictable, in any way be implicated in courtliness? In short, how could unspeakable sexual aberrations manage to infiltrate texts in which the medieval art of love achieves its triumphant apotheosis?

Paradoxical though it may seem, I will argue in this chapter that the marginality of sexual deviance in the *Roman d'Eneas* is in direct proportion to its cultural and ideological centrality. One of the earliest vernacular romances, the *Eneas* (1160–65) is an anonymous Anglo-Norman "translation" [*translatio*] of Virgil's *Aeneid* in which Eneas's voyage from Troy to Rome traces the geographic and historical trajectory of imperial power: from East to West, from ancient to modern times. Though the romance does not explicitly extend that trajectory to the court of the Angevin kings, nonetheless there is an uncanny resemblance between Eneas's imperial descent and the dynastic genealogies of the French and English nobility—genealogies that (like Virgil's) were used to legitimate increasingly autocratic, centralized, and expansionist regimes. In part because genealogy depends upon successful procreation and pure lines of descent, the romance is concerned with the problematic relationship between sexuality and government, the natural body and the body politic. More specifically, it anxiously imagines the possibility that Eneas, future king of Italy and great-grandfather of Romulus (who founded Rome) and Brutus (who conquered Britain), might have used his body in improper ways, contaminating a royal lineage and subverting the legitimacy and continuity of hereditary reign. Twice in the poem Eneas is accused of "evil" sexual practices. His future mother-in-law proclaims to her daughter Lavine that she must not think of marrying Eneas, who is a "sodomite," "traïtor" [traitor], and "coart" [coward] (8583, 8611; 226, 227) and has "gaires de femmes cure" [hardly any interest in women] (8568; 226).[1] Indeed, if all men were like him, the world would come to an end "ainz cent anz" [before a hundred years] (8602; 227). Lavine, briefly convinced that her mother has spoken the truth, imagines lewd acts between Eneas and his "Ganimede" and condemns her future husband for a practice that is "molt par. . .malvés" [extremely evil] (9168; 238).

Both accusations, but especially the mother's (a lengthy passage remarkable for its spectacular obscenity), stand in stark contrast to the refined Ovidian eroticism the romance will eventually use to describe the mutual seduction of Eneas and Lavine. And yet as I will argue in this chapter, these accusations are not at all anomalous but are instead quite typical of the kinds of ideological appropriations of the body that we see in twelfth-century romances, including the conventions of fin amor, or courtly love. Far from being "monosemantic" (to use Peter Haidu's term), medieval courtly literature depicts the body as a particularly complex, even conflictual signifying system.[2] On one hand, it is charged with physically reproducing the existing political order. Through the successful procreation of male heirs, both male and female bodies are brought into alignment with the ideology of twelfth-century feudalism, in which smooth, uncontested succession is critical for maintaining political stability. On the other hand, we are frequently reminded that the body could at any point give rise to disruptive meanings or give way to unruly desires, thereby threatening the very political order it is meant to replicate. Of course, Eneas eventually does father sons and in so doing inaugurates an *imperium sine fine* that is readily appropriated by the Norman kings of England as a myth of political origins. As in the *Aeneid*, Anchises reveals the destiny of the Trojans to Eneas in the Underworld, parading before his son an illustrious progeny waiting to leave their mark on human history. From the perspective of the original courtly audience, this prophecy is always already fulfilled: the very existence of Rome and Britain testifies to the truth value of Anchises' predictions and to the legitimacy and permanence of imperial rule, whether Latin or Angevin.[3] Conformity to the paternal law is thus overdetermined from the outset: Eneas's desires are subordinated to the imperatives of genealogy, which require that he migrate to Italy, marry Lavine, and produce male offspring. The narrator assures us that Eneas's descendents "regnera toz tens senz fin" [will reign for all time without end] (2990), a phrase that the House of Anjou could easily have understood as a prophecy of its own eternal rule. The conclusion of the romance again offers a detailed genealogy of Eneas's male descent, *d'oir an oir:* "Molt furent tuit de grant pooir / et descendirent d'oir an oir, / desi que nez an fu Remus, / de cel linage, et Romulus" [They were all men of great power, and descended from heir to heir until Remus was born of their lineage, and Romulus] (10149–152; 257). Yet even as Eneas's future is apparently assured, nagging doubts remain about his past. His conduct at the fall of Troy could certainly be interpreted as cowardly or even traitorous, and indeed many "authoritative" sources available to medieval readers describe him in precisely this way.[4] Similarly, Lavine's mother's denunciation casts a pall over Eneas's passionate attachment to the beautiful young prince Pallas and calls attention to the sexual ambiguities of epic and of Roman literature in general.[5] In other words, the homosocial bonds and political mythologies that sustain feudal power are themselves potential sources of moral dissipation. Even more crucially, the *Eneas* imagines the possibility that the very person who embodies the state and enforces the law—the king—could use his body to transgress the law and to threaten the survival of his line and the process of state formation. The romance is caught between the law of the father (Anchises' seemingly absolute control over the future of empire) and the highly contingent embodiment of the law in the son, between the eternity of empire and the necessary mediation of that eternity through temporal bodies and unmasterable, unpredictable desires.

I will argue in this chapter that the *Eneas*, like the other so-called antique romances, *Thèbes* and *Troie*, seeks to bolster an ideology of paternal, monarchic, and statist rule not by concealing the weaknesses within that ideology, but, on the contrary, by exposing them to view. Significantly, Lavine's mother's invective finds no real parallel in the *Aeneid* and represents a conspicuous departure from all the various source materials for the *Eneas*.[6] As such, it is plainly meant to awaken, rather than to allay, fears about Eneas's sexual appetites. The poem seeks to define hereditary rule not just as a metaphorical, political body impervious to change, but also as a succession of natural bodies capable of moral failure and as a rhetorical fiction liable to interpretation and revision over time. As a number of critics have argued, the romance repeatedly displaces anxieties about Eneas's culpability onto other characters—characters whose symbolic deaths and entombments signify a kind of ritual purgation of the polity and the political fiction.[7] Yet in defining power as the capacity to curb or extirpate sexual deviance, the romance must continually reinvent deviance in order to eliminate it. Significantly, then, the sexual deviant is not simply acted upon *by* power but is actually a ruse *of* power. Put another way, the sodomite is not radically incompatible with hereditary rule, but rather is an invention of incorporated political structures—structures that signify their own intactness through a repetitive process of projection and displacement, through the continual discovery and annihilation of internal threats. Ultimately the *Eneas* does not wish to cleanse an imperial lineage of the taint of sexual vice, nor does it seek to assuage anxieties about the possible misdeeds of the founding patriarch. Instead it hopes to instill in its readership the paranoid fear that *any* member of the body politic, including the head of state, could undermine civil order through immoral sexual practices. This fear works to consolidate power not through purification or moralization, but through ongoing contamination. Romance conceives of embodiment as a permanent and insurmountable threat to moral and political order and in the process legitimates the constant policing of individual bodies. It constructs courtly subjectivity as both the potential to destroy the world through deviant sexual acts and the obligation to adhere to the law even at the level of intimate desires, acts, and relationships.[8]

Sodomy is thus not at all a peripheral or incidental concern in the *Eneas*, but on the contrary is wholly central to its ideology of incorporated sovereignty. Indeed, as I will argue in this chapter, the romance takes on Eneas's deficiency as its own structural error: it implies that just as Eneas can never entirely live down his past, so the romance that anticipates his (and the courtly audience's) future is incapable of producing a pure signifier of righteous rule or political unity. The *Eneas* foregrounds the instability of rhetorical and textual meaning in order to establish that the body politic, as a metaphorical construct, is constantly subject to destabilization, and in order to reinvigorate forms of social and political coercion that specifically target the body. As we shall see, coercion in romance is not just rhetorical and political, but physical and destructive as well. Deviant or suspect bodies are pierced, dismembered, burned, and buried; and the romance establishes a clear link between threats to sexual, moral, and political order and the need for a violent suppression of those threats.

My argument in this chapter will proceed in three main parts. First, I will examine a number of major episodes in the *Eneas* in which gender and sexual desire are crucially at issue. I will be particularly interested in rhetorical and specular structures in which sexual deviance is simultaneously repudiated and commemorated, circumscribed and disseminated. If the romance seeks to neutralize the threat of sexual deviance rhetorically, it also demonstrates that rhetoric can never be a fully reliable tool for moralization. The failure of moralizing tropes consistently gives rise to violent acts, establishing that, for medieval courtly audiences, the body is a privileged site for ideological coercion. In the second and third parts of the chapter I turn to the relationship between courtly love and sodomy. Specifically, I draw parallels between the refined allegorical portrait of Amor, the god of love, and lewd descriptions of the sodomite and his sexual habits by Lavine and her mother. In both cases, desire is predicated on the indeterminacy of metaphorical meaning and the failure of binary distinctions, including licit/illicit, moral/immoral, and natural/unnatural.

Here, too, the instability of rhetorical and moral meaning leads to the violent, if largely metaphorical, subjugation of individual bodies, including the puncturing of the lovers' bodies by Amor's arrows and the physical symptoms of lovesickness.

The Rhetoric of Specularity

The *Eneas* is, by nearly all accounts, a meticulously geometrized text, one that adheres rigorously, even slavishly, to a formal structural and thematic design. Most critics understand the geometry of the text as linear and irreversible: it is *continuist* in the sense of marking the permanence of certain major institutions and ideologies through history and *progressive* in that it understands the present as a rectification of the moral and political failures of the past. According to these critics, the *Eneas* works to enclose a set of social values and to safeguard those values against contestation or change through fastidious structural order. Ultimately, its goals are to obviate undesirable interpretations and to impose unanimity on the immediate sphere of reception. Lee Patterson, for instance, believes that the *Eneas* presents the

> ideology of continuous lineage. . .in an especially unproblematic form. . . .
> Committed above all else to linearity, the poet accommodates even the
> errancy of Ovidian eroticism: while the past, whether literary or political,
> may harbor dangerous antagonisms and disquieting contradictions, the poem
> bespeaks a will to consistency that disarms all threats.[9]

Aside from an elegiac awareness of the losses incurred through "the triumph of a historiography of continuity," the *Eneas* evinces a powerful forward-looking "optimism" predicated on the "denial of historicity per se."[10] In other words, "Just as Eneas. . .suppresses the discontinuities and errancies of his past, so too does the poet perform a homogenization of his own literary inheritance."[11]

More recently, Renate Blumenfeld-Kosinski has proposed a similar analysis of the structure and ideology of the text. She maintains that, whereas the *Roman de Thèbes* "emphasizes the seriousness of the threat war poses to a civilized human existence," the *Eneas* stages "the move from Theban gloom to Roman glory" and choreographs a lasting victory for both Trojans and Angevins.[12] Anxieties about Eneas's sexual proclivities are erased from memory by his union with Lavine: "At the end of the trajectory from Troy to Rome. . .the threat of homosexuality has vanished in a legitimate marriage."[13] This dénouement is made possible, according to Blumenfeld-Kosinski, by the definitive vanquishing of past dangers and the moralization of past errors.

In my view, the scrupulous systematic design of the *Eneas* does *not* work to impose irreversible linearity and moral teleology on history, to disavow the past, or to suppress difference and deviance through textual closure. On the contrary, it uses overarching formal structures to challenge the ideologies of lineage and statism from within those ideologies, to suggest the inexorable return of a repressed and morally dubious past by dint of repression itself, and to highlight its own contingency and open-endedness as a rhetorical fiction. The *Eneas* implies that processes of repetition, including the procreation of male heirs and the retelling of history *d'oir an oir*, jeopardize the moral and political stability of the courtly milieu. It would therefore be more accurate to describe the geometry of the *Eneas* as reflexive and iterative rather than linear and irreversible. The poem offers a play of reflections, casting back both flattering images of courtly self-sufficiency and stability and deeply unsettling ones of a fragile solidarity that is rhetorical and manufactured, not essential or permanent. As we shall see, when that solidarity is tested, whether overtly or covertly, the outcome is inevitably violent: the brutal puncturing or mutilation of deviant bodies.

Nisus and Euryalus

Jean-Charles Huchet describes the *Eneas* as a "specular romance" and identifies its organizing principle as "narrative chiasmus," a rhetorical inversion whereby one topos mirrors another with respect to which it is roughly equidistant from the physical center of the text.[14] Indeed, it would appear that the first half of the poem evokes various threats to the courtly milieu, while the second half moralizes those threats: Rome is a proud new Troy; the conjugal, procreative union of Eneas and Lavine corrects the adulterous, destructive one of Paris and Helen; and the virginal princess Lavine represents a purified version of the faithless matron Dido (who, in giving herself to Eneas, broke her promise to her dead husband Sicheus). Similarly, on opposite sides of the physical center of the poem, threats to dynastic continuity reflect and seemingly offset one another. Camille, a warrior woman allied with Turnus, is mirrored by Pallas, a beautiful, beardless youth beloved of Eneas. If Camille bears a man's name, refuses women's work, and desires to kill knights rather than make love to them, her gender inversion is in turn inverted by Pallas, who bears a woman's name and whose death on the battlefield marks the demise of his father's lineage (precisely the kind of catastrophe that Lavine's mother associates with sodomy).[15]

   A final mirroring lies at the very epicenter of the poem: the story of the Trojan warriors Nisus and Euryalus, who are comrades-at-arms, the former a *chevalier* [knight], the latter a *damoisel* [youth or squire]. Together Nisus and Euryalus embark on a glorious but ultimately fatal mission to recall

Eneas from Palantee to the embattled Trojan fort in Montauban. They do
so principally in order to glorify their names and "true love":

> Amoient soi de tele amor
> qu'il ne pooient de greignor:
> unques plus voire amor ne fu
> que d'aus, tant com il ont vescu. (4913–16)

[They loved each other with such a love that they could have none greater.
There was never a truer love than that between them, as long as they lived.]
(152–53)

As Huchet remarks, the language they use to describe their love relies heav-
ily, even excessively, on the mirroring trope of chiasmus. Thus Euryalus
declares to Nisus that he will not allow him to travel to Palantee alone:

> Comant remandrai ge sanz toi,
> ne tu comant irras sanz moi?
> Dunc n'iest tu gié et ge sui tu?. . .
> Ne tu n'iras an l'ost sanz moi,
> ne ge ne remandrai sanz toi. (4943–45, 4953–54)

[How will I remain without you, or how will you go without me? For are
you not I, and am I not you?. . .You will not go against the army without
me, nor will I remain behind with you.] (153)

This is, plainly, a narcissistic love defined by the confusion of, and failure
to differentiate between, subject and object. If the two knights can love
only one another (or the self in the other), they are presumably incapable of the kind of erotic, heterosexual attachments that are so crucial
to male subjectivity in romance.[16]

How, then, does narcissistic mirroring and homosocial or homoerotic
desire operate ideologically? On one level, the meticulous self-reflexivity of
the *Eneas* implies that its deviant elements can have no external referent and
are therefore confined to the romance and the dubious history it recounts.
The narrator describes the mutual affection of Nisus and Euryalus as strictly
incomparable ("unques plus voire amor ne fu") and greater than any other
imaginable love ("il ne pooient de greignor"). If that love can reflect only
itself and is promptly extinguished by the knights' deaths, then perhaps it has
no counterpart within or beyond the text. Its threat would therefore be
anomalous and easily managed or eradicated. Once Nisus and Euryalus are
disposed of, the thematic and ideological center of the romance (if not its
actual physical center) could be understood instead as Anchises' prophecy of
eternal Trojan rule: the paternal *ordo* that gives structure and sequence to
history and transforms Eneas's legacy into an *imperium sine fine*.

And yet the narrator repeatedly reminds his readers that the story of Nisus and Euryalus's love survives their death, meaning that the tension between deviance and the law, or between homoerotic *voire amor* and conjugal, procreative *fin amor*, remains unresolved. As the knights prepare to depart on their mission, Nisus proclaims to his companion,

> Se cest besoing poüns fornir
> et de la puissons revertir
> et faire lou si com ge pans,
> an parlera de nos toz tans. (4971–74)

> [If we can supply this need and return from there in the manner that I plan, we will be talked about forever.] (154)

Anchises' prophecy is thus doubled, even rivaled, by another self-fulfilling prophecy. Though Nisus and Euryalus fail in their mission and do not return to the fortress, their daring exploit *is* in fact remembered; and the romance, by speaking of it, stands as the fulfillment of the prophetic words it contains. In this sense, both the author and his courtly audience are responsible for the commemoration of an intimate same-sex love that is otherwise threatening to the moral and political organization of the feudal court.

This odd self-incrimination is all the more striking because the story is quite incidental to the larger narrative of Eneas's journey and could easily have been suppressed. Rather than omit it, the Norman poet greatly exaggerates its importance by placing it *en abyme*, at the structural center of the romance. This "embedded micro-narrative," as Huchet calls it,[17] is more than a step within a progressive history or a symbolic eradication of a threat to the ideology of continuous lineage. I would agree with Huchet that it is, on the contrary, the axis around which all other elements of the "specular romance" turn, and to which they all perhaps refer. Far from associating Eneas's journey with a purification or suppression of the past, the romance suggests that the future will be contaminated by a past it cannot fully disavow and by unsettling desires that are made present precisely through acts of reading.

Even the union of Eneas and Lavine, which looks forward to a glorious future, is contaminated by the errors of a shameful past. In describing their marital bliss and venerable descent, the narrator hearkens back to the adulterous lust that sparked the Trojan War and to the homoerotic love of Nisus and Euryalus:

> Unques Paris n'ot graignor joie,
> quant Eloine tint dedanz Troie,
> qu'Eneas ot, quant tint s'amie
> en Laurente. (10109–12)

[Never did Paris have greater joy when he held Helen in Troy than Eneas had when he held his love in Laurente.]

Though Eneas's love for Lavine clearly reflects his conformity to the paternal command and the imperatives of history and empire, it cannot move forward toward the triumphant founding of Rome without first returning to the shameful defeat of Troy. Moreover, as Huchet observes, the mutual love of Eneas and Lavine plays on the very rhetoric of specular inversion used to describe the love of Nisus and Euryalus. The couple is joined together through "an exchange of looks in which, as in a chiasmus, each plays the role of subject and object in turn."[18] Finally, the language of negative comparison is the same in the two kinds of love: "unques graignor" and "il ne pooient de greignor." The *telos* of the romance thus explicitly carries the reader back to its opening (the fall of Troy) and, implicitly, to its center (Nisus and Euryalus). The morality of the future is compromised by the return of a past that can never be completely repressed.

As if to compensate for the impossibility of erasing homoeroticism completely, the deaths of Nisus and Euryalus stand as a powerful admonition against the consequences of reckless desire—here, not Eros but avarice. During the course of their night sortie, the Trojan knights decide to plunder the enemy camp. Tempted by the sight of a "hialme cler" [bright helmet] (5086; 156) placed near the fire in Mesapus's tent, Euryalus impulsively seizes it and carries it off as a trophy. As he flees, he is spotted by the enemy "par le hiaulme qui resplandi, / contre la lune flanboia" [because of the helmet which glittered, flashing (*flanboia*) in the moonlight] (5100–101; 156). Nisus escapes, but Euryalus wanders into a dense thicket and is captured:

Ne li menbra de l'hialme oster;
cil lo veoient luire cler,
ne lor poeit tant esloignier
qu'il nel veïssent flanboier.
En un espés boison s'est mis,
ne pot avant, iluec l'ont pris. (5131–36)

[He did not remember to take off his helmet, and they saw it glittering brightly. He could not get so far away from them that they would not see it flashing (*flanboier*). He ran into a sort of underbrush and could not go forward. There they seized him.] (156, modified)

Bemoaning the loss of his "dolz amis" [sweet friend/beloved] (5156), Nisus rushes back to the enemy camp, knowing that he is sacrificing his own life:

Por vostre amor perdrai la vie,
soantre vos ne vivrai mie. . . .
Or m'est avis que trop demore

que la moie ame n'est jostee
o la vostre qu'est esgaree;
ele i sera hastivement. (5157–58, 5162–66)

[For love of you I will lose my life: I will never live longer than you. . . .Now I think I am delaying too long, for my soul is not joined with yours, which is suffering; it will be there quickly.] (157)

He is unable to save Euryalus, however, who is decapitated before his very eyes. Nisus, too, is eventually captured and is likewise beheaded: "O son compaignon l'ajosterent, / les chiés ont pris, ses an porterent" [Thus they reunited him with his companion. They took their heads and carried them off] (5253–54; 159). A number of elements in this passage suggest the impossibility of suppressing a deviant past and the need for a violent correction. The gleaming helmet serves as yet another mirror, casting back the blaze of a campfire or the rays of the moon—and perhaps also (as we shall see) Dido's funeral pyre or the flames that light Pallas and Camille's tombs. The helmet signifies a fatal, indomitable temptation and therefore mirrors Nisus's suspect love for his young companion. Just as Euryalus is unable to renounce his desire for shiny loot, so Nisus cannot abandon Euryalus, his "dolz amis" and mirror image. The poem here self-reflexively associates its own overarching specular structure (of which this episode is the center) with a form of desire that is not only perverse but also unconquerable. Huchet believes that the motif of the shining helmet emblematizes a poetics of self-reflexivity that pervades the romance as a whole.[19] Certainly, helmets, flames, and other luminescent images recur throughout. We might conclude, therefore, not only that Euryalus's longing for the helmet mirrors the attachment that joins him to his "dolz amis," but also that the poem highlights its own lurid fascination with homoerotic desire. If, on one hand, the narrator insists that Euryalus is cornered and literally prevented from moving "avant," on the other, it is the romance itself that carries him forward into the present. Likewise, if the courtly audience is fascinated by the story of Nisus and Euryalus, then perhaps it has gazed too long into the mirror of Virgilian epic and has been transfixed by a kind of love that is directly threatening to its own moral and political order.

At the same time, we are reminded that the consequences of indulging such desires are bloody death and public exposure. In a notable departure from Virgil, the bodies of Nisus and Euryalus are decapitated, perhaps signifying a symbolic castration. The soldiers are reunited in death, but only their heads, which are displayed by the enemy mounted on stakes as a warning to the Trojans. Virgilian homoeroticism is thus not expunged from the text but is used to render the act of reading itself suspect. The murder of Nisus and Euryalus becomes a powerful admonition against impulsive, unregulated, or self-indulgent desires. That admonition is reflected throughout the romance, especially in moments when the progress of Eneas toward Italy is disrupted or delayed. Narrative dilation allows the romance audience to ponder the uncertainty of the future and the violent consequences of deviation.

Dido

Eneas's dalliance with Queen Dido in Carthage, which represents an interruption of the larger historical and political movements of *translatio imperii*, provides another clear illustration of the correlation between gender disorder, unregulated desire, and physical violence. The narrator repeatedly describes Dido as a woman of extraordinary political, military, and economic might. Left a widow when her brother murdered her husband, she is exiled from her native Tyre and flees to Libya. Once there, she manages, through a clever verbal ploy, to trick a Libyan prince into giving her enough land for a new city, Carthage, which she rules with remarkable "angin" [cleverness or ingenuity]. Huchet notes that Dido's cleverness allows her to abrogate a form of power that, under feudal law, belongs almost exclusively to men.[20] Indeed, the text obsessively reformulates Dido's sovereignty as a form of gender inversion. We are told that the Queen "avoit tot le païs / et les barons a soi sozmis" [possessed the whole country, and the barons submitted to her] (405–6; 63). Carthage itself is an unassailable fortress, surrounded on all sides by impassable natural barriers and fortified with marvelous magnetic stones (407–70). It is, moreover, a city of incomparable wealth: "Ne se poüst hom porpenser / de richece que el mont fust, / dont en cel leu planté n'eüst" [A man could imagine no luxury in the world that was not plentiful there] (456–58). The use of the masculine impersonal subject ("hom") suggests an anxiety about the failure of men to discover lack in Dido's self-sufficient demesne. While Dido's power and wealth are initially a source of joy for Eneas, his desire for the Queen, inspired by Venus's "flame" (809), poses a clear threat to his heroic mission. When the couple finally gives way to desire, Fame (or "Rumor") quickly spreads the news that Dido "a retenu" [has kept] Eneas and that he holds her "an putage" [in whoredom] (1570, 1572). The idea that Eneas might be captured or waylaid by a woman (whether Venus or Dido) plainly requires some sort of correction. The narrator informs the reader that the nobles of Carthage, feeling "vergondez" [shamed] (1585) by the noble lady's rejection of them as spouses and by her betrayal of the "fience" [promise] (1597) and "covenance" [agreement] (1598) owed to her dead husband, inveigh against women generally: "Antr'els dïent, et si ont droit, / molt par est fous qui feme croit" [They say among themselves, and they are right, that he who believes a woman is very foolish] (1589–90; 88). Their consensus is apparently shared not only by the Libyan nobles, but also by the narrator. Even Fame, herself a *feme*, cannot be believed, since "d'un po de voir dit tant mençonge / qu'il resanble que ce soit songe" [from a little bit of truth she tells such lies that it seems like a dream] (1557–58; 87). Male solidarity is clearly established here through the repudiation of women's speech.

Eneas's weakness and Dido's "felenie" [1568] are seemingly rectified as Eneas is recalled to his destiny and renews his commitment to finding a new fatherland for his people. Eneas "s'an va par estovoir" [went by necessity] (1656; 89), suggesting an inevitable return to a patriarchal grand narrative after a shameful dereliction of duty inspired by the mother (Venus). Dido, however, is not so fortunate. Despairing at the loss of her lover, she commits suicide with his sword: "El tint l'espee tote nue, / soz la memelle s'est ferue" [She holds the naked sword; she has struck herself under the breast] (2031–32; 97). Mortally wounded, she throws herself on a pyre fueled by Eneas's own garments. The striking juxtaposition of present (*el tint*) and past tenses (*s'est ferue*) in this passage suggests the perpetual imminence of Dido's death, while at the same time eliding the moment of penetration itself, which in some sense we do not witness. I would argue that this temporal inconsistency serves several functions. First, it evokes the memory of Eneas's intolerable penetration of Dido's body, a sexual act that impairs rather than affirms his masculinity. Second, it suggests the didactic value of Dido's story as a moral example for women, who may place themselves in Dido's position and see violent retribution as the inevitable consequence of any transgression of feudal or conjugal laws. Finally, it confines Dido to a moment of chronological suspension in which she remains perpetually threatened by the hero's sword. The outlaw is temporally encapsulated by the romance fiction, while the paternal, phallic law continues to loom large. Once Dido's body is consumed by the flames, her sister Anna has the ashes placed in "une asez petite chane" [a very small urn] (2131; 99) and enshrines the urn in a tomb bearing a moralizing epitaph: "Onques ne fu meillor paiene, / s'ele n'eüst amor soltaine" [There would have been no better pagan if solitary love had not seized her] (2141–42; 99). Her body is destroyed and its remains are captured within the tiny urn; Dido's former greatness is reduced to virtually nothing.

Even though Dido is physically destroyed, the romance does not allow her to be removed from memory altogether. On the contrary, as Christopher Baswell aptly remarks, the epitaph on her tomb, with its "self-conscious," anachronistic description of Dido as a "paiene," actually works to collapse time: either it "inscribes the reader in the past, or the ancient inscribers [of the tomb] in the present."[21] Dido is contained in her urn and is therefore "historically ineffectual."[22] At the same time, the epitaph frees her from historical constraints and allows her to infiltrate a moralized, Christian present. The function of Dido's ongoing commemoration is perhaps not to mark a total suppression of female agency but instead to suggest that past misdeeds will continue to haunt the present. As she burns, the queen proclaims:

> Sor ces dras voil fenir ma vie
> et sor lo lit ou fui honie;
> ci lais m'enor et mon barnage,
> et deguerpis sanz oir Cartage,
> ci perc mon nom, tote ma glore,
> mais ne morrai si sanz memore
> qu'en ne parolt de moi toz tens,
> vials non antre les Troïens. (2049–56)

[On these garments, and on the bed where I was shamed, I wish to end my life. Here I have thrown aside my honor and my power, and left Carthage without an heir; here I have lost my name and all my glory. But I will not die so utterly without remembrance that men will not forever speak of me, at least among the Trojans.] (97)

Mirroring Nisus's self-fulfilling prophecy, Dido anticipates the activity of the original readers of the romance, who not only continue to speak of her but consider themselves to be descended from the Trojans themselves. Dido's crime is not simply that she has violated her obligation to Sicheus but also that she has left Carthage "sanz oir." As such, her transgression is not suppressed but rather is reflected episodically throughout the romance, which is obsessed with sexual reproduction and especially the failure to procreate. As with Nisus, Dido's prophecy suggests that her legacy and transgression will follow Eneas's descent forever in the form of language and history ("parolt de moi toz tens"). The only means for regulating immorality and ensuring descent would appear to be the threat of physical mutilation. The piercing of Dido's body at the site of her failed maternity—the breast—may thus offer a model for managing a permanent, inescapable threat through violent coercion.

Camille

Like Dido, Camille also disavows traditional social roles for women. Rather than occupying herself with "ovre a feme" [women's work] (3970; 135), she takes up the sword and lance, betokening a kind of phallic femininity. In two extensive portraits, Camille is rendered as almost completely indeterminate and androgynous. She is, on one hand, a "damoisselle" or "meschine" [young woman], an object of desire whose beauty (like that of so many romance heroines) is virtually indescribable: "Que diroie de sa bialté? / An tot lo plus lonc jor d'esté / ne diroie ce qu'en estoit, / de la biauté que ele avoit" [What shall I say of her beauty? In all the longest summer day I could not tell of it] (4002–5; 135). On the other hand, she is remarkable for her skills as landlord and knight: "A mervoille tenoit bien terre; / el fu toz tens norrie an guerre / et molt ama chevalerie / et maintint la tote sa vie" [She ruled her land wonderfully well. She had been raised always amid warfare, so that she loved chivalry greatly and upheld it her whole life] (3967–70; 134–35). Unlike Lavine, who is repeatedly constructed as a signifier for the land that will be bequeathed to her husband by her father, Camille is herself a landholder and sovereign ruler. Indeed, she rather clearly joins together the functions of man and woman, husband and wife, king and queen: "Lo jor ert rois, la nuit raïne" [During the day she was king, but at night, queen] (3977; 135).

Even Camille's body is a site of gender confusion. Huchet calls it the "very figure of the undecidable. . .a body adorned with the attributes of each sex."[23] The body is indeed largely concealed from view by Camille's magnificent blond hair:

La coife del hauberc fu faite
en tel maniere qu'ele ot traite
sa bloie crine de defors
que el li covri tot lo cors. (6930–32)

[The cape of the hauberk was made in such a way that she had drawn her blond hair outside, so that it covered her whole body.] (191–92)

While the long mane might initially suggest the queen's femininity (as it does with so many Arthurian heroines), it is here plainly also an extension of Camille's armor and therefore remains intimately bound to male, chivalric attire. Huchet argues that the one part of Camille's body that is exposed to view, her right leg, is similarly ambiguously gendered, given that "the right side is, in the Middle Ages, assigned to man while the left is reserved for femininity."[24] It is certainly telling that when Camille is wounded in battle, she is struck in her left breast, the site of her unrealized maternity: "Par som la guige de l'escu, / dejoste la senestre esselle, / la fiert el cuer soz la memelle" [It (the arrow) flew over the handle of her shield and struck her in the heart near the left armpit, below the breast] (7200–202; 196–97). She is then buried with her right hand holding a scepter (emblem of a king's sovereignty), while her left hand is placed on her breast (7641–42). It is undoubtedly true, as Baswell argues, that Camille's androgyny is even more "dangerous to the renascent Trojan empire than was Dido."[25] For not only does Camille subvert traditional gender roles by daring to exercise male prerogatives, but she also embodies a self-sufficiency in which there is no longer any room for gender difference. Whereas Dido cannot survive without Eneas's love, Camille is utterly immune to sexual desire: "La nuit nus hom n'entrast / dedanz la chanbre ou ele estoit" [At night no man entered into the chamber where she was] (3980–81).

One might imagine that the ritual entombment of Camille's body would mark a definitive suppression or containment of her androgynous threat. Her corpse is enclosed within the walls of a mausoleum—walls that are rendered in minute detail by the Norman author in a tour de force of rhetorical, ekphrastic description. With its massive, seamless expanses of stone, the mausoleum is an imposing, unassailable, hermetically sealed monument. The "covercles" [cover] is "molt soltilmant. . .asis" [cemented on very subtly] (7652; 205), and the mortar is an occult mixture consisting of pulverized rock and serpent's blood. Once Camille's body is placed in the crypt,

l'uisserie fu estoupee,
toz les aleors en desfont
qui estoient laissus amont,
par ou Camile i fu portee. (7720–23)

[the doorway was blocked up, and all the passageways by which Camille had been brought there were taken down from the heights.] (207)

The Queen of Vulcane is seemingly immobilized in death, trapped in an ostensibly immovable monolith.

However, the narrator equally draws our attention to the precariousness of the mausoleum both as architecture and as textual monument. The building is shaped like an inverted pyramid, which, like Camille herself, defies the laws of nature and threatens at any moment to collapse under its own weight: "Grant mervoille sanbloit a toz / que graindre ert desus que desoz" [It seemed a great marvel to all that it was larger above than below] (7629–30). In an era of Gothic innovation, in which verticality depends on increasingly sophisticated supports, Camille's mausoleum would doubtless have appeared to be not merely marvelous but improper and unviable. The instability of this architecture is summed up in the description of a magical lamp hanging near the crypt. This lamp "toz tens ardra, toz tens durra" [will burn for all time, will last for all time] (7678), except in the event that the lamp is broken or struck. The lamp hangs from a chain, the other end of which is held in the beak of a golden dove. Across the mausoleum, a sculpted archer holds an arrow to his bow and aims it directly at the bird. If anyone were to enter the tomb and trip a delicate switch, the archer would release his arrow, hitting the bird, smashing the lamp, and extinguishing the flame. A single breath could cause this to occur: "A un sofle fust tot perdu" [At a breath all would be lost] (7712; 206). We are told that the archer "pot longues viser / et toz tens mes l'arc anteser" [can aim for a long time and can forever stretch the bow] (7705–06). The monument is therefore not immobile and stable, but instead constantly anticipates unsettling movement. Camille is not removed from time, but coexists with, and threatens the eternity of, Trojan rule: "toz tens."

Even more importantly, the bent bow hearkens back to Camille's violent death on the battlefield. After handily killing Tarcon, who taunted her for her "desmesurance" [arrogance] (7081; 194) in daring to fight men and who offered her gold coins in exchange for sexual favors, Camille's attention is immediately drawn to Cloreus. The latter is described as magnificently armored and "trestoz dorez" [entirely gilded] (7166; 196). In particular, he sports "un hialme tant cler / que nus nel pooit esgarder: / contre soloil reflanbeot" [a helmet so bright that none could gaze upon it as it glittered (reflanbeot) in the sunlight] (7169–71; 196). Anticipating Euryalus's demise, Camille irrationally and fatefully longs to possess the radiant, flaming helmet in which she sees a reflection of her own glory: "S'el ne l'a / malvesement se prisera" [If she did not get it, she would value herself poorly] (7179–80; 196). Camille kills Cloreus and then alights from her horse to claim her trophy, foolishly leaving herself vulnerable to attack. While she stands over the corpse, Arranz, the most cowardly of the Trojans, hurls a dart at her "par grant vertu" [with great strength] (7199; 196), killing her instantly. The narrator here offers a moralization, explaining that Camille has been occupied "de grant noiant" [with a great nothingness] (7189; 196) and has sacrificed her life to "coveitise" [covetousness] (7190; 196). This moral is doubled by a violent correction of Camille's gender insubordination. Not only is she wounded in the site of her unrealized maternity, but also the perforation of her body endows the faint-hearted Arranz with virile strength (vertu, from the Latin virtus and vir, "man"). Arranz's virility is admittedly short-lived: though he is "liez" [delighted] (7205; 197) with his deed, still he "paor ot, fuiant s'an vait" [was afraid and ran in flight] (7206; 197). One of Camille's maidens pursues and fells him, proclaiming, "Ceste joie a duré petit; / de ma dame ai pris la vanjance, / vos n'an ferez ja mes vantance" [This joy has lasted little; I have taken vengeance for my lady: you will never live to boast] (7210–12; 197). However, the killing of Camille offers a clear model for rectifying gender insubordination and reestablishing male supremacy through violent aggression.

This model is affirmed by the image of the archer in Camille's tomb. With his arrow nocked and his bowstring perpetually stretched at the ready, the archer signifies ominous, looming dangers—both the threat of a disruption of structural and political order (as evidenced in the verbal architecture of the mausoleum) and a compensatory threat of violence toward those who are responsible for unsettling order. If Camille proclaims her emancipation from "ovre a feme," the *Eneas* seeks to control her unruliness by transforming her hermaphroditic body into a site of ongoing correction and always-impending violence. Equally, if the unnatural rhetorical architecture of the tomb does not contain but instead imitates Camille's insubordination, it nonetheless illustrates the brutal consequences of violating gender norms.

Pallas

The rigorous specular geometry of the *Eneas* plainly designates Pallas as Camille's mirror image and therefore as the flip side of her gender inversion. Huchet provides a detailed account of the two characters' numerous parallelisms, some borrowed directly from Virgil and others invented by the Norman author.[26] Each character has blond hair and is referred to as a "meschin" or "meschine" [young man, young woman]. Camille appears on the battlefield in a purple tunic embroidered in gold by three fairies, while Pallas is buried in a purple tunic embroidered in gold by three goddesses. Weeping over his friend's dead body, Eneas refers to Pallas as the "flor de jovente" [flower of youth] (6147; 176), while Turnus, in similar circumstances, proclaims that Camille was "d'autres fames. . .flor" [the flower of all women] (7400; 200). When the knights are returned to their respective homelands for burial, they are carried on nearly identical biers, adorned with matching ornaments and described in equivalent terms. The obsequies are also in many respects analogous. Both bodies are preserved from decomposition through elaborate embalming processes; both knights are buried holding a scepter and wearing a crown; and both mausoleums are lighted by eternal flames (lamps hanging from gold chains) and ornamented with common motifs: a golden bird, three apple-shaped orbs, and a golden plaque bearing an epitaph. According to Huchet, the effect of these specular repetitions is further enhanced by "the order of appearance and death" of Camille and Pallas, which establishes a relationship between the "embedded micro-narrative" (Nisus and Euryalus) and the "reflected macro-narrative" (Camille and Pallas). Just as Nisus is named before Euryalus in the text but is killed after him, so Camille appears in the text before Pallas but dies and is buried after him. Pallas does not simply mirror Camille but is surrounded by her. The story of his life and death is, moreover, physically proximate to the story of Nisus and Euryalus and (given his passionate, fatal love for Eneas) thematically linked to their "voire amor."

Pallas is therefore profoundly threatening to the gendered economy of the romance, indeed considerably more so than Camille, since he is allied directly with the future ruler of Italy. Like Camille, Pallas is coded as an androgynous fusion of chivalric prowess and alluring beauty; and Eneas's heartfelt devotion to Pallas draws attention to both. When Pallas is felled on the battlefield, Eneas eulogizes his friend as a valiant warrior: "Tu avoies mult bon corage / et graignor pris de vasalage" [You had much courage and greater worth in arms] (6161–62). Later, though, he laments the passing of Pallas's delicate, pale beauty:

> Molt par est flaire ceste vie;
> tant estïés biaus ier matin,
> sos ciel n'avoit plus gent meschin,
> en po d'ore te voi müé,
> pali et tot descoloré:
> ta blanchor est tote nercie
> et ta color tote persie. (6186–92)

[This life is extremely fragile. Yesterday morning you were so handsome that there was not a more seemly youth under the heavens. In a short time I see you changed, paled and all discolored: your whiteness is all darkened, your color all turned to perse.] (177)

That beauty seems to hold particular value for Eneas, who bemoans the premature end to "nostre amor" [our love] (5853; 171) and bitterly laments the loss of this "bele faiture, gente chose" [handsome creature, seemly youth] (6193; 177). Invoking a symbol traditionally associated with the female beloved, Eneas likens that loss to the withering of a rose by the sun (6194). Here the Norman poet is more restrained than Virgil, who describes Pallas as "most like a flower a girl's fingers plucked, / Soft-petaled violet or hyacinth,"[27] Hyacinthus being one of Apollo's young male lovers. Still, it is clear that Pallas, who is endowed with great beauty and fragility as well as "bon corage" and "vassalage," should be taken as an androgynous fusion of masculine and feminine.

Though the mutual love of Eneas and Pallas is less intimate and detailed than that of Nisus and Euryalus, it would be difficult to overlook suggestions of latent eroticism in their relationship. First, there is the pairing of an older, bearded man and a younger, beardless one—the homoerotic love of *senior* and *iuvenis* that medieval readers knew from Virgil and Ovid and that is invoked again when Lavine speaks of Eneas's "Ganimede." Additionally, Eneas adorns Pallas's corpse with garments belonging originally to Dido and to Eneas's dead wife Creüsa (6121–29), thus linking Pallas to those women who were lost or abandoned as Eneas made his way from Troy to Italy. Finally, we are told that Eneas does not kill Turnus in order to win Lavine's hand but instead to avenge the death of Pallas. Forced into submission, Turnus willingly renounces his claim to Lavine and her father's lands, and pleads with Eneas for mercy: "Lavine est toe, ge l'otroi, / o li te les tote la terre" [Lavine is yours: I grant her to you, and with her I give up all the land] (9786–87; 250). Eneas is briefly appeased until he spies a ring on his opponent's finger, a trophy Turnus claimed from Pallas after killing him. Recalling that Turnus was responsible for his friend's death, Eneas retorts, "Ne t'ocirra mie Eneas, / mais de toi se venche Pallas" [Eneas will not kill you, but Pallas avenges himself on you] (9809–10; 250). Pallas is temporarily resurrected in order to take Turnus's head, thus claiming the life that claimed his own. But even more importantly, Eneas here *becomes* Pallas, collapsing the difference between himself and his friend just as Nisus and Euryalus repeatedly claim to be both "I" and "you." In other words, the very gesture that fulfills Eneas's heroic destiny and his father's prophecy of an *imperium sine fine* hearkens back to the "voire amor" that unites Nisus and Euryalus together "toz tans."

As with Camille, the mausoleum that encloses Pallas's body signifies a monumental containment of the threat of homoeroticism, but also a precariousness that lives on through the very rhetoric of containment. On one level, we are led to believe that the tomb can never be opened or disturbed. The vault is structured like an impregnable, monolithic fortress: "N'i ot fenestre ne verriere / ne mes une sole desriere" [it had neither opening nor window, except a single one in the rear] (6421–22). The exterior wall, which is "saine et antiere" [sound and integral (untouched)] (6426), is fashioned from "bon marbre" [good marble] (6426). The flame that lights the tomb similarly suggests perfect self-sufficiency and exemption from change:

> D'abesto an estoit la mece,
> d'une pierre que l'an alume;
> tel nature a et tel costume:
> ja puis estointe ne sera,
> ne nule foiz ne deffera. (6514–18)

[Its wick was of asbestos, a stone which one lights. Asbestos has this nature and property: after it is lit it will never be extinguished, nor at any time will it be consumed.] (184)

The inextinguishable lamp commemorates a death but does not itself succumb to loss. It is, moreover, able to signify an anomaly within nature ("une pierre que l'an alume") without compromising its own nature ("tel nature a"). It would therefore seem to be the perfect emblem to memorialize Pallas: it encapsulates the threat of gender disorder without itself succumbing to unnatural aberration.

And yet the eternal flame also draws attention to the mausoleum's instability as a verbal construct. Even though the flame signifies timelessness, it is also a textual artifact that must be repeated in order to signify and that is therefore subject to interpretation and revision in time. Indeed, the mausoleum is not a real edifice but an intertext: the *Eneas*-poet has borrowed much of his description from William of Malmesbury's account of the opening of Pallas's tomb in the *De gestis regum anglorum*.[28] Though the narrator insists on the tomb's marvelous intactness, in fact the tomb is nothing more than a literary representation of a monument that has already been opened and plundered. This plundering carries with it a clear threat of sexual deviance. We are told that Pallas's crypt is carefully sealed against the elements using a magical substance, "betumoi d'Alfalte" [bitumen from the Asphalt Lake] (6496; 183). This seal can be broken by only one thing: "Il n'est pas gent ne bel ne bien / que l'en le nont apertement, / s'a consoil non priveement" [It is not polite or well or good to name this thing openly, but only secretly, in private] (6502–4; 183). The reference here is either to Solinus's *Collectanea rerum memorabilium* or to Isidore of Seville's *Etymologiae*, both of which stipulate that menstrual blood is the one substance that can dissolve asphalt.[29] Since menstruation would be evidence of failed conception, menstrual blood is precisely that which will be spilled on the soil of Laurente if the tomb fails to warn adequately against gender inversion. Indeed, the notion of an unspeakable pollution no doubt also evokes sodomy, which, as Lavine's mother will later proclaim, could quickly bring an end to the world. The breaking of the seal on Pallas's tomb (which has already been broken, according to William of Malmesbury) would indicate that the temptation of deviance had escaped its encasement in stone.

The porousness and instability of Pallas's tomb suggest that sexual deviance is never entirely distinct from the embodiment of the law in a ruler or future ruler. The law can only retain its validity by repeatedly condemning transgressions. Such condemnation can be found in the lament uttered by Evander, Pallas's father and king of Palantee, upon hearing of his son's death:

N'ai mes anfant qui mon regne ait
ne nul baron qui me manait,
car tuit sevent bien mon pooir,
que vialz hom sui, si n'ai nul oir;
n'avront mes roi de mon linnage
qui sire soit par eritage;
por toi cherrai an grant vilté
toz les jors mes de mon aé. (6307–14)

[I have no other child to have my kingdom nor any baron who will remain with me, for they all know well my power—that I am an old man and have no heir. They will never have a king of my lineage, who would be lord by inheritance. Because of you, I will fall into great contempt all the remaining days of my life.] (179)

Evander not only weeps over his son's lifeless body but also over the body politic, which has been deprived of a legitimate heir. Indeed, quite unlike Virgil's character (who makes no mention of succession and offers only praise for his son's self-sacrifice), the Evander of the *Eneas* excoriates his dead son for disgracing his father and causing the catastrophic demise of his line. What is at stake here is land and rule: "Qui maintandra or mon païs, / mon realme, tote m'enor / dunt tu fusses eir aucun jor?" [Who will now sustain my country, my realm, my entire domain, to which you would one day have been heir?] (6304–05; 179, modified). Once the news of Pallas's death spreads, Evander's kingdom will be as vulnerable to insurrection and attack as Pallas's body was to Turnus's sword.

Pallas's weakness is thus linked to a form of violence far more brutal than any other in the romance, precisely because it targets the body politic as a whole. The feebleness of Pallas's flesh, a rose withered by the sun, becomes the feebleness of his "linnage" and of the kingdom of Palantee. That feebleness will eventually be transformed into great strength through a much-anticipated regime change: Palantee is the future site of Rome,

qui tot lo mont ot an destroit:
de tot lo siegle fu raïne,
tote terre li fu acline. (4805–8)

[which held the whole world in its grip: she was queen of the entire world, and the whole earth was subject to her.]

And yet the mausoleum that holds Pallas's body signifies the coeternity of perversity and empire, weakness and power, Pallas and Palantee. The rhetorical monument that houses Pallas's deviant body is not capable of containing the threat of gender disorder, but can be broken open by the failure to procreate. Equally, the romance cannot moralize the past (including Eneas's suspect love for Pallas) simply by auguring the founding of Rome. On the contrary, the instability of the ekphrastic monument (or of the genealogical narrative) suggests a permanent threat to Trojan, Roman, and Angevin rule. If the law itself is embodied in a frail and wayward ruler, then the law can only exert force by repeatedly subjecting (or threatening to subject) bodies to violent correction. This is perhaps nowhere more obvious than in the Norman poet's reflections on Eneas and Lavine's conjugal, procreative, and allegorical love, as well as his foregrounding of the various forces that thwart that love, most notably sodomy.

The Allegory of Love

If the five characters discussed above represent obstacles to the fulfillment of Eneas's destiny, Lavine and Amor are construed as the keys to dynastic renewal and textual closure. Early on in the romance, Anchises describes Lavine as the woman who will bear Eneas's progeny and inaugurate a lineage of kings. Showing Eneas the future of the Trojan bloodline waiting "prendre mortel vie" [to take on mortal life] (2924; 114), Anchises points out Silvius and proclaims, "Lavinia l'avra de toi, / qui est fille Latin lo roi. . . .il sera roi et de rois peres" [Lavine will bear him to you, Lavine who is the daughter of King Latinus. . . .He will be king and father of kings] (2937–38, 29941; 114, modified). The narrator later confirms the accuracy of that prediction when, at the very end of the romance, he describes the succession of Roman rulers descended from Eneas:

> Et puis fu si com Anchisés
> a Eneas *ot aconté*
> an enfer, et bien demostré
> les rois qui aprés lui vendroient,
> si com il dist que il nestroient:
> l'un avant l'altre ansi sont né
> com a son fil *l'ot aconté*. (10142–47, emphasis added)

[Then it happened just as Anchises in hell *had told* Eneas it would, when he had shown well the kings who would come after him. Thus they were born, one after another, as he *had told* his son.] (257, modified)

If the significance of this genealogy is to legitimate the expansionist, imperial rule of the Angevins, Lavine must certainly play a crucial role. Specifically, she lends validity to Eneas's ancestral claim to Latium (through Dardanus) by bringing that land to the marriage as a dowry. As a virgin, she signifies the purity of the new lineage, which is conceived in an immaculate, unsullied vessel. Moreover, the mutuality and fervor of Eneas and Lavine's love signifies, at least initially, Eneas's conformity to a paternal command and the imperatives of exogamous marriage and procreation. Here, the sexual ideology of courtly love is made plain: the lover/prince's desires and acts must conform to the law he is meant to embody, a law predicated on agnatic descent and unswerving obedience to patriarchy.[30] The love that joins Lavine and Eneas is thus overdetermined from the outset: well before either sets eyes on the other, Anchises has predicted their union and its outcome. Indeed, the father's mastery over future contingencies is emphasized by the twofold repetition of "ot aconté": in his hands, narration becomes truth, and prophecy reality.

Love's Awakening

And yet as the scene of Lavine's awakening to love makes clear, Lavine also exemplifies female sexual agency and a kind of dialogism that is directly threatening to the paternal grand narrative. Spying Eneas for the first time from her high castle window, she is overcome with desire and decides to communicate her love to the Trojan warrior·by writing a letter "tot an latin" [all in Latin] (8777) in which she declares "tot...son talant" [all her desire] (8786; 231). The exact content of the letter is left ambiguous, prompting Stephen Nichols to see in this "suppressed text" a form of "soft-core" eroticism that is both necessary to the goals of the romance as well as unsettling to them.[31] The *Eneas*-poet certainly emphasizes the titillating danger of Lavine's confession: the princess wraps the letter around a "saiete barbelee" [barbed arrow] (8809; 231) and then asks an archer to shoot the arrow into the Trojan encampment, an act that is initially interpreted as a sign of aggression and nearly jeopardizes a cease-fire between the two armies. Although Lavine's gesture is almost immediately reinterpreted metaphorically as a sign of love (the barbed arrow becomes Cupid's dart), its impact on the Trojan forces is devastating nevertheless. Eneas is physically debilitated by his figurative love wounds and is unable to mount his horse the next day. His infirmity demoralizes his troops, who predict the dissolution of the Trojan cause. That Lavine's desire objectifies and emasculates Eneas is evidenced in one of the extant manuscripts of the romance (manuscript A) through a highly suggestive and unusual inflection of the hero's name:

> Lavine fu an la tor sus,
> d'une fenestre garda jus,
> vit *Eneam* qui fu desoz,
> forment l'a esgardé sor toz. (8048–51)
>
> [Lavine was up in the tower. She looked down from a window and saw Eneas, who was below. She gazed intently at him above all.] (215)

A bit later, "Vers *Eneam* a atorné / tot sun corage et son pansé" [She turned all her desire and her thought toward Eneas] (8063–64; 215). Finally, the letter is handed to Eneas by a messenger: "Uns d'aus corut, et si l'a prise, / a *Eneam* el poing l'a mise" [One of them ran and took it, and placed it in Eneas' hand] (8861–62; 232). Here, the inflection of the patronymic (elsewhere declined as *Enee* or not declined at all) marks Eneas as the passive recipient of Lavine's desire: the reconstituted final "m" in *Eneam* is a stylistic use of a Latinate morpheme expressing inactiveness or passivity.[32]

As with Camille and Pallas, Lavine's gender inversion is immediately countered by rhetorical strategies that appear, at least at first, to restore traditional gender order. The Trojans perceive the lovesick princess gazing longingly at Eneas from a vantage point in her father's castle and transform her metonymically into a fortress longing to surrender to the enemy:

> Tel gardant a en cele tor,
> se ses consalz an ert creüz,
> tost nos avroient receüz:
> se tuit li autre l'an creoient,
> molt hastivement se randroient. (9236–40)

[There are such glances in that tower that—if their messages might be believed—the Latins will soon receive us in the city: if all the others think as she thinks, they will surrender themselves very quickly.] (239)

Dido's impervious, literal stronghold here becomes Lavine's pervious, metaphorical one; and Lavine's earlier appropriation of the phallic arrow is transformed rhetorically into a yearning for penetration and capitulation.

If it is the Trojan soldiers, and not Eneas himself, who translate and correct Lavine's threatening gesture, Amor (or Cupid) ultimately works to ensure his half brother's future: "Por lui l'a molt Amors navree: / la saiete li est colee / desi qu'el cuer soz la memelle" [For his sake Love has wounded her (Lavine) severely; the arrow struck her as deep as the heart beneath the breast] (8065–67; 215, modified). After Eneas recovers from his bout of lovesickness, Amor endows him with fantastic strength in preparation for his battle with Turnus. Eneas's surrender to Amor, marked by a dramatic use of anaphora, results in a dramatic physical renewal:

> Se Turnus la velt desraisnier
> molt le quit forment chalongier,
> molt li cuit randre grant estor;
> quatre mains m'a doné Amor.
> Amor molt fait ome hardi,
> Amors l'a molt tost anaspri.
> Amors, molt dones vasalages!
> Amors, molt faiz croistre corages!
> Amors, molt es roides et forz!
> Amors, molt es de grant efforz!
> Amors, tu m'as molt tost conquis! (9057–67)

[If Turnus wishes to do battle for her, I think I will challenge him very strongly. I expect to give him a great battle, for Love has given me four hands. Love makes a man very bold; Love inflames him most quickly. Love,

you grant many feats of bravery! Love, you increase men's courage much!
Love, you are very firm and strong! Love, you are of very great power! Love,
you have most quickly conquered me!] (236)

Even after this triumphant speech, Eneas will remain vulnerable to attack:
he is gravely wounded in the arm by a stray arrow and is once again inca-
pacitated and unable to fight. Yet his body, now endowed with four hands,
has been fortified by love. He is ready to challenge Turnus's claim to
Lavine and Latium and to fulfill the duty his father assigned to him.

As for Lavine, her own injury at the hands of Amor is described as an
explicit loss of self-determination. Unlike Dido and Camille, who die as a
result of their very literal wounds, Lavine is injured only metaphorically.
Those injuries serve a similar ideological purpose, however. The allegory
of love subordinates her desires to the overarching design of Anchises'
prophecy: Lavine has fallen "es laz d'amors, / voille ou non, amer l'estuet"
[into the snare of love: whether she wishes it or not, she must love]
(8060–61; 215). The allegory of love forces her into submission and
requires that she conform unreservedly to the goals of empire.

The Temple of Love

It would be a mistake to assume, however, that the *Eneas* uses allegory
exclusively to verify its grand narratives. For the poem equally draws our
attention to the unpredictability of allegorical meaning and the instability
of rhetorical constructions of power. Thus Lavine's mother, defying her
husband's wishes and thwarting Anchises' prophecy, marshals the allegory
of love in an attempt to convince her daughter to marry Turnus rather
than Eneas. The queen (who remains conspicuously nameless in the *Eneas*
but is known as Amata in the *Aeneid*) employs a variety of rhetorical
maneuvers to teach Lavine how to love. At first she insists that no one can
learn about love "par parolle" [by words] (7895; 211); it can only be understood through experience. Subsequently, however, she offers an extensive
series of metaphors that describe love figuratively as a sickness. If love is not
literally an "anfermetez" [infirmity], she explains, "molt petit an falt" [it is
not far short of that] (7916, 7917; 211). "Pire. . .que fievre agüe" [worse
than an acute fever] (7919; 211), love produces a number of grave physical
symptoms: perspiration, chills, shaking, trembling, sighing, and gasping.
For her part, Lavine misconstrues her mother's description as strictly literal
and refuses to accept that she will ever love if it means to suffer such pain:
"N'an ai que faire" [I will have nothing to do with it] (7935; 212). The
queen rejoins that "Amors n'est pas de tel nature / com autres maus" [Love
is not of the same nature as other ills] (7939–40) and proposes an oxymoronic

description instead: "Cist maus est buens, ne l'eschiver" [This evil (or ache) is good; don't avoid it] (7937).

To illustrate her point, the queen gestures toward an icon in the temple and offers her daughter an ekphrastic description of the portrait of Amor. Whereas she earlier maintained that love is ineffable and purely experiential, Lavine's mother here insists on the transparency and immediacy of the allegory's meaning:

> Garde el tenple comfaitement
> Amors i est *poinz* solement,
> et tient dous darz en sa main destre
> et une boiste an la senestre;
> li un des darz est d'or en som,
> qui fet amer, l'autre est de plom,
> qui fet amer diversement.
> Navre Amor et *point* sovant,
> et si est *point* tot par figure
> por demostrer bien sa nature:
> li darz mostre qu'il puet navrer
> et la boiste qu'il set saner;
> sor lui n'estuet mire venir
> a la plaie qu'il fet garir. (7975–88)

[Look in the temple, how Love is painted there alone, holding two darts in his right hand and a box in his left; one of the darts is tipped with gold, which causes love, and the other with lead, which makes love alter. Love wounds and pierces (*point*) often, and is thus painted figuratively (*point tot par figure*) to show clearly his nature. The dart shows that he can wound, and the box that he knows how to heal. With him it is not necessary that a doctor come to treat the wound which he heals.] (213)

The queen's description implies that the icon's meaning can be revealed without mediation or gloss; the portrait has only to be seen or shown for its "nature" and meaning to be revealed. Yet the queen also points to crucial ambiguities in the allegory of love, especially through the pun on *point* (from the Latin *pungere*, meaning "to puncture or stab") and *poinz*, the past participle of *poindre* or *peindre* (from *pingere*, "to paint or draw"). The literal meaning (Amor pierces lovers with darts) is doubled by a metaphorical one (Amor causes lovers to fall in and out of love), and the phrase "point tot par figure" offers a clear indication for how the allegory should be interpreted. Yet we might also understand Amor as himself a producer of metaphors ("point sovant") or as pierced *by* metaphor ("point tot par figure"). A slippage of meaning between the two verbs leaves us to wonder whether Amor's function is to pierce or to paint, to cause love or to produce figures.

The allegory of love seemingly cannot be reduced to a singular gloss, nor is its meaning immediately discernable. Rather than the ideal convergence of form and content implicit in the phrase "Amors fet amer," the allegory points to a diversity of meanings, and perhaps also desires. Indeed, the queen's explanation that Amor can either "fet amer" or "fet amer diversement" suggests the allegory's liability to interpretive difference. The word "diversement" (which is borrowed directly from Ovid)[33] stems from the Latin *diversus*, meaning "differing or opposing" but also "varied or variable." "Amer diversement" could suggest a separation of lovers, but it could equally be read as the kind of semantic shifting and polymorphous desires for which Ovid was widely known. Above all, it is clear that in spite of her statements to the contrary, the queen's depiction of Amor does not produce a stable, conventional doubling of sense (saying one thing and meaning another), but is on the contrary polysemous and undecidable.

Of course at this particular moment in the text, the flexibility of allegorical meaning is useful for advancing the romance's ideological ends. In order to ensure her future, Lavine must resist her mother's demands through misinterpretation, whether deliberate or unintentional. Moreover, the allegory of love eventually does take on more decisive meaning. Immediately after her mother leaves her chambers, Lavine sees Eneas for the first time and is struck by Amor's dart. Amor clearly refuses to work on behalf of a "false" maternal power but sides instead with father and fatherland. The allegory thus sustains the illusion of Anchises' mastery over the course of history and also, apparently, over the figuration of desire. Yet this same episode also makes clear that the allegory can never be definitively resolved or completed and that its incompletion can give rise to another, equally dangerous form of agency: female sexual desire. Thus Lavine, after having been wounded by a metaphor, invents one of her own:

Ge sui une meschine fole,
novelement m'as a t'escole,
tot ai apris an moins d'un jor,
les maus, la poine, la dolor;
forment me plain, griément me deuil.
Amors, car retorne ton foil,
de l'autre part me fai garder! (8211–17)

[I am only a foolish maiden, and you (Amor) have me newly in your school, but I have learned in less than a day all the ills, the pain, and the sorrow. Bitterly I complain, grievously I lament. Love, turn over your page (*retorne ton foil*), make me look in another place!] (218)

When her mother taught her about Amor, Lavine naively misread the pangs of lovesickness as literal and sought the meaning of love in physical illness. Under Amor's tutelage, however, she invents tropes of her own: school and lesson, page and book. Lavine depicts herself as a disciple instructed by her master in the ways of love and subordinated to a teaching she is forced to learn against her will. Yet her submission to Amor is also the starting point for her own brand of authorship, and the skills she requires "a t'escole" are clearly defined as a form of literacy (indeed *Latin* literacy, the privileged domain of the medieval clerical elite) that would normally have been withheld from women.

This literacy is in fact as much about linguistic and intellectual training as submission to the beloved. Instructed by Amor or awakened to love, Lavine acquires the ability to invent her own metaphorical and erotic fictions. Thus she expresses her yearning to confide her love to a friend, implying that love is not just a desire to be joined to the beloved but a desire to speak about love itself:

> S'or trovoie qui m'escotast
> et de mon consoil me celast,
> g'en savroie maint bon trait dire. (8315–17)

> [If now I should find someone who would listen to me, and who would hold my words in confidence, I would know how to speak many good things about it.] (220)

Since Lavine has no confidant, her love takes the form of extended passages of interior monologue replete with the very Ovidian metaphors she had previously misunderstood: darts, wounds, joy, pain. In spite of this accumulation of figures, Lavine is unable to explain the nature of her love fully:

> La meschine ert a la fenestre,
> ne pooit dire tot son estre,
> ne ce que sent de son ami. (8381–83)

> [The maiden stood at the window. She could not express all her condition (literally, her entire being), nor what she felt toward her beloved.] (221–22)

Love is here quite conspicuously a rhetorical and fictional invention, one that is desirable precisely because it is incomplete and open to interpretation. Amor represents, in other words, an unfulfillable desire for an adequate representation of love and self: Lavine cannot say "ce que sent de son ami" nor "tot son estre." The *Eneas* demonstrates that the allegory of love has no internal coherence or formal unity; on the contrary, love and the lover are disrupted through acts of loving and speaking. Contradicting her mother's earlier statement that love cannot be learned "par parolle,"

Lavine reveals instead that love actually *is* "parolle," a desire *for* and *in* language.

Naming the Beloved

Though Lavine cannot speak of her love in concrete terms, she does identify her beloved by name. In doing so she manages to dismember the patronymic, thereby suggesting the unsettling effects of women's speech and desire on patriarchy, genealogy, and history. After first glimpsing Eneas from her window, she spends a sleepless night tormented by love pangs. The following day she is confronted by her mother, who notices that Lavine is pale and asks after her health. Echoing her mother's descriptions of Amor, Lavine responds that she has a fever. Yet "bien sot la mere qu'el mentoit, / altrement ert que ne disoit" [the queen knew well that she was lying, that it was otherwise than she said] (8451–52; 223). Lavine strategically echoes her mother's allegorical discourse, speaking of her love "altrement" but hoping she will be taken literally. The queen easily guesses that her daughter loves, however, and indeed, that "tu l'aimes par amor" [you love him *par amour*] (8530; 225). At her mother's insistence, Lavine names her beloved. Whereas Anchises consistently addresses his son as "Fils Eneas" (2169, 2839, 2879, and 2889) and thus links the name to filial duty and piety, Lavine speaks haltingly, dividing the name into its constitutive syllables:

> Il a non "E . . ."
> puis sospira, se redist: "ne . . . ,"
> d'iluec a piece noma: "as . . . ,"
> tot en tranblant lo dist en bas.
> La raïne se porpensa
> et les sillebes asanbla.
> Tu me diz "E" puis "ne" et "as";
> ces letres sonent "Eneas."
> Voire, dame, par foi, c'est il. (8553–60)

> ["He is named E." Then she sighed, and added, "ne," then after a while, "as." She spoke it softly, all trembling. The queen thought and assembled the syllables. "You tell me *E*, then *ne*, and *as*; these letters spell Eneas!" "True, mother; in faith, it is he."] (226)

As Michel Zink argues, Lavine, in naming Eneas as the object of her affections, denies him three times.[34] First, the three syllables in Eneas's name produce the phrase "e ne as," meaning "and you have not." Second, the effect of liaison and nasalization in Old French could transform the phrase *il a non e* into *il a non ne*, or "he has the name 'not' (the particle *ne*)." Finally, we can add to this a pun on the word *non*, which can mean either "name" or "no." Simon Gaunt maintains that this passage should be read as Lavine's challenge to her mother's "pseudo-authority," since the queen herself remains conspicuously nameless in the Eneas.[35] He further notes that the queen's repetition of the syllables pronounced by Lavine could be read as her "composition" of Eneas's name, "the assembly of his identity" rather than its "disintegration."[36] And yet Lavine certainly also exposes a flaw within the patronymic: rather than simply a signifier of the *imperium sine fine*, it is also a sequence of syllables that is uttered in time and that contains unsuspected, destabilizing meanings: not plenitude and sufficiency but nothingness, fragmentation, and lack. Even more crucially, it names namelessness, which is both Lavine's mother's predicament (she is never called Amata, as she is in the *Aeneid*) and a common trope for sexual perversion (*nefandum*). In an attempt to name its protagonist as a conqueror of lands and a woman, the romance (through the words of its heroine) instead transforms him into the embodiment of a crisis: an unspeakable defect in speech (which does not contain its object but instead points to its lack) and a hideous crime "unfit to be named among Christians."

Of course, it is also the case that Lavine is inflamed with desire for the appropriate love-object and ultimately fulfills the destiny that has been scripted for her by Anchises. And yet perhaps this, too, is not a truly normative form of desire, but rather a threatening form of gender inversion. After all, it is Lavine who desires Eneas and initiates the seduction. She is pierced by Amor's darts and subjugated to the allegorical fiction, but in turn she usurps the phallic instrument for her own purposes, whether the arrow, the pen, or the gaze. The allegory of love thus affords the possibility of a deviant inversion of gender order, or even (as is so often the case in the *fabliaux*) the mobility of the phallus: a metaphorical, detachable, and floating signifier rather than a literal member. The *Eneas* uses Lavine and the allegory of love to suggest that female desire, literacy, and agency may have unpredictable effects, including the appropriation of language and metaphor to produce meanings that are fundamentally destabilizing to patriarchy.

Sodomy

As a number of critics have argued, this acknowledgment and apparent valorization of female sexuality require a compensatory gesture: the erasure of Lavine from the very genealogy she helps to create and the bracketing of her desire through strategies of rhetorical and narrative control. Huchet writes, "Once married, Lavine brutally disappears from the fiction; the romance is completed through a rapid evocation of Eneas's descent, thus inscribing in reality and History the truth contained in the paternal word."[37] Baswell similarly believes that Lavine's " 'independent' desire for Eneas" only serves to align her "with a preference that her father, guided by the pantheon, has already expressed. This narrative containment of Lavine climaxes a whole series of strategies by which the poem contains feminine challenges to the order of patriarchal will or divine power."[38] In effect, Lavine's desire is never entirely her own: Anchises' prophecy scripts both her marriage to Eneas and her removal from the genealogy she is responsible for producing. The fact that the love is fully reciprocal also serves to exonerate Eneas: in spite of past failings, the Trojan prince is capable of fulfilling his duty to his father and the fatherland through conquest, marriage, and procreation.

Yet if Lavine's role is to moralize the founding of a new dynasty, it is also the case that before her marriage she is herself responsible for tarnishing her future husband's reputation, perhaps irremediably. The union of Trojan prince and Latin princess, and the genealogy that results from it, are preceded by two extensive diatribes in which Eneas is accused of sexual immorality, first by Lavine's mother and subsequently by Lavine herself. Lavine will eventually retract her accusation, and in some sense that retraction exonerates Eneas and (as Gaunt puts it) repudiates the "type of male bonding exemplified. . .by Pallas and Eneas, and Nisus and Eurialus."[39] And yet I would argue that these accusations also work to conflate desire, whether normative or deviant, with linguistic slippage and to demonstrate that even fictions of patriarchal power are subject to the vicissitudes of interpretation and unpredictability of desire. Discourse itself, including the moralizing tropes used to condemn the sodomite and to arrive at a normative closure, is revealed to be perilously indeterminate. Even as the romance attempts to name and disavow the unnamable vice, it spawns a profusion of rhetorical figures that are ultimately more seductive and proliferating than moralizing and restrictive.

Lavine's Mother

Thus in her bilious denunciation of Eneas, Lavine's mother condemns sodomy as a heinous, world-destroying vice but at the same time fails to explain what precisely the word "sodomite" means. Though the language of the passage is meant to be morally and tactically effective (excoriating the Trojans for their vice and transforming Lavine's love into hate), it also offers a titillating play of meanings in which stable referents and transparent meanings are conspicuously absent. When Lavine acknowledges her love for "E. . .ne. . .as," the queen asks:

Que as tu dit, fole desvee?
Sez tu vers cui tu t'es donee?

Cil cuiverz est de tel nature
qu'il n'a gaires de femmes cure;
il prise plus lo ploin mestier;
il ne velt pas biset mangier,
molt par aimme char de maslon;
il priseroit mialz un garçon
que toi ne altre acoler;
o feme ne set il joër,
ne parlerast pas a guichet;
molt aime fraise de vallet;
an ce sont Troïen norri.
Molt par as foiblemant choisi.
N'as tu oï comfaitement
il mena Dido malement?
Unques feme n'ot bien de lui,
n'en avras tu, si com ge cui,
d'un traïtor, d'un sodomite.
Toz tens te clamera il quite;
se il avoit alcun godel,
ce li seroit et bon et bel
quel laissasses a ses druz faire;
s'il lo pooit par toi atraire,
nel troveroit ja si estrange
qu'il ne feïst asez tel change,
que il feïst son bon de toi
por ce qu'il lo sofrist de soi;
bien lo lairoit sor toi monter,
s'il repueit sor lui troter;
il n'aime pas poil de conin.
De cest sigle seroit tost fin,
se tuit li home qui i sont
erent autel par tot lo mont;
ja mes feme ne concevroit,
grant sofraite de gent seroit;
l'an ne feroit ja mes anfanz,
li siegles faudroit ainz cent anz.
Fille, molt as lo sens perdu,
quant de tel home as fait ton dru
qui ja de toi ne avra cure
et qui si fet contre nature,
les homes prent, les fames let,
la natural cople desfait.
Garde nel me dïes ja mes;
ceste amistié voil que tu les,
del sodomite, del coart. (8565–8611)

[What have you said, foolish mad woman? Do you know to whom you have given yourself? This wretch is of the sort who have hardly any interest in women. He prefers a wholly different trade (*lo ploin mestier*): he will not eat hens (*biset mangier*), but he loves very much the flesh of a cock (*char de maslon*). He would prefer to embrace a servant-boy rather than you or any other woman. He does not know how to play with women, and would not parley at the wicket gate (*parler au guichet*); but he loves very much a young man's ass (*fraise de valet*). The Trojans are raised on this (*an ce sont norri*). You have chosen very poorly. Have you not heard how he mistreated Dido? Never did a woman have any good from him, nor do I think you will have, from a traitor and a sodomite. He will always be ready to abandon you. If he finds a debauched minion (*godel*), it will seem well and good to him that you should give yourself to his favorites. And if he can attract the boy by means of you, he will not find it too outrageous to make an exchange, so that the boy will have his pleasure from you, while in turn sufficing for him. He will gladly let the boy mount you (*toi monter*), if he in turn can ride him (*lui troter*): he does not love coney fur (*poil de conin*). It would quickly be the end of this life if all men were thus throughout the world. Never would a woman conceive; there would be a great dearth of people; no one would ever bear children, and the world would fail before a hundred years. Daughter, you have completely lost your senses, since you have taken as your love such a man, who will never have a care for you, and who acts so against nature that he takes men and leaves women, undoing the natural union. Take care that you never speak to me of him again. I wish you to give up the love of this sodomite, this coward.] (226–27, modified)

In a celebrated essay, Erich Auerbach argues (somewhat obtusely, it must be said) that Lavine's mother here "accuses Aeneas and the Trojans of homosexuality in *very plain language*."[40] And yet the most cursory reading of the text reveals that there is precious little that is plain in the queen's invective. To be sure, the passage is striking for its obscenity; but that obscenity depends upon equivocalness and polysemy rather than any transparent evocation of sexual acts. Indeed, the acts and desires the queen evokes here (whether "natural" or "contre nature") are so ambiguous that strict distinctions between norm and transgression or literal and figurative meanings are virtually impossible. In order to grasp the obscenities of the passage, we must read it on literal and figurative levels simultaneously. *Biset*, for instance, literally means "pigeon" or "dove" and figuratively suggests a woman (one of the common metaphorical uses of the term in Old French). Here, it is also a synecdoche (not the woman but her genitals) and therefore suggests a metaphorical "meal" or oral stimulation. The queen is suggesting, first, that Lavine will be disappointed in her husband's refusal to offer her pleasure with his mouth and tongue; and second, that having an interest in women (*avoir de femmes cure*) implies an appetite for cunnilingus.

To take another example, *poil de conin*, like *biset*, can be understood literally as the fur of a coney or rabbit; yet in this context it should presumably be understood both as a metaphor (Eneas does not like "cunt hair") and as a synecdoche (simply, he does not like "cunt"). This reading is confirmed by a salacious pun: *conin* (rabbit, from the Latin *cuniculus*) evokes *con* (from *cunnus*, the basic Latin obscenity for the vagina).

Though not strictly speaking a metaphor, the term *char de maslon* certainly should be read as a pun and synecdoche. *Char* can refer to animal meat or human flesh, while *maslon* means either "wild duck" or "male," especially a diminutive man or perhaps a boy. Eneas's desire is therefore directed either at a duck dinner, at male flesh, or at the part of a man's body that confers masculinity, presumably the genitals. Since the word *char* suggests a meal, and since Lavine's mother claims in the very next line that the Trojans are actually nourished (*norri*) on such things, the implication is that Eneas enjoys performing fellatio. Still more complex is *fraise*, which means either "tripe" or "ribbon." *Fraise de vallet* could be interpreted literally as the bowels of a young man or as an ornate or effeminate garment or undergarment. It could also be taken metaphorically as his ass (that which the undergarment covers). Since the word *fraise* primarily evokes animal guts (the stomach, pancreas, and intestines of a ruminant), the queen is perhaps referring to another metaphorical "meal"—that is, not just anal intercourse but anilingus as well. This reading is certainly corroborated by the juxtaposition of *fraise de vallet* with *parler au guichet*, which could be interpreted either as a tryst in the garden or as cunnilingus. Taken literally, *parler au guichet* simply means chatting at the wicket gate (a door within a door) or even through a chink in the wall (perhaps a reference to Ovid's story of Pyramus and Thisbe). Here, though, it clearly has a scabrous, figurative sense. *Parler* is a common euphemism for sexual intercourse in the Middle Ages, and doorways or openings are traditional metaphors for the vagina. The phrase could therefore be understood as vaginal penetration or even cunnilingus. The word *parler* indeed suggests that this act involves the tongue, and the queen's overriding concern in the passage seems to be oral copulation.

It is certainly telling that this particular signifier should literally refer to speech and metaphorically to a nonprocreative sexual act. Here as elsewhere, the *Eneas* points to a close but fraught relationship between language and desire, rhetoric and the body, a figurative tongue (the faculty of speech) and a literal one (the fleshly member). Crucially, that relationship involves the proliferation of alternate or competing meanings rather than any straightforward act of denotation. Far from succinctly and categorically condemning forbidden acts or sanctioning licit ones, Lavine's mother deploys a particularly oblique, varied, and playful erotic vocabulary, one that gives rise to multiple possible readings and that locates deviant sexual pleasure of various kinds in the involutions of metaphorical interpretation. More to the point, the queen's tirade operates *both* as a limitation or repression of difference (for instance, designating Eneas's conduct as fundamentally negative, i.e., "contre nature" or world-destroying) *and* as an unstable production of difference through figure (signifying multiple taboo acts through metaphorical transfer).

I would argue that both of these operations serve to advance the romance's ideological agenda. On one hand, Lavine's mother voices a concern of the romance as a whole, perhaps even its overriding concern: that the future ruler might betray his responsibilities to the feudal monarchy and might use his body to violate the law he will be expected to embody and uphold. On the other hand, the romance uses the queen's titillating and highly equivocal erotic language to point to dangers intrinsic to the act of interpretation itself and to suggest that even a moralizing discourse could give rise to improper, unanticipated meanings and desires. Indeed, Lavine's mother here renders discursive contingency wholly perverse: she verbosely names forbidden acts, betrays her own rather too intimate knowledge of deviant sexual acts, and puts her "tongue" in every orifice she can imagine as erogenous. In maligning her future son-in-law as a sodomite, the queen speaks not just of unnatural desires but also of her own prurient interests in speaking about "speaking." By demonstrating, moreover, that the possibility for impropriety is intrinsic to language itself (including, or perhaps even especially, the language of moralization and censorship), the *Eneas* suggests that interpretation could give rise to a profusion of "immoral," socially unacceptable meanings and desires.

Lavine's mother's conception of sodomy is thus paradoxically both sterile and fertile. Though she claims it thwarts nature and could lead to the demise of human generations, sodomy nonetheless parodies procreation through a particularly fecund form of semiosis. Scrupulously avoiding a strictly literal, denotative, or anatomical vocabulary, and reveling in the myriad ways of naming what she forbids to be named ("garde nel me dies ja mes"), the queen allows the word *sodomite*, its cognates, and synonym group to ramify in many different directions at once. Not unlike an allegory, *sodomy* is both an abstract representation of moral failure (a defect in nature and even the potential to destroy nature itself) and a signifier pointing toward an ineffable meaning so outrageous it can only be spoken of "otherwise," through circumlocution.

If this incompatibility of signifier and signified is somehow procreative (leading to a flowering of alternate meanings), and if sodomy is never fully distinguished from "natural," procreative acts, then deviance is all the more difficult to recognize and control. Indeed we might conclude that the queen here renders *all* desire perverse, since the libido (whether "natural" or "unnatural") is directed not toward bodies but toward a regression of signifiers, tropes that metamorphose the body and its members into beasts (birds, rodents, horses). More to the point, Cupid (the god of love) and Eneas (the alleged sodomite) are literally brothers, both offspring of Venus, whose erotic machinations are notoriously unpredictable and unsettling. This alternate, maternal genealogy, which is internalized within the romance's official, paternal one, links desire not to the procreation of male heirs but to alternate meanings spawned by venereal desire and perpetuated in language. As we have seen, the internalization of defect in language fuels ideologically useful fears of instability, including the failure of dynastic renewal, the collapse of the sovereign state, and the end of the world itself. It also suggests that those fears can never be fully quieted, that moral and immoral, productive and destructive desires can never entirely be separated, and that they require constant vigilance. The sodomite is thus not radically incompatible with the feudal state or courtly romance but is, on the contrary, a construction of feudal ideology and an enemy internal to it.

Lavine

Lavine's own attack on Eneas suggests the insidious power of this internal enemy. Temporarily swayed by her mother's invective, Lavine, too, accuses Eneas of sexual crimes and calls into question the sexual virtue of the founding patriarch. In the process, she demonstrates that moral deviance is internal to the language of moral outrage and compromises her own purity through metaphorical play. Though the Trojan prince has succumbed to her charms, Lavine becomes confused when he does not appear beneath her window one day. The reality is that Eneas has been struck down by Amor and is wasting away from lovesickness. However, Lavine takes his absence as proof of debauchery:

> "Ce est," fait ele, "verité,
> que ma mere m'a de lui dit;
> de feme lui est molt petit,
> il voldroit deduit de garçon,
> n'aime se males putains non.
> Son Ganimede a avec soi,
> asez li est or po de moi;
> il est molt longuement an ruit,
> a garçon moine son deduit;
> quant a mené o als son galt,
> de nule feme ne li chalt.
> Buer sera or la dame nee
> qui a tel home ert mariee;

molt avra de lui bon confort
et bele amor et bel deport:
il l'esparnerat longuement,
ne l'en prendra longues talant.
Bien voi que de feme n'a soing;
il n'a de tel deduit besoig;
unc puis que sot quel vols amer,
ne deigna ceste part garder;
puis qu'il me vit a la fenestre,
que li ai fait savoir mon estre,
n'i esteüst il a nul fuer:
de moi veor ot mal al cuer.
Molt me prisast mialz Eneas,
se j'aüsse fanduz les dras
et qu'eüsse braies chalcies
et lasnieres estroit liees.
Il a asez garçons o soi,
lo peor aime mialz de moi,
fandue trove lor chemise;
maint an i a an son servise,
lor braies sovant avalees:
issi deservent lor soldees.
Maldite soit hui tel nature
d'ome qui de femme n'a cure;
il est de ce toz costumiers.
Molt par est malvés cist mestiers
et molt par a fol esciant
qui feme let et home prent." (9130–170)

["What my mother told me about him is the truth," she said. "Women mean very little to him. He would like his pleasure from a man, and will love no one except evil whores. He has his Ganymede with him, and a very little of me is now enough for him. He is very long at his pleasure (*ruit*), and is enjoying his delight with a man. Since he has enjoyed his amorous pleasure with them, no woman matters to him. Happily born will be the lady who is married to such a man! She will have much good comfort and fair love and fine pleasure indeed from him! He will spare her for a long time, and will not often take his pleasure with her. I see well that he has no care for women, and no need for such pleasures. Never since he knew that I would love him has he deigned to look in this direction. Since he saw me at the window where I have made my feelings known to him, he would not stop there for any price: he is repulsed at the idea of seeing me. Eneas would have prized me much more if I had split my clothes and if I had hose breeches and tightly tied thongs. He has plenty of men with him, and loves the worst of them better than me. He finds them with their shirts split. He has many of them at his service, and their breeches are often lowered: thus they earn their wages.

May that kind (*nature*) of man who has no interest in women be cursed today; and he follows that custom completely. The business is extremely evil, and he who leaves women and takes men is wholly mad in his judgment."] (237–38, modified)

Whereas earlier Lavine coyly misconstrued her mother's portrait of Amor as literal, here she demonstrates that she has fully grasped the significance of the queen's obscene, metaphorical description of the sodomite's crimes. Indeed, she makes use of that description for her own purposes, which are simultaneously moralizing and libidinous. On one hand, she is bitterly censorious, perhaps even more so than her mother. She reviles Eneas for his "mestiers," which she describes as evidence of mental derangement ("fol esciant") and extraordinary evil ("molt par est malvés"). The crime is indeed so wicked and destructive that she curses anyone of that "nature": "maldite soit." On the other hand, even as she moralizes, Lavine belies any claim she might have had to virginal innocence. At first she simply and somewhat modestly restates her mother's claim that Eneas desires men rather than women. When she recalls the "truth" her mother told her (that the Trojan will have little interest in pleasuring a wife), she adds only a touch of sarcasm and a passing reference to the myth of Ganymede (in which she no doubt sees herself playing the part of Jupiter's misused wife). The implicit reference to Juno may even have the effect of casting Lavine as virtuous protector of monogamy and fertility. When it comes to imagining what specifically constitutes Eneas's perversion, however, Lavine is much more creative, taking full advantage of the ambiguity of the alleged crime in order to devise a number of erotically charged and highly ambiguous scenarios. Like her mother, she describes Eneas's lust as bestial in nature, though here the image is not so much a knight trotting his "horse," rather a grotesque rutting ("ruit," from the Latin *rugire*, "to bray, neigh, or roar, especially in heat") that transforms Eneas into a bellowing animal.

Faced with a lover who prefers goatish humping to "bele amor" and "bel deport," Lavine fantasizes about cross-dressing in order to suit her lover's taste.[41] Whereas Camille donned male attire in order to perform extraordinary feats of *chevalerie*, Lavine here rather more perversely imagines playing the role of a male subordinate in order to fool Eneas into satisfying her sexual needs. Though it is clear she has little intention of following through on her proposal, nonetheless the fantasy points to crucial gaps within the representation of desire. First of all, Lavine's descriptions of revealing dress indicate her awareness that the gendered body is mediated through external and potentially deceptive signs, rather than through the physical fact of the flesh itself. Indeed in Lavine's mind, it would seem that gaping or form-fitting garments attract Eneas more than the nakedness they simultaneously conceal and reveal. "His" desire (obviously a projection) for his "Ganimede" is aroused by a kind of striptease in which garments substitute for body parts: a "chemise fandue" that offers a glimpse of the chest underneath, "braies avalees" that allow the genitals to peek through, and body-hugging "braies" and "lasnieres" that reveal the outline of the buttocks by clinging to them.

Tellingly, the flesh itself is never fully visible in this passage. Lavine seems to imagine that even a woman could be concealed beneath male attire and could somehow manage to fool an unsuspecting sodomite into offering her sexual pleasure in place of a man or boy. The passage suggests, in other words, that gender is a metaphorical construct rather than a material fact, and that desire is invested less in the body than in the difference between clothing and body, gender and genitals, words and things. Ultimately, neither Lavine's rendering of Eneas's "mestiers" nor her mother's can expose an objective or uniform "verité" about what precisely constitutes sodomy or the unnatural. Instead it offers us words that substitute for the body and at the same time proliferate its meaning in a perverse series of metaphorical substitutions.

Indeed, though Lavine's obloquy is less obviously metaphorical than her mother's, she here evokes one of the most common figures for figuration in medieval culture: clothing. If the "braies" and "lasnieres" are nothing like the "modest veil of allegory" that adorns Macrobius's Lady Nature, the two garments share a common semiological structure. They are representations of an impossible representation—a process of meaning that begins with the evasiveness of the signified. Allegory designates figuratively and elliptically that which is ultimately ineffable (an affirmative presence), and implies that language is inadequate to express a truth that lies beyond the contingencies of discursive meaning. Not dissimilarly, sodomy signifies, through circumlocution, that which must not be spoken for moral reasons, and conveys the anxiety that speaking the unspeakable might well contaminate the language of moralization. Allegory and sodomy both point to difference as an unavoidable, and potentially unsettling, by-product of speaking the unspeakable. Thus if the *Eneas* deploys the allegory of love in order to consolidate power within dynastic genealogies and guarantee the validity and permanence of patriarchal rule, it also reveals the indeterminacy and unpredictability of its own meaning. In Lavine's case, indeterminacy leads to various forms of gender insubordination and the disarticulation of the patronymic. Likewise, sodomy points to a meaning antithetical to language and nature, yet all the while it eroticizes the dissemination of alternate meanings and parodies procreation. Ultimately, the *Eneas* seeks not only to distinguish between normative and deviant loves, but also to demonstrate that the two are never entirely distinguishable from one another, that desire may have the effect of blurring the difference between natural and unnatural, lawful and unlawful, good and evil. As Lavine's mother declares when she describes lovesickness: "Cist maus est buens" [This evil (or ache) is good] (7937).

The fact that the "maus" of love could be understood either as a moral value or as an actual, physical pain suggests that the ramifications of this blurring of binaries or of the unsettling of categories (whether ethical, discursive, or political) are ultimately played out through the body. As we have seen, violent ideological appropriations of the body are more or less constant in the *Eneas*. If the romance fails to discriminate between homosocial and homoerotic bonds, it provides a brutal correction of that error in the wounding, destruction, and subsequent commemoration of the deviant bodies of Nisus, Euryalus, and Pallas. Likewise, if the poem reveals the fact that gender is a cultural construct subject to interpretation and revision, it acts out anxieties related to gender mobility and insubordination through the piercing and entombment of the bodies of Dido, Camille, and Pallas. Finally, if Amor has the capacity either to weaken empire (by effeminizing the patriarch and thwarting procreation) or to fortify it (by ensuring normative, conjugal desire and a continuous line of progeny), he does so by perforating the lovers' bodies, forcing them into submission, and causing them to ache. Eneas is only granted the physical strength to defeat his enemies once he has acknowledged that he has been handily defeated by the figuration of his own desire: "Amors, tu m'as molt tost conquis" [Love, you have most quickly conquered me] (9067; 236). If Eneas and Lavine's role is to regenerate dynastic, imperial power, they are also implicitly and explicitly linked to desires that might be thought to place that power—and the social and political cohesiveness of the romance audience—in jeopardy.

* * *

In all these cases, violent appropriations of the body do not actually resolve the problem of discursive, moral, or political undecidability; nor in the end does the text understand its constructions of racial, political, or gendered identity as truly monological. Instead violent acts are themselves coded as symbolic or allegorical fictions—and therefore as contingent, indeterminate performances of power. Still, a consistent pattern or strategy can be observed throughout the text: the ambivalence of cultural signifiers, especially those linked to masculine privilege and political sovereignty, consistently yields some form of violent redress. Thus the romance affirms the validity of an imperialist, expansionist monarchy by demonstrating that the state is in fact profoundly and perilously embodied, that both political bodies and natural bodies require constant surveillance and discipline in order to ensure the validity and continuity of hereditary rule. Certainly the grand design of the *Eneas* suggests that the body politic could be conceived as a closed system in which future contingencies are rigorously subordinated to a grand paternal design (Anchises' prophecy). And yet that design is simultaneously revealed to be a rhetorical fiction, one that is constantly threatened by bodies that may or may not perform their civic duty, or that may be conquered by perverse desires rather than normative ones. In the end, the romance shows that even its symbolic triumphs over unlawfulness, immorality, or weakness are just that: symbolic fictions that do not govern stable, uniform meanings but instead are subject to the vagaries of interpretation. Far from seeking to disavow the flaw intrinsic to representation, the *Eneas* foregrounds it instead, emphasizing that the censoring or subordination of otherness through fictional means does not in fact eradicate its threat, but merely gives shape to it temporarily. Ultimately difference and deviance regenerate themselves through speech. Compensating for the inescapability of difference, the romance proposes that the body can be appropriated as a site of violent ideological control: the mutilation or puncturing of deviant bodies demonstrates to the reader his or her own corporality and vulnerability to the state, even if sovereignty is itself a rhetorical fiction.

In the final analysis, the *Eneas* does not seek to construct the body politic as a consensual unity but instead as a fragmentary, disorderly manifold in which a seemingly limitless potential for error paves the way for menacing, coercive displays of power. Eneas is unsuccessful in rectifying his moral errors over the course of his voyage from Troy to Italy and does not manage to erase the memory of a checkered past. Indeed, in spite of its careful structuring of the future, the genealogy prophesied by Anchises and inaugurated by his son ultimately fails to quiet anxieties about political stability. Nor should it be understood as a naive attempt to forge a bounded collective identity beyond discursive or historical contingencies. The *Eneas* is certainly an ideological fiction, and as such it interpellates its readership through models of collective identification. Yet in my view, it does so primarily by defining the norm itself as perverse and by representing all bodies as potential sources of corruption or failure. The result of this normalization of perversion and transgression is a paranoid awareness that bodies must be subject to constant surveillance and repressive controls. The sovereign ruler himself is not exempted from oversight, but on the contrary is coerced all the more for being the very embodiment of political power and dynastic continuity. The internalization of deviance within the law, of evil within the good, or of sodomy within the body politic anticipates a process of displacement, moralization, and scapegoating that is coeternal with empire itself and will endure, like the Trojan line, "toz tens senz fin" [for all time without end] (2990).

This vision of eternity is not at all an "extolment of stability, co-inherence in the body politic, peace on earth," which is how Raymond Cormier describes the closure of the romance.[42] Nor should we mistake the *imperium sine fine* as evidence of the obliteration of "homosexuality in a legitimate marriage" or of "a will to consistency that disarms all threats."[43] On the contrary, the *Eneas* suggests that its ideological opponents can never be fully vanquished but will live on through acts of commemoration, indeed through the genealogies and metaphors of the romance itself. If, halfway through the romance, Nisus declares to Euryalus, "An parlera de nos toz tans," this prophecy is the starting point for a tortured, paranoid, but also highly effective ideological strategy whereby moral error is located at the very heart of the body politic and its foundational history. The effort to rectify and fortify this allegorical body against internal enemies—a moral and political obligation that can never be entirely fulfilled and is therefore endlessly renewed—leads inexorably to the violent marking of literal, natural bodies. Pierced, mutilated, burned, and buried but never fully obliterated, these bodies serve to define state sovereignty as the power to render human life vulnerable to violent forms of discipline.

CHAPTER 3

ALLEGORY AND PERVERSION IN
ALAN OF LILLE'S *DE PLANCTU NATURAE*

In moving from the Old French verse romance *Eneas* to Alan of Lille's Latin prosimetrum *De planctu Naturae* [*The Plaint of Nature*],[1] I am making a somewhat radical departure. Both texts were written by learned clerics during the same period (the 1160s or 1170s) and in the same rough geographical area (England or Northern France).[2] Both are interested in questions of desire and morality, figuration and power. And as critics like Edmond Faral and Reto Bezzola long ago established, there are many indications that vernacular romance and the Latin poetry of the schools drew from a common literary and intellectual heritage.[3] From a sociological and thematic perspective, however, the two texts could scarcely be more different. The *Eneas* was composed for a seigniorial or royal court and addressed itself to a largely illiterate, mixed gender audience. Its themes are inherently secular: erotic love, marriage, warfare, and statesmanship. By contrast, the *De planctu* addressed itself exclusively to male ecclesiastical readers trained in theology and the liberal arts. Its themes are intellectual and philosophical: the natural world and its laws, cosmology and ethics, language and figuration, sin and redemption.

The purpose of this chapter will be to demonstrate that different as these texts are, they still share a common set of rhetorical and ideological strategies. Just as the *Eneas* uses the allegory of love to consolidate power within an incorporated feudal monarchy, so the *De planctu* uses Nature and Genius to naturalize the ideology of a postreform, "monarchic" Church and to signify the authority of the clergy to interpret and enforce natural and divine laws. Similarly, if the *Eneas* internalizes deviance within the law and sodomy within the body politic, so the *De planctu* locates perverse slippages of meaning within its principal allegorical and ecclesiastical figures. Finally, if the *Eneas* temporarily resolves the instability of its rhetorical and ideological system through the violent subjugation of deviant bodies, the *De planctu* suggests that unnatural evil can only be attenuated through penitential discipline, including procedures for ostracizing evildoers from the order of nature and the community of faith. Put simply, my argument in this chapter will be that the *De planctu* uses contradictory but ultimately cooperative strategies to shore up the power of a ruling class, in this case the intellectual clergy. On one hand, Alan allegorizes essential forms of being and conflates them with the moral and spiritual authority of the Church. On the other hand, he uses the semantic and moral ambivalence of allegory to legitimate the assiduous policing of desire, especially the sexual drives.

The association of Nature and Genius with Church hierarchics and disciplinary tactics is writ large in the *De planctu*. Nature describes herself as "vicaria Dei" [God's vicar] (8.224), a title that recalls the pope's own: *vicarius Christi* or *vicarius Filii Dei*. Like the Supreme Pontiff, she is charged with mediating between man and God, reminding humanity of its moral and spiritual obligations, and restraining the flesh and its appetites. The opening sections of the *De planctu* are devoted to an extensive description of Nature's diadem and robes, a virtual catalogue of *naturalia*. Nature then speaks directly to the poet, explaining to him that of God's creatures, man alone has broken with the order of nature, alienating himself from the creation and the Creator. In order to punish these sinners *contra naturam*, Nature calls upon Genius, her priestly consort whose edict will close the work. Like Nature, Genius is plainly endowed with an ecclesiastical and tutelary role: armed with the "pastoral staff" (206) or "punitive rod of excommunication" (208), he curses and casts out unnatural sinners, including first and foremost effeminate and homosexual men. This "anathema," which the poet describes as a "devastation" or "destruction" [exterminium] (18.159), is clearly meant to evoke the official liturgy of excommunication.[4] In his role as officiant, Genius exiles unnatural sinners from "the harmonious council of the things of Nature" (220), while the Virtues, standing in for the congregation, ratify the act with "ready words of approbation" (221) and lower their candles, signifying the loss of the excommunicates to Satan.

Larry Scanlon argues that Alan's fascination with "procedural detail" in this passage suggests that the rhetorical and ideological function of the *De planctu* is in part to project "the institutional power of literacy onto the created universe" and to read "the discursive disciplines of the Church into the process of natural reproduction."[5] Indeed, he is correct: both vicar and priest, *planctus* and *anathema* are used to find confirmation of the Church's moral and spiritual authority in the realities of natural processes, and to render the cosmos itself as an abstruse fiction intelligible only to an intellectual elite. The external design of the natural world is rendered as a highly ornate and learned ekphrasis on Lady Nature's diadem and robes, while the moral and religious significance of that world is revealed through a *lectio* or *disputatio* in which Nature plays Scholastic *magister* to the poet's *discipulus*. If this vision of Nature is intelligible only to those who can comprehend its rarified language, it plainly serves to naturalize the role of the schoolmen as arbiters of moral integrity, spiritual purity, and intellectual truth. Like the rules of sacred science, the secrets of nature are withheld from *rudes* [the uncultured] and revealed only to *periti* [experts]: those who have renounced worldly desires, who are "guided by a purer mind," and who can "climb toward ineffable things and see with a purer eye."[6]

And yet as Scanlon is quick to note, Alan's poetic visions are by no means uncomplicatedly orthodox.[7] On the contrary, Alan often locates unnatural desires and improper deviations of meaning within his allegorical figures. The *De planctu* is, as Scanlon puts it, "a relentlessly self-conscious text" in which allegory exposes its own "artifice" in order to complicate its own "claims."[8] The blurring of reality and representation, truth and falsehood, natural and unnatural in the *De planctu* cannot simply be attributed to intellectual incoherence or latent, unexpressed desires. On the contrary, Scanlon maintains that the text's ambivalence constitutes a strategy by which Alan authorizes, and even eroticizes, the disciplinary or penitential strategies of the Church in the period following the Gregorian reform movement. In ideological terms, the value of allegory is precisely its ambivalence—its liability to a titillating play of meanings that threatens to destabilize orthodoxy by revealing its status as a rhetorical, cultural, and even erotic fiction. Scanlon contends that the *De planctu* in fact has no "orthodox core that resists the play of language," as some critics have suggested. Rather, the text's "orthodoxy is the product of its transgressive figurations," such that "even the semiotic gaps in this text help motivate its regulatory desires."[9] Put another way, the "movement of Alain's narrative is not from pleasure to renunciation, but indeed from one sort of pleasure to another, as the unnamable pleasure of the homoerotic is displaced by the unnamed pleasure of power."[10]

My own thesis builds on Scanlon's: I will claim in this chapter that the improprieties of Alan's allegorical poetry ultimately motivate more concerted efforts to exclude or eliminate sexual deviants and to consolidate moral authority and political power within Church hierarchies. In his *Ars praedicandi*, Alan argues that the confusion of virtue and vice in the sublunary world demands that we "look in the glass of wariness, in case a vice is hiding itself under the guise of a virtue."[11] In the *De planctu*, he seems acutely aware that Nature and Genius, as rhetorical fictions rather than verifiable rules of theology, are similarly vulnerable to the unpredictability of verbal and figurative meaning. Nature may initially appear to overcome her status as poetic artifice by uttering "quasi archetipa uerba idealiter preconcepta" [virtually archetypal words that had been preconceived ideally] (6.12–13; 116, trans. modified).

But the limiting adverb *quasi* suggests a form of contingency that is particularly damaging to allegory's transcendental claims—namely, the unbridgeable gap between the personified figure and the ineffable essence it purports to signify, between the robes that clothe Nature and the truth they ostensibly conceal. Even as Nature gestures in the direction of ultimate truths and spiritual restoration, she exposes her status as a rhetorical fiction that is *not* essentially natural (and therefore good) but rather simulated and constructed (and therefore morally uncertain). Though the poet describes Nature as the "bond of the universe and its stable link," a "mirror for mortals," and a "light-bearer for the world" (128), she is clearly incapable of comprehending ultimate truths and is deeply compromised by her association with the flesh. Genius, too, is a morally uncertain figure. He is described as an ambidextrous writer who produces *orthography* with his right hand (actual, divinely created species perpetuated through lawful propagation) and *pseudography* with his left (shadowy, perverse images that lack substantial being and moral purity). These writings are in turn received either by Truth (a dutiful, chastely conceived daughter) or by Falsehood (a misbegotten, misshapen hag who disfigures Genius's script). Thus even orthographical inscriptions are potentially false, since they are liable (like all human signs) to reading and misreading.

And yet despite this confusion of truth and falsehood (or, rather, because of it), Nature's plaint and Genius's curse are endowed with tremendous ideological force. Indeed, though the violence of the anathema is itself mostly latent and symbolic (it is described as a "devastation," but it is unclear what kind—physical or metaphysical, corporeal or spiritual), its broader significance should not be overlooked. In keeping with the solemn rite of excommunication, which places the sinner in the hands of the devil, Genius's edict implies that the person excluded from the order of nature will be left utterly vulnerable to evil—nothingness or annihilation. One might conclude from this that the excommunicate will not only suffer alienation from his embodied, natural state and debarment from the visible church but will also cease to exist in a more radical sense or will be subject to degradation and dehumanization. As Boethius's Lady Philosophy explains (in a prosimetrum that served as a model for Alan's own), "Whatever falls from goodness, ceases to be"; a man who gives himself over to evil ceases "to be a man, since he cannot pass over into the divine state" and instead "turns into a beast."[12]

There is considerable evidence to suggest that medieval readers construed the *De planctu* as an eliminationist text. Several manuscripts append a colophon that reads, "Let the profane sodomite perish."[13] In the context of a fire-and-brimstone reading of Sodom and Gomorrah, the Dominican Robert Holcot praises the *De planctu* as a particularly effective tool in the campaign against sodomy, "the most unspeakable vice."[14] Walter de Burgh adds three verses on sodomy (including a vicious *ad hominem* attack) to a copy of *Vix nodosum* (a poem erroneously attributed to Alan), and explains that his verses are inspired by "the plaint of Nature against a sodomite prelate."[15] Though the evidence is purely circumstantial, Scanlon suggests that traces of Alan's influence may also be found in official Church pronouncements, most notably the canon of the Third Lateran Council that officially prohibited the "vice against nature" for the first time. While there is no proof of Alan's influence here, it is clear that Alan anticipated the direction the Church would subsequently take: using threats of excommunication (and eventually also extermination) to claim regulatory authority over desire.

In this chapter, I propose to examine how the subversion of intellectual, allegorical, and moral coherence in the *De planctu* is used to shore up ecclesiastical power and to legitimate aggressive disciplinary and penitential practices. I will argue that Alan's text pursues its ideological goals in part by internalizing transgression within the law, all the while suggesting that the purging of the community of faith is both a sacred responsibility and an inexhaustible labor. For Alan, the authority to excommunicate always retains its associations with, and in fact clearly depends upon, the very deviant practices it proscribes. Locating unnatural, malevolent desires within normative models of the natural and the good, the *De planctu* gives rise to fears regarding the vulnerability of the Church's moral authority and political stability. In turn, it motivates an ongoing struggle to bolster ecclesiastical power through disciplinary techniques. I explore this argument in four sections. First, I examine Alan's sign theory, paying particular attention to the moral ambiguities of the language arts. I then offer a reading of the opening meter of the *De planctu* and discuss the relationship between poetry and semantic, moral, and sexual deviation in the work as a whole. In the two remaining sections, I discuss Nature and Genius. I demonstrate that the *De planctu* uses a variety of techniques to shield Nature from responsibility for unnatural evil, but ultimately foregrounds her rhetorical excesses and moral aberrations. I then consider—and reject—the possibility that Genius, as an allegory of the priesthood, might represent a viable alternative to Nature's semantic and moral deviations. I conclude by arguing that the ideological value of Genius's anathema is precisely its failure to extirpate the unnatural vices it condemns.

Language and Ethics

In order to grasp the ideological complexities of the *De planctu Naturae*, we must first grapple with Alan's understanding of the relationship between the *artes sermocinales* (grammar, logic, and rhetoric) and *theologia moralis* (both theoretical and practical). It cannot be emphasized enough that as an ethicist, Alan is preoccupied with moral frailty and its catastrophic effects. As Maurice Gandillac explains, Alan, like Augustine, conceives of man as a "spiritus vadens ad peccatum et non rediens ad bonum" [spirit moving toward sin and not returning toward the good].[16] It should come as no surprise, then, that Alan similarly describes human, postlapsarian sign systems as both semantically and morally equivocal. Verbal signifiers are subject not just to repetition and difference in time, but also to sensual desires and moral devolution. On one hand, Alan believes that signs can inspire the mind to ascend toward sublime truths, notably through the three- or four-fold structure of scriptural hermeneutics. On the other hand, he is adamant that the interpretation of signs (including even scriptural hermeneutics) can lead in the opposite direction as well, toward moral degeneracy and spiritual alienation. Indeed, for Alan, words are always at least partially signifiers of human weakness and depravity, especially insofar as they fail to fulfill their function as indices of moral, intellectual, or spiritual truth.

As Jan Ziolkowski argues, the notion that grammar and ethics were complexly intertwined would have been a familiar one for Alan's readers: "Grammar and ethics were, in effect, two aspects of the same discipline," and indeed were considered to be so by pagan, Jewish, and Christian thinkers alike from antiquity on.[17] More than simply the art of correct usage, medieval grammar sought to impose norms for moral conduct along with prescriptive rules governing orthography, phonetics, morphology, syntax, prosody, and exegesis. This is not to say, however, that for medieval thinkers grammatical correctness would necessarily imply moral health. Nor, conversely, would moral rectitude alone yield correct grammar. Some of the strictest moralists of the period go so far as to denounce the study of grammar on moral and doctrinal grounds—or at least insist on strict distinctions between correct usage and the holy wisdom of theology. The most famous example is the eleventh-century reformer Peter Damian, who argues that grammar is a kind of apostasy that perverts holy truths by blindly insisting on form over content, morphology over theology: "Look, brother, do you wish to learn grammar? Then learn to decline God in the plural; for the devil, as he founds anew the art of disobedience, introduces in the world an unheard-of rule of declension, to guarantee that many gods will be worshiped."[18] In an effort to counter the excesses of his contemporaries, Peter declares, "My grammar is Christ," by which he means that to privilege the language arts over traditional Christology is to lapse into heterodoxy.

Alan of Lille's position on grammar is by no means as extreme as Peter's, though he, too, is ambivalent about its value. In the *Anticlaudianus*, he describes the maiden Grammar in respectful but oddly paradoxical terms. She is both a chaste virgin and a body ravaged by "lost nulliparity," a lactating mother who nurtures her young with properly crafted words and a whip-wielding father who "punishes the faults which youth in its way absorbs." Strained though they may be, these antinomic metaphors are clearly meant to signify the nobility of Grammar's role. Simultaneously harsh and comforting, exacting and compassionate, she "teaches infants to speak, looses tied tongues and shapes words in the proper mold." She then cleans and polishes the metaphorical "teeth" of her young charges, correcting their mistakes and guiding them toward wisdom.[19]

Nevertheless, Grammar's androgyny and dubious chastity may also suggest that Alan, like Peter, believes in the inherent limitations, deficiencies, and even perversities of grammar, especially insofar as its methods are used to make sense of religious mysteries. In his *Rhythmus de incarnatione Christi*, Alan writes that in the case of the utterly pure and self-identical "Word of the Father," the copula "confounds every rule," including case inflection and voice.[20] Commenting on this passage, G.R. Evans writes, "The moral Alan wishes to draw is that the rules of the *artes* must never be overextended in their application without being adapted for theology."[21] Indeed Alan will elaborate this point at length in the *Regulae Theologicae* and the *Summa quoniam homines*. And yet there is perhaps a bit more to Alan's reticence than simply a desire to distinguish between predication and the divine presence, between the methods of grammar and those of theology. Alan also claims that human sign systems are by their very nature morally ambivalent and, in a postlapsarian world, generally tend toward error. As grammarians attempt to cull truths from texts, they must arm themselves with reason in order to avoid egregious, schismatic misreadings. In a famous passage from the *Contra haereticos*, a text meant to defend Catholicism against pagan and heretical doctrine, Alan writes, "Since authority has a wax nose, that is it can be diverted to the opposite position, it must be reinforced by the faculties of reason."[22] As they seek out holy truths from Scripture, grammarians must constantly measure their findings against the laws of reason and the tenets of orthodoxy. It is not simply that authoritative or sacred texts can be misappropriated or falsified; it is also that grammar is itself indeterminate and bends according to the free will of the grammarian. Whereas "the other branches of learning have their own rules upon which they rely," grammar "depends wholly upon man's good will and wishes. . .and. . .its rules. . .depend upon the decisions of men."[23] If the morality of grammar is not grounded in necessary, self-evident principles, it must be guided by other kinds of rules and must orient itself toward higher goals. Thus Alan's allegorical depiction of Lady Grammar in the *Anticlaudianus* excludes those "base grammarians who rejoice in mere husks, whom the richness of the marrow within does not set apart."[24] These scholars have studied grammar for its own sake and have read only according to the letter, which kills. If they are to discover the life-giving spirit beneath the letter, they must use grammar as a tool for achieving wisdom rather than as an end in itself.

Though logic (unlike grammar) is governed by formal, axiomatic rules and does not depend wholly upon the good will of the logician, Alan is similarly reticent about its moral valence and religious orthodoxy. To be sure, Alan belongs to an intellectual tradition that valued logic not just for its instrumentality, but also for its innate integrity. Like Boethius, Alan believes that logic is more than simply a tool for constructing viable arguments but has the capacity to distinguish intellectual truths from superficial falsehoods. As Marie-Dominique Chenu observes, Alan and some of his contemporaries transformed the role of logic in radical ways, using ratiocination to shape "doctrinal concepts" and even allowing logic to enter into "the structuring of the faith itself."[25] If John of Salisbury used Aristotle's Organon to furnish "the necessary and fertile apparatus for a deep penetration into the faith," Alan went a step further, bringing "the faith to a reasoned fullness" by borrowing liberally from Aristotle, Cicero, Boethius, and Porphyry.[26] Describing theology as the "supercelestial science,"[27] Alan insists that it is governed by self-evident, universally acknowledged rules offering a reliable means for structuring theological questions and evaluating the accuracy of responses. This systematic, rational approach to theology prompts Chenu to conclude that Alan's *Regulae Theologicae* represents "a nearly unique attempt in the West to weave the free wills of God and the disparate moments of man's salvation into a deductive and axiomatic system."[28]

In spite of his belief in the compatibility of logical deduction and theological speculation, Alan still expresses considerable anxiety about the potential for logic to lapse into paralogism, heterodoxy, and evil. In the *Anticlaudianus*, Alan personifies Logic as an "ingenious," "assiduous" maiden whose "comeliness" is nonetheless marred by "a certain leanness": "deep hollowed and dry skin" wedded to "fleshless bones."[29] Logic's beauty is not to be found in her outward appearance but rather in her "never-sleeping mind," which outshines the other arts and indeed casts them "into the shade."[30] Though she is not beautiful like Rhetoric and though her hair is snarled "in a tasteless brawl," Logic is nonetheless endowed with a "power of vision" that exceeds that of the eagle or the lynx and that holds the key to unlocking "the secrets of Sophia," who sees "all that the divine world embraces."[31] And yet Alan also insists that Logic is inherently unpredictable and labile. To begin with, her techniques are vulnerable to misappropriation by the "pseudo-logician," who imitates the "outer aspect" of the art form (the entanglements of eristic disputation) and uses "certain stunts" to "sell falsehood packaged as truth."[32] If it is Logic herself who "cuts down" the sophist's falsehood and exposes his hypocrisy, still the disease and its cure are called by the same name and can be exceptionally difficult to distinguish. Master logicians like Zeno and Boethius were able to reveal truth through reasoning; they exposed the "innermost recesses of the art" and brought "the dark back to light."[33] But Logic (not unlike Genius in the *De planctu*) is herself divided between positive and negative qualities, a right hand and a left: "The gift of flowers decorates her right hand; a scorpion encircling her left threatens with pointed tail. One hand savours of honey, one bears the juice of venom; one promises laughter, the other ends in tears; one attracts, the other repels; one salves, the other stings; one smites, the other soothes; one graces, the other taints."[34] If the logician is inexpert or dishonest, his reasoning may do more harm than good, perverting sacred wisdom rather than revealing it. Ultimately, however, it is Logic herself that is divided between good and evil; and ambivalence plainly begins with the art, not the artist.

For Alan, rhetoric, even more so than the other *artes*, plays a contradictory, morally dubious role. Himself a master rhetorician and preacher, Alan freely admits that oratory is a necessary skill for proclaiming the Gospel and for ensuring conformity within the community of belief. Yet he also insists that by its very nature as eloquent, euphonious speech, rhetoric offers aesthetic, worldly, and even carnal pleasures that interfere with moral and religious instruction. In the *Anticlaudianus*, Alan distinguishes Rhetoric for her physical beauty: she endows "things previously produced" with "added embellishment" and "further refinement," and she "enfolds in her bosom the complete art of the painter."[35] The enticements of rhetorical language are directly linked to, and no doubt also compromised by, erotic allurements, notably those of the female body. If the rhetorician is to harness the seductive power of rhetoric for penitential and evangelical purposes, his speech must be guided by reason and orthodoxy. Thus in the opening chapter of his *Ars praedicandi* [*Art of Preaching*], Alan argues that for sermons to provide "knowledge of spiritual matters" and guidance in "the living of a good life,"[36] they must consistently seek out *gravitas* and *mediocritas*, and must avoid the indulgent use of playful, mellifluous, or theatrical language. Preachers ought to persuade their congregations with rhetorical flair, but tropes must only be used to shape morals, never to make a display of the preacher's skill or to indulge the congregation's desire for pleasure:

> Preaching should not contain jesting words, or childish remarks, or that melodiousness and harmony which result from the use of rhythm or metrical lines; these are better fitted to delight the ear than to edify the soul. Such preaching is theatrical and full of buffoonery, and in every way to be condemned. Of such preaching the prophet says: 'Your innkeepers mix water with the wine' [Is 1.22]. Water is mingled with wine in the preaching in which childish and mocking words—what we may call 'effeminacies'—are put into the minds of the listeners. Preaching should not glitter with verbal trappings,

with purple patches, nor should it be too much enervated by the use of colorless words: the blessed keep to a middle way.[37]

If rhetoric is pursued for its own sake, it will lapse into degenerate stylistic games rather than signifying spiritual truths. By mixing water with wine, the "faithful city" of Isaiah 1 will become a whore and will incur God's wrath. As Michel Zink explains, there is more at stake here, however, than simply an ethics and aesthetics of *mediocritas*. Alan ultimately approaches the topic of eloquence from two blatantly incompatible positions. On one hand, he believes that rhetoric is little more than "literary vanity," "incidental ornament," and "effeminate softness," that rhetorical figures can be opposed to essential ideas just as "the materiality of the letter" (which kills) can be opposed to "the spirit" (which gives life).[38] On the other hand, he never fully acknowledges that the "art of figures" is the "very foundation of his own poetry" and that he himself indulges in rhetorical excesses, especially in the *De planctu*.[39] Alan the moralist refuses to admit that an "edifying work" like the *Ars praedicandi* is a treatise on rhetoric, while Alan the writer cannot conceive of the possibility of "a mode of expression that would be stripped of rhetoric."[40] Though a necessary skill for evangelical preaching and theological speculation, rhetorical figures are thus inherently unpredictable and potentially perverse.

Even the eloquence of Scripture is subject to perverse misreading, though its intention is obviously unimpeachable: "For very often those who discuss the words of sacred eloquence more than they ought slip into the carnal sense."[41] Depicting the Bible figuratively as *vestimenta*, or "clothing," he proclaims,

> The sacred Scriptures and the sacraments of the Church are said to be the vestments of Christ, whence David said: "They divided my garments among themselves" [Ps. 22.18]. Those who divided his garments are understood to be those who pervert the Scriptures. Just as they literally divided the garments [Mar. 15.22–24], so do those who do not aim at unity corrupt the spiritual sacraments and sacred Scriptures through heresies and depraved exposition.[42]

Holy signs are metaphorically rendered as the garments worn by Christ on the Cross and are therefore as close to the divinity himself as clothes are to the body. And yet these signs are nonetheless vulnerable to mistreatment, those who deform Scripture being analogized to the Roman soldiers who tormented the Son of God. If Jesus' very clothing could be sullied by cruelty and greed, signifying not just the fulfillment of a prophecy, but also the egregiousness of human sin, certainly the Gospels themselves must be liable to misuse. In essence, the polysemy of Scripture is simultaneously a means for transcending the "carnal sense" and a perverse division of that which is undividable, God. In effect, to speak of God is to run the risk of pluralizing the Monad. If the faithful wish to avoid proliferating heretical meanings, their understanding of Scripture must be constantly and rigorously supervised.

Perhaps the most destabilizing aspect of Alan's conception of the *artes*, however, is his notion that the moral and spiritual condition of the speaker cannot be determined by the form or content of his speech. Alan argues in the *Ars praedicandi* that we can easily mistake statements of religious orthodoxy for true piety, when in fact they are evidence of the deepest hypocrisy, affectation, and malevolence. It is possible, for instance, that men may utter righteous speech and yet inwardly revolt against righteousness: "There are many who have God in their mouths and the devil in their minds, who praise God with their voices but blaspheme in their minds, and although their tongue is singing hymns, their spirit is in the stewpot. What they vow with their mouths, they disavow in their spirit."[43] Heresy itself is so perilous precisely because it has the outward appearance of truth and piety, even though it is in fact the work of deceivers and evildoers. Again, like Augustine, Alan believes in the intrinsically defective, corrupt nature of human morality. Saddled with the legacy of the Fall, man is incapable of curing himself or even of perceiving the defects in his own nature. The signs by which he strives to reach God (or by which he *claims* to do so) are themselves profoundly ambivalent, simultaneously a means to enlightenment and a repository and symptom of alienation and evil.

The Poet's Complaint

Alan's ambivalent attitude toward the *artes sermocinales* generally and rhetorical and poetic representation specifically is nowhere more obvious than in Meter 1 of the *De planctu*, a proem in elegiac verse that is, as Kathryn Lynch observes, "a kind of prospectus for the rest of the poem."[44] The poet here sermonizes in the manner of scriptural parenesis and denounces human sexual depravity using figures drawn from the standard Scholastic curriculum. At the same time, it is clear that his language is morally suspect—less a tool for the remediation of sin than a vector for moral corruption. Alexandre Leupin describes this ambivalence as Alan's "antithetical poetics": "The enunciation of the text which gives way before everything that it denounces as hermaphroditic provokes the return of the literary exception *in* a theology that is otherwise completely orthodox."[45] Indeed, the poet consistently chooses tropes that render his own gender identity and sexual desires uncertain. A paradoxical juxtaposition of moralization and moral failure is established immediately in the opening lines:

> In lacrimas risus, in luctus gaudia uerto,
> In planctum plausus, in lacrimosa iocos,
> Cum sua Naturam uideo decreta silere,
> Cum Veneris monstro naufraga turba perit;
> Cum Venus in Venerem pugnans illos facit illas
> Cumque sui magica deuirat arte uiros.
> Non fraus tristiciem, non fraudis fletus adulter,
> Non dolus, immo dolor, parturit, immo parit.
> Musa rogat, dolor ipse iubet, Natura precatur
> Vt donem flendo flebile carmen eis. (1.1–10)

[I turn from laughter to tears, from joy to grief, from merriment to lament (*planctu*) from jests to wailing, when I behold Nature's silence about her own decrees, when large numbers are shipwrecked and lost because of a Venus turned monster, when Venus wars with Venus and changes "hes" into "shes" and with her witchcraft unmans man. It is not a case of pretence begetting a show of grief or faked tears giving birth to deceit: it is not an act, but rather an ache, that is in labour or, rather, actually giving birth. The Muse implores, grief itself orders, Nature begs that with tears I give them the gift of a mournful ditty.] (67)[46]

To a great extent, these verses assign to Lady Nature—and by extension to the poet himself—a certain moral, doctrinal, and even juridical authority. The term *decreta* evokes canon law and suggests a set of disciplinary edicts pronounced by an ecclesiastical council or even (as with the decretals) by a sovereign pontiff. Given Nature's silence about her decrees (or her tearful pleading), the poet takes it upon himself to inveigh against unnatural perversity on her behalf and to deplore man's immorality with echoes of the Letter of James 4.9: "Lament and mourn and weep. Let your laughter be turned into mourning and your joy into dejection." The poet's *planctus* is, however, quite a bit more severe than James's moral exhortations, and it should be understood not just as a lament, but also as a legal claim seeking redress. It anticipates Nature's own *planctus*, in which the goddess censures man's "accursed excesses" and ponders "what kind of penalty should answer such an array of crimes" (138). Moreover, the closing lines of Meter 1 foreshadow Genius's anathema in the closing lines of Prose 9. If Genius demotes unnatural sinners "from the harmonious council of the things of Nature," the poet declares that men "who refuse Genius his tithes and rites [meaning, presumably, those who impede procreation] deserve to be excommunicated from the temple of Genius" (72). Ostensibly, then, Genius's anathema transforms the poet's "mournful ditty" and Nature's plaint into an official injunction against unnatural vice. It thereby forges a moral, legal, and even institutional alliance between the poet (who first gives voice to Nature's grievance), the vicar (who is aggrieved), and the priest (who announces and enforces the law).

And yet this passage also clearly evinces the moral pitfalls of figuration, which seems to have the effect of contaminating both the poet and his proem with the very same crimes they deplore. Even as he excoriates unmanned men, the poet metaphorically translates the authenticity of his grief, and the process of literary creation it gives rise to, into the painful throes of childbirth. More than simply offering a conventional trope for the agonies of literary invention, the poet repeatedly insists on the authenticity of his suffering, which is not pretense or deceit but real. His words thus paradoxically transform his moral anguish into the very crime that is the source of that anguish and his writing into the perversity he seeks to counteract through writing: the unmanning of men, a biologically impossible act of male parturition. Not only does the play of literal and figurative meanings implicate the poet in unnatural acts, but it also suggests that speech inevitably revolts against the authority of the speaker, producing meanings that thwart his stated moral intentions and lapsing into immorality. Indeed, it is the impossibility of fixing meaning in discourse or controlling the sphere of reception that makes language and the language arts so appropriate as figures for sexual deviance. As Elizabeth Pittenger argues, the "two dominant concepts" in the *De planctu* are "writing and perversion, which at various times and in various ways stand for one another."[47] Orthography, like desire, can easily go astray and lapse into pseudography, which is likened to illicit forms of sexual intercourse. The irony, of course, is that in linking moral error to words, moralizing language fails to distance itself from the sins it denounces and is permeated by deviance even as it signifies a desire to extirpate it. Slippages within moralizing language must be understood as themselves immoral, which means that an attentive reader like Pittenger will repeatedly find "sodomitical penetration in the textual recesses of [Alan's] diatribe against sodomitical penetration."[48]

If the opening lines of Meter 1 immediately establish the inseparability of poetry and perversion, moral language and moral deviation, it quickly becomes apparent in what follows that these tensions will not be diminished but will continue to plague the text. After explaining the intentions behind his *planctus*, the poet uses metaphors drawn from the *artes* in order to describe the vices he wishes to censure. At the same time, the poet manages to suggest an entanglement whereby the *artes* are bound to the very perversions they are meant to regulate and abolish:

Heu, quo Nature secessit gracia, morum
Forma, pudicitie norma, pudoris amor?

Flet Natura, silent mores, proscribitur omnis
Orphanus a ueteri nobilitate pudor.
Actiui generis sexus se turpiter horret
Sic in passiuum degenerare genus.
Femina uir factus sexus denigrat honorem,
Ars magice Veneris hermafroditat eum.
Predicat et subicit, fit duplex terminus idem.
Gramatice leges ampliat ille nimis.
Se negat esse uirum, Nature factus in arte
Barbarus. Ars illi non placet, immo tropus.
Non tamen ista tropus poterit translatio dici.
In uicium melius ista figura cadit.
Hic nimis est logicus per quem conuersio simplex
Artis nature iura perire facit.
Cudit in incude que semina nulla monetat.
Horret et incudem malleus ipse suam.
Nullam materiem matricis signat idea
Sed magis in sterili litore uomer arat. (1.11–30)

[Alas! Where has Nature with her fair form betaken herself? Where have the
pattern of morals, the norm of chastity, the love of modesty gone? Nature
weeps, moral laws get no hearing, modesty, totally dispossessed of her
ancient high estate, is sent into exile. The active sex shudders in disgrace as
it sees itself degenerate into the passive sex. A man turned woman blackens
the fair name of his sex. The witchcraft of Venus turns him into a hermaphrodite. He is subject and predicate: one and the same term is given a double
application. Man here extends too far the laws of grammar. He denies that
he is a man, becoming a barbarian with respect to the grammar of Nature.
Grammar does not find favour with him but rather a trope. This transposition, however, cannot be called a trope. The figure here more correctly falls
into the category of defects. That man, in whose case a simple conversion in
an Art causes Nature's laws to come to naught, is pushing logic too far. He
hammers on an anvil which issues no seeds. The very hammer itself shudders
in horror of its anvil. He imprints on no matter the stamp of a parent-stem:
rather his ploughshare scores a barren strand.] (67–69)[49]

On one level, the poet clearly invokes the *artes* as a body of rules that is
compatible with natural and moral law and that serves as a standard against
which to identify deviations and transgressions. Borrowing from the termi-
nology of grammar, the poet describes a passive or effeminate man as a
subject turned into a predicate.[50] Though a sexual agent by nature, this man
has illicitly transformed himself into a sexual object, or rather has become a
"barbarian" and a "hermaphrodite" by fusing the two roles together,
making subject and object case inflections the same. Invoking Boethian
logic, the poet in turn describes unnatural vice as a "simple conversion"

whereby the subject and predicate are inverted: "All A is B" changes to "Some B is A."[51] Though the meaning of the analogy is obscure, the poet probably intends to suggest that deviants reverse sexual roles in such a way that some members of the "active" class assume the "passive" role during intercourse. Finally, the poet uses metaphors drawn from rhetoric to describe the sterility of this union. The unnatural sinner contaminates grammar through the use (or abuse) of a trope [*tropus*]; yet his sin is so utterly improper that it cannot be a trope, rather a transposition [*translatio*] whereby figure [*figura*] degenerates into defect [*uicium*]. Perhaps seeking to avoid the redundancy and obscurity of these figures *for* figuration, the poet turns to more material metaphors to describe the sterility of improper couplings. The anvil that "issues no seeds" and the "barren strand" that yields no harvest presumably stand for the anus of a male partner; the hammer and plowshare for the penis; and, by extension, the fruitful anvil and fertile field for the vagina or uterus, the "proper" or "natural" object choice. If the hammer "shudders" [*horret*] at the thought of the improper anvil or if the active sex "shudders" at being rendered passive, it is presumably because the anus, which excretes waste, has supplanted the vagina, which yields new life. The hammer is a phallic instrument intended for imprinting form [*idea*, "eternal prototype"] on matter [*matrix*, "womb"]. If, for medieval philosophers, the world itself is the product of a hylomorphic, heterosexual union, any other pairing is not simply unnatural but malignant and moribund.

And yet there is certainly a sense in this passage that the metaphors and disciplines the poet invokes are not capable of distinguishing moral and immoral conduct in any absolute way. Indeed, as Pittenger suggests, perversion can be found throughout the "textual recesses" of the poet's invective. The verb *horrere* is a particularly telling example. The literal meaning of the term is "to be stiffly erect," and it is only figuratively that it denotes horror or dread. The notion that anything other than a heterosexual pairing must be thoroughly repugnant is thus contradicted by the very word used to describe that repugnance. In effect, the active sex does not simply shudder but actually hardens at the prospect of being rendered passive. The phallic hammer is simultaneously bristling and stiff, revolted and aroused, while the seedless anvil would, by extension, be simultaneously monstrous and seductive. Elizabeth Keiser is quite right to wonder whether the poet could possibly find unnatural vice as revolting as he pretends: "Apparently, same-sex union is thought to be so desirable that only the severest threats. . .can deter the human male from finding it preferable to heterosexual intercourse."[52]

The moral ambiguity is merely amplified if we take seriously the poet's references to the *artes*. Twelfth-century readers would have been well aware that the laws governing grammar, logic, and rhetoric do not necessarily prohibit the practices the poet disparages. Quite the opposite, they may even encourage them as legitimate or necessary. To begin with, the rules of Latin grammar do allow for subject and predicate forms to be identical, even if it is rare. Likewise, simple conversion is not necessarily an improper maneuver in logic but can, on the contrary, yield truthful deductions.[53] As for rhetoric, several scholars have argued that the slippage between *tropus, translatio, figura,* and *uicium* frustrates the poet's attempts to differentiate between proper and improper figuration, licit and illicit desire.[54] Scanlon remarks, "The first three terms all mean basically the same thing in this context, a rhetorical figure. *Translatio* and *figura* are each slightly more general than the term succeeding, as Alain struggles to identify homoeroticism with figuration, while at the same time conveying its complete illegitimacy."[55] As a strategy, however, the approach is clearly flawed: "This equivalence could itself be described by all of these terms. If troping and homoerotic sex are equivalent, then Alain becomes guilty of the very sin he decries by making the comparison."[56]

As if to confirm his guilt by figuration, the metaphors the poet subsequently chooses to describe natural and unnatural intercourse are themselves highly irregular and improper. The hammer and anvil in particular are so utterly incorporeal that they denature the body and sexual difference and destroy the very principle of similitude that is the basis for metaphor. As James Sheridan observes, it is rather strange "to speak of an anvil producing seeds"; the only gloss he can offer, "seeds of fire," is so strained as to be ridiculous.[57] Keiser notes a similar problem with the hammer-and-anvil metaphor: the pounding of "a (male) hammer" on the "hard, flat surface of a (female) anvil" renders sexual intercourse as a "violent, percussive, and unpleasurable process" and provides an "ironic contrast to conventional references to heterosexual intercourse as irresistibly attractive."[58] The poet seems intent on offering "a vision of sex which lacks all erotic zest and seems completely violent and unpleasurable for either party."[59] Perhaps this can be chalked up to clerical asceticism, as Keiser suggests; yet the poet's vision may be considerably more perverse than Keiser allows. If the anvil transforms the vagina and uterus into an impervious plane rather than a vessel for enveloping new life, the union of hammer and anvil should be understood as impeding procreation and thwarting Nature's design. Moreover, if the anvil is a hard surface struck by an equally hard hammer, then the metaphor tends toward the pairing of like with like—precisely the error it is meant to correct. Perhaps, then, the anvil should be taken less as a metaphor than a catachresis or *uicium: all* pairings of hammer and anvil are improper, defective figurations and therefore morally deviant. By using metaphors *for* metaphor to describe natural and unnatural intercourse, the poet renders all sexual unions and the language of sexual morality scandalously ambiguous and contingent.

If the poet turns to Ovidian exempla and moralizing exegesis in the remainder of the poem (activities that would fall under the rubric of grammar in the medieval curriculum), his goal would seem to be to make the fatal consequences of unnatural intercourse more immediately intelligible to his reader. He praises the beauty of women, notably Helen of Troy, whose "godlike form" inspires gods and men alike. Of course, Helen's beauty can never be fully dissociated from the crime of rapacious, adulterous love, and the poet (probably following Ovid, *Heroides*, 1.6) scornfully dubs Paris "the Phrygian adulterer." Still, the sins of modern men exceed even Paris's wickedness: "Non modo Tindaridem Frigius uenatur adulter / Sed Paris in Paridem monstra nefanda parit" [Not only does the Phrygian adulterer hunt the daughter of Tyndareus, but Paris also performs monstrous and unspeakable acts on Paris] (1.51–52; trans. mine). The language of the passage in fact suggests a number of sexual crimes at once. To begin with, Paris's prey is as monstrous as the deed he commits with that prey: "monstra nefanda" could signify either "monstrous, unspeakable acts" or "unspeakable monsters." Moreover, the reflexive, narcissistic copulation of Paris with Paris, however monstrous and unnatural it may be, is far from unproductive: the verb "parit" might well denote both the doing of monstrous misdeeds and the begetting of monstrous offspring, here through homosexual intercourse and male parturition. Indeed, the passage plainly recalls the poet's description of his own act of writing ("non parturit, immo parit"), which is now inextricably linked to the depraved acts he purports to loathe. It seems the poet can scarcely speak of those unspeakable acts without implicating himself and his speech in monstrosities.

In an apparent attempt to align himself with those men who do still long for women's beauty, the poet laments the fact that the "crop" of women's kisses has not been harvested from their willing lips. And yet this metaphor almost immediately takes on a life of its own:

> Virginis in labiis cur basia tanta quiescunt,
> Cum reditus in eis sumere nemo uelit?
> Que michi pressa semel mellirent oscula succo,
> Que mellita darent mellis in ore fauum.
> Spiritus exiret ad basia, deditus ori
> Totus et in labiis luderet ipse sibi,
> Vt dum sic moriar, in me defunctus, in illa
> Felici uita perfruar alter ego. (1.43–50)

> [Why do so many kisses lie fallow on maidens' lips while no one wishes to harvest a crop of them? If these kisses were but once planted on me, they would grow honey-sweet with moisture, and grown honey-sweet, they would form a honeycomb in my mouth. My life breath, concentrating entirely on my mouth, would go out to meet the kisses and would disport itself entirely

on my lips so that I might thus expire and that, when dead myself, my other self might enjoy (*perfruar*) in her (*in illa*) a fruitful life.] (70–71)

As Mark Jordan observes, "Kissing takes two, and the kisses lying on virgins' lips are the kisses of their otherwise preoccupied male lovers."[60] We may wonder, then, "whose kisses. . .our narrator mean[s] to harvest," male or female. Either way, it would appear that "the effect of harvesting the kisses is to impregnate not the maidens, but the narrator himself. In him they grow into honeycomb."[61] Certainly, these kisses yield fruit: *felix vita* denotes not just a happy life but also a sexually active, fecund one. Similarly, the verb *perfruor* [to enjoy, including sexually] contains the root word *frux*, meaning "crops." The poet's delivery of his poem and Paris's begetting of monsters on Paris are thus doubled by the ambiguous kisses the poet imagines receiving. There are perhaps other obscenities lurking here as well, especially given that the mouth usually associated with fecundity is the *os matricis*, or female genitalia. Could we understand this passage as referring to cunnilingus? That very act is suggested only a few lines later when the poet recounts the story of Pyramus and Thisbe and offers a pun on *rimas* [cracks in the wall], *rimatur* [to search for; literally, to probe the crevices for], and *rimula Veneris* [little cleft of Venus]: "Non modo per rimas rimatur basia Thisbes / Piramus, huic Veneris rimula nulla placet" [No longer does Pyramus search for Thisbe's kisses through the cracks; no little cleft of Venus pleases him] (1.53–54). The precise meaning of the metaphorical cracks and cleft is left ambiguous, however, as indeed are the referents for "alter ego" and "illa" in the passage cited above. Will the other self enjoy sexually, and then live on in, the woman he kisses? Will the kisses the poet exchanges yield a female child? Or will his death transform him into an other, female self?

The poet seems to have obscured his meaning deliberately here, and has located deviant forms of desire within that obscurity. It would be difficult to read the poet's *planctus* as anything other than a repetition of the errors it purports to condemn, as an unsettling of the authority of the *artes*, and (scandalously) as an impious parody of the Letter of James. The homoeroticism of the *De planctu* can hardly be understood as unacknowledged or repressed desires that lie hidden in the text's ambiguous language. In this first *planctus*, the plaintive poet is inextricably and conspicuously linked to the very "monstrous and unspeakable acts" he denounces. More seriously, the discourse prohibiting those acts is itself the fruit of a monstrous, unspeakable union: a perverse poem rather than a misbegotten child. The fact that the *planctus* denouncing unnatural acts as immoral and sterile should itself spawn immoral meanings can be taken as evidence that, for Alan of Lille, Nature is not a stable ontological or moral order, but instead a signifying process and verbal creation liable, like all texts, to semantic and moral deviation.

Nature's Complaint

It should be clear at this point that the sexual ethics outlined in the opening meter of the *De planctu* is indelibly marked by the legacy of Augustine. The "stirring" of the flesh and slippages of meaning in signs are, for both Augustine and Alan, symptoms of the damage incurred through the Fall.[62] Even in his attempts to achieve redemption, man remains mired in wickedness and lives out his moral defects in language and the body, rhetoric and desire. If Augustine believes that a redeemed rhetoric, in spite of its intrinsic limitations, can mediate between man and God and can lead eventually to salvation, that rhetoric inevitably reflects the alienation and ambivalence of postlapsarian existence. Indeed, Augustine's sign theory depends upon a constant moral tension between the instrumental and self-referential, transitive and intransitive properties of signs. He defines signs as things used to signify "something else" and distinguishes between *use* and *enjoyment:* "Those things which are to be enjoyed make us blessed. Those things which are to be used help and, as it were, sustain us as we move toward blessedness in order that we may gain and cling to those things which make us blessed."[63] It would seem that the only legitimate object of enjoyment is the Trinity, which alone is "worthy of love."[64] If, however, we enjoy things *other* than the godhead, including those things that are meant to guide us back *to* the godhead, then "our course" toward blessedness "will be impeded and sometimes deflected."[65] We may even find ourselves permanently exiled from "our native country."[66]

Meter 1 of the *De planctu* exhibits a similarly antinomic conception of signs. On one hand, the poet uses rhetorical figures as an instrumental, orthographic language that serves to moralize human behavior and to guide man back to a lost state of purity. On the other hand, as we have seen, his rhetoric contains alternate, perverse meanings that contravene his moral message and indulge in the circular, self-referential pleasures of pseudography: the enjoyment of signs for their own sake. If Augustine worries that such enjoyment will shackle men to the world and impede the quest for God, Alan demonstrates that language and desire are both so thoroughly compromised by human desire and depravity that one can scarcely speak about ethics without lapsing into deviant, wicked pleasures.

Alan's allegory of nature is itself clearly divided between use-value and enjoyment, moral rigidity and semantic play. As Jon Whitman argues, Nature is as much a speaker as a character in the *De planctu*, and is defined as much by what she *says* as what she *is*. Alan's poem "dramatizes how the problem of characterizing the natural world finally converges with the problem of assessing its mode of discourse."[67] The allegory of nature cannot simply be subsumed to the category of integumental poetry that Nature herself describes: a temporary concealment of the "sweeter kernel of truth" beneath "the outer bark of the composition" (144). Instead, as Whitman observes, Nature is a discursive construct in which we may locate a permanent tension "between conditions of integrity and disintegration," just as the language of the *De planctu* as a whole tends "to modulate between states of proficiency and deficiency."[68] The fact that Nature's *modus loquendi* "does not just depend upon turns of expression" but actually "luxuriates in them" leads Whitman to the apt conclusion that "the very elaboration of Nature's argument tends to attenuate it. The more expansively she talks, the more she betrays the constriction of her activity. In part, that is, her extended speech is not just a lament *about* her limitations, but a repetition *of* them."[69] The result of Nature's prolixity is an allegory in which cosmology merges with ethics but in which the moral dimension of the allegory is undermined by its tendency to refer to itself rather than to a sublime truth or transcendental signified. The ambiguous meanings and desires implicit in the poet's "mournful ditty" should not, therefore, be understood as temporary aberrations that are corrected by Nature's appearance before the poet or by Genius's edict of excommunication. On the contrary, the allegorical visions the poet describes are themselves implicated in perversity and remain so throughout the poem.

As a number of scholars have argued, medieval readers would have been predisposed to view Nature's moral authority and religious orthodoxy with skepticism, especially given her intimate associations with the flesh and its desires. Certainly, as we saw in chapter 1, there is an association in medieval intellectual traditions between being and goodness, the inherent structure of the created world and moral virtue. Hugh White explains, "Within the Christian moral tradition from very early on it was possible to see the natural as pointing to the right and to think of what was unnatural as wrong."[70] For Alan of Lille, the foundations for virtue are inherent in human nature, even if "these natural dispositions to the good are not in themselves true virtue."[71] However, there is also "a far from negligible strain in medieval thought [that] associates the natural with the animal and the irrational and recognizes that there is a sense of nature in which nature can move to the bad."[72] This does not invalidate Nature's role as moral guide, at least not completely. The natural is always morally superior to the unnatural and so offers a set of basic guidelines for what behaviors must be avoided. At the same time, the relationship between the natural and the good is far from stable or absolute. If, for Alan and other of the Chartres scholars, Nature typically works to achieve the good (by overseeing procreation, participating in the divine plan, or encouraging virtuous conduct), her complicity with Venus is also inescapably problematic. Sexual desire, which is necessary for "the activity of generation" and is "at the centre of Nature's purpose," is unpredictable and morally ambivalent, giving rise to "what is bad as well as what is good."[73] Nature may seek to blame others for her own intrinsic flaw; indeed, she does so repeatedly in the *De planctu*, indicting both man and Venus. However, doubts remain about whether "the sexual system which she initiated could ever be wholly satisfactory" or whether Nature herself could ever be truly "blameless."[74] As White observes, it is not simply that for medieval thinkers Nature lacks "salvific reach in comparison with the direct activity of the divine through Grace"; it is also that "her associations with the body and sex" obscure "her moral glory."[75]

In point of fact, Alan does not expend much effort seeking to buttress Nature's moral authority against these prejudices. On the contrary, he repeatedly undermines Nature's own efforts to dissociate herself from evil and even suggests that Nature is guilty of the very crimes that injure her. For instance, though Nature is repeatedly described as a woman and mother, Alan also consistently depicts her assuming masculine roles. By pronouncing *decreta* and arrogating the power of a high-ranking ecclesiastical official, she in effect transforms a "she" into a "he" and inverts the crime of inversion ("hes" into "shes") that the poet associates with "a Venus turned monster." Similarly, if Nature plays the role of *magister* or *doctor* to the poet's *discipulus*, she thereby signifies her membership in an elite intellectual class that is defined in large measure by its absolute exclusion of women. (Some medieval manuscripts make the androgyny of Lady Nature visible by depicting her as a woman dressed in male clerical garb and/or lecturing at a podium.)[76] Finally, as Jordan observes, Nature is rendered androgynous by the very symbols she uses to describe the perpetuation of species. In explaining her appointment as *vicaria Dei*, she says that God commanded her to "put the stamp on the different classes of things," molding "the images of things, each on its own anvil," so that "the face of the copy should spring from the countenance of the exemplar" (146). Guided by "the right hand of the supreme authority," she uses her "writing-reed" to produce images of the exemplars so that like will yield like in keeping with God's design (146). Jordan wonders why "the female Nature" is allowed to "wield hammers and write with a stylus," and concludes that Nature has perversely appropriated "the approved male role in copulation."[77] This apparent betrayal of the law by the embodiment of the law is all the more remarkable in that it occurs at the precise moment when Nature explains her relationship to the sublime source of all justice, authority, and rectitude: the right hand of God. Nature's unnaturalness is not an incidental breach, then, but a fracturing of her moral authority at its source.

I do not mean to suggest (nor does Jordan) that Alan's allegory lacks didactic or moral value altogether. On the contrary, Nature offers a number of highly orthodox teachings on physics, metaphysics, and ethics, drawing attention in particular to the moral significance of cosmic hierarchies. In

Prose 3, she describes the harmonious relationship between macrocosm and microcosm in which Platonic cosmology merges with Pauline and Augustinian theology. Her account of these hierarchies suggests not only that the rational organization of the universe can help to determine human morality, but also that it privileges spirit over flesh and subordinates the individual will to the will of God.[78] Whereas the "movement of reason" is fixed and singular, the "movements of sensuality" are plural and unstable, slipping "with twisted course. . .to the destruction of earthly things" (119). Reason draws man to "the source of virtue," transforms him "into a god," "illuminates the dark night of the mind with the light of contemplation," allows man "to hold converse with angels," and shows him "in exile how to get back to his fatherland" (119). Sensuousness, by contrast, "draws man's mind down to the destruction arising from vice," corrupts and "changes him into a beast," "removes the light of the mind by the dark night of concupiscence," "drives him to wanton with brute beasts," and forces him "into exile" (119).

Nature indicates that in spite of her link to the body and its restless appetites, she bears no responsibility for evils that arise from them. She asserts that the capacity to choose evil is itself a good:

> Nec in hac re hominis natura mee dispensationis potest ordinem accusare. De rationis enim consilio tale contradictionis duellum inter hos pugiles ordinaui, ut, si in hac disputatione ad redargutionem sensualititas ratio poterit inclinare, antecedens uictoria premio consequente non careat. Premia enim uictoriis comparata ceteris muneribus pulcrius elucescunt. Munera enim empta laboribus iocundius omnibus clarescunt gratuitis. (6.64–70)

> [Nor in this matter can the blame for man's nature be laid on my order and arrangement. It was on reason's advice that I arranged such antagonism and war between these contestants, so that if in this dispute reason should be able to turn to refute sensuality, the victory so gained may not lack the due reward. For rewards obtained from victories shine more fair than all other gifts. Rewards purchased by toil bring more honour and delight than all gifts given gratis.] (119–20)[79]

Man's principal responsibility in this cosmic struggle between reason and sensuousness, virtue and vice, is to obey the angels, who are in turn obedient to God:

> In hac ergo republica deus est imperans, angelus operans, homo obtemperans. Deus hominem imperando creat, angelus operando procreat, homo obtemperando se recreat. Deus rem auctoritate disponit, angelus actione componit, homo se res operantis uoluntati supponit. Deus imperat auctoritas magisterio, angelus operatur actionis ministerio, homo obtemperat regenerationis misterio. (6.82–88)

[In this state, then, God gives commands, the angels carry them out, man obeys. God creates man by his command, the angels by their operation carry out the work of creation, man by obedience re-creates himself. By his authority God decrees the existence of things, by their operation the angels fashion them, man submits himself to the will of the spirits carrying out the operation. God gives orders by his magisterial authority, angels operate by ministerial administration, man obeys by the mystery of regeneration.] (120–21)

In short, man must not simply find moral guidance in the macrocosm but must submit to the hierarchies that are inscribed upon the macrocosm and that call for subordination to God's law. Thus Wisdom, who "rests in the citadel of [man's] head," must subdue Magnanimity, who fends off injustice either from without or from within the body (121). In turn, Magnanimity must subdue the "loins and willful desires," which "do not dare to oppose the orders of Magnanimity but obey her will" (122). In imitation of the cosmic hierarchy—God/angels/man—Wisdom assumes the role of "commander-in-chief," Magnanimity that of "administrator," and Desire "the image of the one obeying" (122). In this and other respects, "the form of the human body takes over the image of the universe" (122). By emulating the order of nature and by *using* things of nature rather than *enjoying* them, man may avoid evil and find his way back to blessedness.

If at first glance the content of Nature's arguments appears quite orthodox, a closer examination of her rhetorical style reveals plentiful ambiguities and pitfalls. To begin with, Nature's description of cosmic harmonies is entirely out of keeping with what it purports to describe. As Sheridan observes, Nature does not achieve balance and moderation in the passages cited above but instead indulges in arresting, but apparently superfluous, forms of wordplay. Most notable is her "use of words with similarity in sound but difference of meaning: *imperans, operans, obtemperans; creat, procreat, recreat; disponit, componit, supponit; magisterio, ministerio, misterio.*"[80] It is counterintuitive, to say the least, to privilege sound over sense in a text concerned with the subordination of matter to spirit. Inverting the very hierarchy she describes, Nature plays with the physicality of the signifier rather than striving to grasp a transcendental signified. To put it in Augustinian terms, Nature is rather clearly *enjoying* what ought to be *used.*

As if to confirm the inappropriate playfulness of her own language, Nature almost immediately acknowledges, "Our chain of reason extends too far when it dares to lift our discourse to the ineffable secrets of the godhead, although our mind grows faint in sighs for a knowledge of this matter" (121). Emphasizing her imperfect connection with the godhead, she declares that she does nothing but "follow closely in the footprints of God in His operations" (124). If the poet is seeking confirmation of her deficiencies, he should listen not to her but to Theology, with whom she shares "no close kinship" (125): "Consult the authoritative teaching of [T]heology on whose trustworthiness you should base your assent rather than on the strength of my arguments" (124). Whereas Theology "understands the incomprehensible," Nature sees only "what is visible"; whereas Theology "marches in the hidden places of heaven," Nature walks "around the earth like a brute beast" (125). Nature's most significant failing with respect to Theology is her inability to comprehend the mystery of baptism, of rebirth in Christ: "Ego Natura huius natiuitatis naturam ignoro" [I, Nature, am ignorant of the nature of this birth] (6.146–47; 125). Even as she humbly acknowledges her limitations, though, Nature manages to insinuate herself where she does not belong. Her redundant use of "ego" (in Latin, personal pronouns are expressed as subjects only for emphasis) and her self-naming are immediately doubled by a playful alliteration and the mapping of Nature's name onto a supernatural mystery: "huius natiuitatis naturam." Far from being self-effacing, Nature is almost completely self-regarding: even as she defers to a mystery beyond language and the world, she returns repeatedly to her own name.

Rather than an incidental defect, Nature's self-reflexivity is repeatedly linked to sexual perversities, most notably in Prose 4. Here, Nature responds to the poet's inquiry about why she has appeared before him weeping. She explains that lesser creatures than man have held themselves "bound in voluntary subjection to the ordinances of my decrees according to the rank of each's activity" (131). Yet man, "who has all but drained the entire treasury of my riches, tries to denature the natural things of nature and arms a lawless and solecistic Venus to fight against me" (131). She then offers an account of human depravity that echoes the poet's own *planctus*:

> Solus homo, mee modulationis citharam aspernatus, sub delirantis Orphei lira delirat. Humanum namque genus, a sua generositate degenerans, in constructione generum barbarizans, Venereas regulas inuertendo nimis irregulari utitur metaplasmo. Sic homo, Venere tiresiatus anomala, directam predicationem per compositionem inordinate conuertit. A Veneris ergo orthographia deuiando recedens sophista falsigraphus inuenitur. Consequentem etiam Dionee artis analogiam deuitans, in anastrophen uiciosam degenerat. Dumque in tali constructione me destruit, in sua syneresis mei themesim machinatur. (8.54–61)

> [Man alone turns with scorn from the modulated strains of my cithern (*citharam*) and runs deranged (*delirat*) to the notes of mad (*delirantis*) Orpheus' lyre (*lira*). For the human race, fallen from its high estate, adopts a highly irregular (grammatical) change when it inverts the rules of Venus by introducing barbarisms in its arrangement of genders. Thus man, his sex changed by a ruleless Venus, in defiance of due order, by his arrangement changes what is a straightforward attribute of his. Abandoning in his deviation the orthography of Venus, he is proved to be a sophistic pseudographer.

Shunning even a resemblance traceable to the art of Dione's daughter, he falls into the defect of inverted order. While in a construction of this kind he causes my destruction, in his combination (*in sua synderesis*) he devises a division in me (*mei themesim*).] (133–34, slightly modified)

Orpheus is, of course, the father of lyric poetry, trained by Apollo himself in the art of the lyre. Nature attacks the excesses of Orphic poetry with a pun on *lira* and *delirare*: man rejects orthography and Nature's well-regulated song, lapsing instead into the madness of pseudography and unnatural intercourse. Scanlon interprets *delirare* as "to delyre" and argues that "as an essentially Orphean vehicle, the lyre characteristically 'delyres' itself—that is, it dissolves harmony in the course of attempting to produce it."[81] Of course, Alan doubtless also knew the etymology of *delirare* (*de–* + *lira*, or "furrow"), whether from Isidore of Seville or some other source.[82] Man's unnatural delirium and Orpheus's deranged lyric clearly recall the metaphor of the plowshare that deviates from its path or that finds a deviant new furrow. Above all, it is clear that Orpheus should be understood here not just as a poet but also as a pederast and teacher of pederasts. This is certainly how Ovid describes him in the *Metamorphoses*: "Orpheus preferred to centre his affections on boys of tender years, and to enjoy the brief spring and early flowering of their youth: he was the first to introduce this custom among the people of Thrace."[83] Orpheus is, moreover, the narrator who recounts some of the most celebrated pederastic myths in the *Metamorphoses*, including Apollo and Cyparissus, Apollo and Hyacinthus, and Jupiter and Ganymede—all characters mentioned in the *De planctu*. As Susan Schibanoff has recently argued, for Alan of Lille, lyric and pederasty merge in the figure of Orpheus and indeed are inextricably linked to one another.[84]

This association of poetry and perversity certainly explains Nature's attempts to dissociate her "modulated strains" from Orpheus's delirious ones and to articulate once again the distinction between orthography and pseudography. And yet as always, the distinction is not simply drawn. Nature chooses the *chitara* as her instrument and assigns the *lira* to Orpheus; but the difference between two instruments is far from obvious. Moreover, just as Ovid's Orpheus is both a poet and a character in a poem, so Nature both declaims lyric and is herself a lyric creation. If Orpheus recounts and emulates Apollo and Jupiter's pederastic desires, might Nature not also be implicated in the sexual madness she describes? Certainly, her status as a rhetorical, fictional, and poetic creation links her more to pseudography than to orthography. If man's improper combination of genders (*syneresis*: the merging of two syllables into one) betrays Nature and devises a division within her (*tmesis*: the separation of a compound word by an intervening word or words), we are reminded by these grammatical metaphors that

Nature is not an essential being but a verbal contrivance. Indeed, her redundant claim that Man "tries to denature the natural things of nature" points to the fact that Nature is herself no more than a figure of speech: a common noun rendered as a proper name. Far from embodying or purveying truth, Nature is a blatantly deceptive fiction. It is starting to become difficult to believe that there could be any meaningful differences between her and "mad Orpheus," the "sophistic pseudographer."

These tensions are merely amplified as Nature continues her attack on sexual deviance, recounting a number of negative exempla from the *Metamorphoses*. Strikingly, though Nature's intention has been to denounce gender inversion and male same-sex love, she here chooses myths that have little to do with either. She refers first to Helen's "harlotry" and Pasiphae's "bestial marriage" (135). She then cites the stories of Myrrha, who played a "mother's role" with her own father, and Medea, who played a murderous "stepmother" with her own "natural son" (135–36). When she does finally mention a male hero, Narcissus, Nature describes his crime of self-love principally in terms of the play of illusions and reflections: "Narcisus etiam, sui umbra alterum mentita Narcisum, umbratiliter obumbratus, seipsum credens esse se alterum, de se sibi amoris incurrit periculum" [Narcissus, when his shadow faked a second Narcissus, was reflected in a reflection, believing himself to be a second self, and rushed headlong to his destruction by loving himself] (8.76–78; 136, modified). From this description, we might conclude that the crime of Narcissus is less same-sex desire than self-reflexivity and verbal play. As Wetherbee observes, Ovidian myths in the *De planctu* are not merely "conventional moralizations"; rather, "mythology and its perilous ambiguities are a major theme" of the work.[85] If Nature refers only obliquely to the homoeroticism of Ovid's Narcissus, it is no doubt because his concern is not deviant sexuality alone, but also the pleasurable, playful, and self-referential dimensions of rhetoric and poetry—what Leupin calls "the deadly threat of circular writing."[86] Whereas "Orphism emblematizes homosexuality and a certain art of writing characterized by the primacy of its own movement," Leupin says that Narcissus embodies a "sophistic writing" that "can only allegorize (in the deviation of the simulacrum) captivation by the self."[87] In Augustinian terms, the crime of Narcissus is *enjoying* visual images and metaphorical substitutions for their own sake rather than for what they might be *used* to signify—that is, a moral condemnation of unnatural desire. In describing Narcissus, Nature finds herself indulging yet again in playfully repetitive language, language that privileges sound as much as, if not more than, sense: *Narcissus–Narcissum, sui–seipsum–se–sibi, umbratiliter–obumbratus*. Apparently seduced by her subject matter, Nature imitates in language the very reflexivity she condemns. Indeed, she seems to admit as much when she warns the poet that he should not be surprised if her words are cousin to the deeds she condemns: "Non igitur mireris si in has uerborum prophanas exeo nouitates, cum prophani homines prophanius audeant debachari" [Do not be surprised, then, that I go beyond limits in my use of this strange and profane language when impious men dare to revel in wicked manner] (8.94–97; 137). By Nature's own admission, it is impossible to dissociate her moral language from the moral failure it deplores. Moreover, the fact that the passage she is describing here reiterates much of the content of Meter 1 (the grammar of Venus, the "interchangeability of subject and predicate," and so on) suggests that Nature is little more than a mirror reflecting the text in which she appears. William Burgwinkle certainly reads Nature in this way, as a cross-dressed double of the author: "Nature is no lady; she is a surface, a reflection of Alain himself."[88]

The poet draws further attention to the imbrication of poetry and perversity when he asks Nature why she attacks man alone and does not condemn the gods also for their improprieties:

> Miror cur poetarum commenta retractans, solummodo in humani generis pestes predictarum inuectionum armas aculeos, cum et eodem exorbitationis pede deos claudicasse legamus. Iupiter enim, adolescentem Frigium transferens ad superna, relatiuam Venerem transtulit in translatum. Et quem in mensa per diem propinandi sibi prefecit propositum, in thoro per noctem sibi fecit suppositum. (8.115–22)

> [I wonder why, when you consider the statements of the poets, you load the stings of the above attacks against the contagions of the human race alone, although we read that the gods, too, have limped around the same circle of aberration. For Jupiter, translating (*transferens*) the Phrygian youth to the realms above, transferred (*transtulit*) there a proportionate love for him on his transference (*translatum*). The one he had made his wine-master by day he made his subject in bed by night.] (138–39)

The rape of Ganymede is here rendered metaphorically *as metaphor*. Pittenger notes that the words *transferens, transtulit,* and *translatum* all "depend on the complexity of the 'grammatical' notion of *translatio,*" which Chenu defines as "a transference or elevation from the visible sphere to the invisible through the mediating agency of an image borrowed from sense-perceptible reality."[89] This Augustinian notion of an instrumental language that rises above the world and returns the reader to the fatherland is here betrayed by the poet's reference to Jupiter's ascent from earth to Olympus with the "Phrygian youth" in his clutches. Ganymede's dual roles (cupbearer and beloved) indeed suggest that the *artes* are transformed into deviant sexual positions. *Propositus*, a proposition in logic or a general question in rhetoric, is doubled by *suppositus*, that which has been placed beneath.

Suppositus may in turn suggest a pun on *suppositorium*, or "suppository," in which case Jupiter would be the penetrated partner.[90] Weighted down with double entendres, the passage suggests less a moralization of the sexual misdeeds of the gods than the intrinsic immorality of poetry, rhetoric, and signs in general.

Nature's response is telling: she denounces the poet not for his insubordination or his obscenely playful references to same-sex love, but rather for his misunderstanding of the nature of exegesis. In a much quoted passage, she offers a reminder of the Scholastics' integumental theories of reading:

> An ignoras quomodo. . .in superficiali littere cortice falsum resonat lira poetica, interius uero auditoribus secretum intelligentie altioris eloquitur, ut exteriori falsitatis abiecto putamine dulciorem nucleum ueritatis secrete intus lector inueniat? (8.128–36)

> [Do you not know how. . .the poetic lyre gives a false note on the outer bark of the composition but within tells the listeners a secret of deeper significance so that when the outer shell of falsehood has been discarded the reader finds the sweeter kernel of truth hidden within?] (140)

Though this account of the usefulness of pagan *fabulae* may run counter to a strict Augustinian orthodoxy, it is certainly in keeping with contemporary theories of moral exegesis, which used allegorical interpretation to uncover spiritual truths in texts whose literal meanings were considered perverse or immoral.

And yet Nature here seems to want to overlook the fact that she has herself used poetry in a very different way. As Wetherbee observes, Nature does not decouple external falsehoods from internal, encoded truths, but rather teaches moral lessons through the literal recounting of myth: "For there are human problems to which poetic fable and its mythological apparatus, gods and goddesses representative of cosmic and psychic forces, lend themselves naturally. Nature herself employs such resources, and has used their imagined corruption to illustrate the corruption of human nature."[91] More to the point, Nature's "account of poetry gives no indication of *how* the true and false instances of poetic mythology are to be distinguished."[92] This is a "crucial omission" and will assume "thematic significance almost at once."[93] The very distinction between instrumental and self-referential uses of language begins to blur, suggesting that a return to the fatherland may not be possible after all. Wetherbee explains,

> The corruption of man's nature is reflected in the corruption of his art; the only artist capable of genuine metaphor, the *poeta platonicus*, was Adam in the Garden, giving names to his subject creatures and in the process realizing his own true dignity as man. That the artistic resources employed by Alain bear

within them the germ of their own corruption is thus a telling instance of the distortion of man's self-awareness.[94]

Scanlon takes the argument a step further, noting that the lyre has already been linked to Orpheus and homoeroticism: "When the lyre reappears in the defense of allegory as the vehicle of the one acceptable form of poetic fiction, the vehicle whereby exegetical labor can work through fiction to the truth, it does so as a vehicle already tainted by the very disorder it would escape."[95] Scanlon observes that the "figural *nucleum veritatis*" is itself a metaphorical fiction: an integumental falsehood posing as the inner truth concealed beneath another integumental falsehood. Clearly, the path to spiritual regeneration is exceedingly difficult (if not impossible) to locate within signs. Rhetoric and allegory, poetry and the cosmos are thus symptomatic of the waywardness of desire and the alienation of humanity from its original state of grace. Scanlon's conclusion is a wholly apposite one: Alan's question about the sexual habits of the gods "suggests there is something fundamentally queer about poetry; *Natura*'s response acknowledges he is right, even in the course of denying it."[96]

A final passage from Prose 4 tells us just how seriously compromised Nature is by her own status as a poetic and allegorical figure. Strikingly, the passage is also Nature's most elaborate conceit for deflecting responsibility for unnatural vice. The poet asks his teacher, "Miror cur quedam tue tunice portiones, que texture matrimonio deberent esse confines, in ea parte sue coniunctionis paciantur diuorcia, in qua hominis imaginem picture representant insompnia?" [I wonder why some parts of your tunic, which should approximate the interweave of a marriage, suffer a separation at that part in their connection where the picture's phantasy produces the image of man] (8.161–63; 142). Nature replies,

Iam ex prelibatis potes elicere quid misticum figuret scissure figurata parenthesis. Cum enim, ut prediximus, plerique homines in suam matrem uiciorum armentur iniuriis, inter se et ipsam maximum chaos dissensionis firmantes, in me uiolentas manus uiolenter iniciunt et mea sibi particulatim uestimenta diripiunt et, quam reuerentie deberent honore uestire, me uestibus orphanatam, quantum in ipsis est, cogunt meretricaliter lupanare. Hoc ergo integumentum hac scissura depingitur quod solius hominis iniuriosis insultibus mea pudoris ornamenta discidii contumelias paciuntur. (8.164–72)

[From what you have already sampled you can deduce what is the symbolic signification of the representation of the parenthesis-like rent. For since, as we have said before, many men arm themselves with vices to injure their own mother and establish between her and them the chaos of ultimate dissension, in their violence they lay violent hands on me, tear my clothes in shreds to have pieces for themselves and, as far as in them lies, compel me, whom they should clothe in honour and reverence, to be stripped of my clothes and to go like a harlot to a brothel. This is the hidden meaning symbolised by this rent—that the vesture of my modesty suffers the insults of being torn off by injuries and insults from man alone.] (142–43)

The parenthesis-like tear in Nature's garments could initially be understood as an elision of the unnatural, unspeakable sin in the discourse and figuration of Nature. As Macrobius argues, Nature envelops herself "in variegated garments" and conceals "a decent and dignified conception of holy truths" beneath "a modest veil of allegory."[97] Presumably, then, the tear in the garment represents a violent attempt to corrupt Nature's purity and expose her body to view. And yet the language of the passage thwarts this or any other kind of straightforward gloss. Nature says that the meaning of the tear can be deduced on the basis of what she has already said; but for the moment at least, Nature refuses to describe the acts that have injured her, preferring to use figures to insulate herself from the damage that has been done to her by men. The "symbolic signification of the representation of the parenthesis-like rent" indeed places the unspeakable vice at four degrees of distance from Nature herself: similitude, representation, signification, and symbol. And yet this layering of representation also prevents us from glimpsing the truth of Nature: a body that is never described but is instead passed over in silence. On one hand, this elision might be attributed to chastity and virtue: Nature's garments have been torn and her body prostituted, so both she and the poet protect that body from prying eyes by covering it in a "vesture of modesty." On the other hand, the body and truth of Nature become, through antiphrasis and periphrasis, remarkably similar to the unnatural vice: that which cannot be spoken directly but must be spoken otherwise, a gap within representation.

By her very condition as an allegorical creation, Nature is embroiled in the deviations she seeks to repudiate. She cannot reveal her truth openly for fear that it will fall into the wrong hands, and indeed that truth seems to have been exposed to unscrupulous, violent sinners. Yet in speaking her truth otherwise and concealing it beneath multiple layers of representation, she suggests that it is ultimately unspeakable and therefore homologous with unnatural sin. Though she promises to reveal the "hidden meaning" of the tear in her garment, providing for the poet and reader the correct gloss, she merely repeats what she has already said: "that the vesture of my modesty suffers the insults of being torn off by injuries and insults from man alone." The tautological phrase "figuret figurata" [figured by figures] can be completed only by another tautology: the integument depicts what has already been depicted.

Ultimately, this redundancy exposes the vulnerability of allegory's moral and transcendental claims. Allegory cannot contain its truth but suggests instead that it lies beyond the text—or indeed is a *nucleus* embedded deep within it. The only means it has to designate that truth is, however, verbal and metaphorical, meaning that the transcendental signified is constantly displaced along a chain of imperfect verbal signifiers. The authoritative speech of the *vicaria Dei* amounts to an infinite regression of citations or self-citations in which there is no pure, truthful meaning and no obvious moral utility. Nature is a poetic creation, and poetry, as Wetherbee argues, is in this context rather clearly "an index to the limits of man's power to realign himself with the natural order."[98] Whitman makes a similar point: Nature's

> turns of language, no sooner seeking to control defection than collapsing into it, suggest the moral complications of her turn to man. Her narrative fable, developing its own wayward momentum, reenacts the insubordination in her natural order. If personification is "the fashioning of a character and speech for inanimate things," both the imaginative technique and the world it animates seem to have come to a dead end.[99]

Many scholars have sought a way out of this impasse. Whitman argues that Nature's discourse is "a still undetermined realm with its own potentialities" and is therefore open to moral transformation and reform.[100] Lynch reads the *De planctu* "as a kind of metapoetry, a poetry that seeks, in the tradition of the Boethian or philosophical vision, to define the terms of its own existence, to establish a true and viable basis for its authority."[101] However, many other scholars, most notably Leupin, Jordan, and Burgwinkle, offer less optimistic readings. Leupin argues that "the contagious force of hermaphrodism" cannot be "easily dismissed" and plagues the *De planctu* from beginning to end.[102] The final lines of the work are indeed notable for the dense layering of illusions rather than any revelation of truth or awakening to moral enlightenment: "Huius igitur imaginarie uisionis subtracto speculo, me ab extasis excitatum insompnio prior mistice apparitionis dereliquit aspectus" [Accordingly, when the mirror with these images and visions was withdrawn, I awoke from my dream and ecstasy and the previous vision of the mystic apparition left me] (18.164–65; 221).[103] It seems clear from these lines that we will never discover the "kernel of truth" in Alan's poem, only a circular logic whereby the poem refers to itself and its status as imaginative fiction. Thus Leupin refers to these closing lines as a "vertiginous closure" in which "all scriptural forms seem to originate in the left hand, the hand sinfully brimming with phantasmal images."[104] Jordan makes a similar observation: the poem's denouement suggests that its "didactic sections" and the teachings of Lady Nature were never anything more than a dream [*insomnium*], an ecstasy [*exstasis*], and "figures of our narrator's fantasy."[105] If "the narrator means *insomnium* in the technical sense known to twelfth-century readers from

Macrobius's commentary on the dream of Scipio," then the dream is neccs-sarily deceptive: "For Macrobius, an *insomnium* is a disturbance of sleep that brings no truth with it. To call the whole of the previous text *insomnium* is to call it a deceit."[106] Certainly, the status of dreams has already been compro-mised, since Nature associates them "with the errors of the most voluptuous and mendacious philosophy—'the dreams of Epicurus.' "[107]

Burgwinkle goes a step further than Leupin or Jordan, and his reading is, to my mind, the most convincing:

> Only at the end of the text do we learn to what extent we have been drawn into a multilayered voyeuristic trap, a structuring device which undercuts the serious message Alain claims to have been imparting. The dreamer peers beneath a gap or tear in Nature's dress; his alter ego, the narrator/poet, watches on and inscribes himself in the act of gazing; and we, the unwitting voyeurs, are encouraged throughout to invest a sleeping man's vision with a mantle of reality that is only lifted, rhetorically, in the final sentence.[108]

Certainly, given Nature's elaborate blurring of the boundary between reality and representation, it is not difficult to imagine that the poem's "contagion" might extend beyond its own boundaries, infecting the reader himself with the very desires and crimes that the text is meant to denounce and extirpate.

Genius's Anathema

Might Genius, as a representative of the priesthood, offer an alternative to Nature's distortions of rhetoric and poetry or a more reliable means for accessing intellectual and spiritual truths? Many critics have suggested as much. Guy Raynaud de Lage argues that Genius's anathematization and exclusion of unnatural sinners marks the reconciliation of man and nature, nature and God. For the sake of "decency," Alan entrusts the priestly func-tion of excommunication to a male figure only; but here Genius serves as Nature's mouthpiece, articulating a solution to the moral problems that Nature has raised with her plaint.[109] Reading the *De planctu* within the tra-dition of the "philosophical vision," Lynch similarly believes that the poem "details a profoundly meaningful progression of experience" from "confu-sion to spiritual health."[110] Unlike Wetherbee, she does not find that the *De planctu* ends in ambivalence but rather in harmony: the reconciling of previously dissonant forces, notably nature and grace. Harmony is "reflected in the appearance of Genius," who embodies and is knowledgeable about the links between creation and Creator, nature and faith.[111] Lynch under-stands the anathema as particularly significant in that it provides "a more complete resolution of the problem of evil" than previous thinkers were able to conceive. The anathema is like "a culminating chord" that "harmonizes all at once the poem's many notes and melodies, resolving all previous discords" and excommunicating evildoers from the realm of Nature.[112] Genius does not necessarily effect an eradication of evil, in Lynch's view, nor indeed does he emblematize a moral force. He is instead the personification of human imagination, of "the Dreamer's *ingenium*," and his role is to illustrate the Dreamer's final "comprehension of the role evil plays as part of God's plan."[113] More recently, Schibanoff has assigned a similar meaning to Genius's edict, drawing attention especially to the move from writing to orality, from the proliferation of unnatural desires in poetry to the "new oral discourse of morality" in which perversity is more strictly circumscribed.[114] Ultimately, she does not believe that Genius is capable of separating poetry from perversity. However, she does see his oral edict as an "earnest," if "frustrated," attempt to resolve that difficulty.[115]

Though each of these arguments has its merits, each should also be carefully qualified. Certainly, it is true that Genius's maleness (which is repeatedly emphasized in the opening of Prose 8) accords him privileges that Nature cannot (or should not) have. Nonetheless as we have already seen, Nature regularly performs the functions of a male ecclesiastic—indeed, the very same functions that Genius performs. Both characters make official pronouncements, with Nature's address to Genius being specifically marked as such.[116] Both write with reed-pens, in Nature's case an *arundo* (16.185), in Genius's a *calamum* (18.68). Genius himself declares that he and Nature are "administrators" of a single "office" (220). And though it is Genius who pronounces the excommunication of unnatural sinners, he makes clear that the edict ultimately derives from Nature: "O Nature, it is not without the divine breath of interior inspiration that there has come from your balanced judgment this imperial edict" (219). Nature explains that her resemblance to Genius is far from incidental:

> Quoniam similia cum dissimilium aspernatione similium sociali habitudine gratulantur, in te uelut in speculo Nature resultante similitudine inueniendo me alteram, tibi nodo dilectionis precordialis astringor aut tecum in tuo profectu proficiens aut in tuo defectu equa lance deficiens. Quare circularis debet esse dilectio, ut tu, talione dilectionis respondens, nostram fortunam facias esse communem. (16.189–94)

> [Since like, with disdain for unlike, rejoices in a bond of relationship with like, finding myself your alter ego by the likeness of Nature that is reflected in you as in a mirror, I am bound to you in a knot of heartfelt love, both succeeding in your success and in like manner failing in your failure. Love, then, should be a circle so that you, responding with a return of love, should make our fortunes interchangeable.] (206–07)

Man's foremost crime, the joining of like with like, is here doubled by Nature's bond with her other self. The vice of Narcissus is mirrored by Nature's love of her own likeness, her self–conscious naming of herself, and her typically (and needlessly) playful, repetitious language: *similia– dissimilium–similium–similitudine, profectu–proficiens, defectu–deficiens.*

Schibanoff's claim that the anathema, as oral discourse, represents an attempt to rise above the association of poetry and perversity is a more solid argument. Genius speaks last in the *De planctu* and, with characteristic terseness, goes a long way toward curbing Nature's prolixity and rhetorical extravagance: "Dum hoc uerborum compendio Genius sue orationis frenaret excursum, sue exclamationis quasi aurora nascente tristicie tenebras paulisper absentans, saluo sue dignitatis honore Natura Genio graciarum iura persoluit" [While Genius was reining in the running commentary of his speech in the above short-cut of words and removing to some extent the darkness of gloom by what might be called the rising dawn of his outburst, Nature, mindful of his honour and dignity, returned him due thanks] (18.135–37; 220). If, as Whitman suggests, Nature's limitations are inseparable from the expansiveness of her speech, then it is undoubtedly significant, first, that Genius is capable of bridling his own speech and, second, that Nature's expression of gratitude is rendered only in indirect discourse. Nature does not speak again in the *De planctu*, and it is clear that her silence can be attributed in part to Genius's dignity and concision. Genius is a man of few words, and his words apparently function as performatives: they enact what they describe.

And yet this argument is complicated by the fact that, as Burgwinkle observes, "writing precedes speech" in the *De planctu*: the signifier takes "temporal precedence over" and "obscures" the signified.[117] The performative does not refer to an exterior reality or stable meaning but to itself and perverse slippages of meaning within signs. Scanlon's argument about the "kernel of truth" substantiates Burgwinkle's claim. The *nucleum veritatis* is itself a form of literary deception: a metaphor substituting for the truth that supposedly lies beneath the "outer bark" of metaphor. Likewise, Genius's oral speech is known only through multiple levels of mediation: first, through the dream vision itself (or, rather, the "dream and ecstasy" in which the poet experiences a "vision" of a "mystic apparition" [221]); and, second, through writing and text, the writing down of the poet's vision as a poem. If writing and perversion are inextricably linked in the *De planctu*, then even Genius's anathema must contain perverse meanings.

As for Lynch's argument that the anathema effects a resolution to the problem of evil, it would be difficult to imagine that Genius, whose existence is so emphatically ambivalent and phantasmic, could possibly arrive at this kind of philosophical or theological truth—or even that he could be associated with a mode of consciousness through which that truth might be intuited.

Lynch understands Genius as initially an "ambiguous" figure but argues that ambiguities fade with the arrival of his daughter Truth, who allows him to celebrate "a newly sacramental reality."[118] Lynch concludes, "The theme of imagination. . .becomes the tertium quid, the middle term, capable of giving fullness to this poet's vision, capable of mediating successfully between his desire for a truth that is of this world and one that finally transcends it."[119] And yet a close examination of the text does not support this claim. Truth is *not* privileged over Falsehood. Instead, the former seems to overcome the latter and deconstruct her claims: "Lying in wait for the picture of truth [*pictura Veritatis*]," Falsehood "disgraced by deformity whatever truth graced by conformity" (218). In essence, Truth is not merely vulnerable to Falsehood's distortions but is herself a species of falsehood. We are told that her "garments had been joined to [her] body by a bond so close that no separation by removal [*dieresis*] could ever make them Separatists from [her] body" (218), meaning, presumably, that the covering (signifier) and that which is covered (signified) are virtually identical. And yet *pictura Veritatis* is a provocatively ambiguous genitive. It suggests not only that Truth produces representations but also that she is herself a depiction: an allegory that signifies a coincidence of signifier and signified but that is itself always a signifier, one that covers and conceals the truth even as it claims to reveal it.

Exactly like his daughter, Genius is described as a regression of mimetic, metaphorical, and vestimentary illusions. When Genius first appears in the *De planctu*, the poet describes his clothing as a shifting, ephemeral textual surface:

> Vestes uero nunc grossioris materie uulgari artificio plebescere, nunc subtilioris materie artificiosissima contextione crederes superbire. In quibus picturarum fabule nuptiales sompniabant euentus, picturatas tamen ymagines uetustatis fuligo fere coegerat expirare. Ibi tamen sacramentalem matrimonii fidem, connubii pacificam unitatem, nuptiarum indisparabile iugum, nubentium indissolubile uinculum, lingua picture fatebatur intextum. In picture etenim libro umbratiliter legebatur, que nuptiarum iniciis exultationis applaudat sollempnitas, que in nuptiis melodie sollempnizet suauitas, que connubiis conuiuarum arrideat generalitas specialis, que matrimonia Citheree concludat iocunditas generalis. (16.23–33)

> [You would imagine that his clothes at one moment were inferior, the product of common workmanship on rather coarse material, at another moment that they were showing their pride in a highly skilled weave of finer material. On these clothes tales, told in pictures, showed, as in a dream, the circumstances connected with marriage. The black paint of age, however, had almost forced the images in the pictures to fade out. Yet the picture's message kept insisting that there had been woven there the faithfulness proceeding from the sacrament of matrimony, the peaceful unity of married life, the inseparable bond of marriage, the indissoluble union of the wedded

parties. For in the book of the picture there could be read in faint outline what solemn joy gives approval to marriage at its beginning, what sweet melody gives a festive, religious tone to the nuptials, what special gathering of guests shows their approbation of the marriage, what general delight rounds off the Cytherean's ceremonies.] (197–98, slightly modified)

Initially, we might understand the message on Genius's garments as a wholly orthodox one. Indeed, it offers clear echoes of Augustine's moral treatises on marriage, especially *The Excellence of Marriage*. The "tales told in pictures" remind the reader of the three goods Augustine attributes to marriage: first, the union of man and wife, which allows for "the procreation of children"; second, the fidelity [*fides*] that allows for "mutual service" and enables the couple to "avoid illicit unions"; and finally, the sacrament itself, which guarantees the indissolubility of marital unions and serves as "a symbol that in the future we shall all be united and subject to God in the one heavenly city."[120] Just as Augustine used the idea of sacraments to endow the Church with the power to administer and determine the mysteries of faith, so Alan believes that the clergy ought to be empowered to regulate marriage and sexual ethics. Indeed, he suggests that this power has always belonged to them: in spite of the passage of time, which has caused the images on Genius's robes to fade, the "lingua picture" continues to affirm the permanence of the sacrament and the unions it solemnizes. A part of the delight that marriage affords is certainly venereal; but "suauitas" and "iocunditas generalis" are qualified by "sollempnitas," meaning in accordance with religion and law. If Nature's garments are torn by "diuorcia" [separation, divorce] where there should be the "the interweave of a marriage," Genius's garments appear to mend that rift, joining together husband and wife and solidifying the religious doctrine that is the basis for a higher unity with God.

However, as always in the *De planctu*, this orthodox message is unquestionably at odds with the language through which it is communicated. Genius's robes, like Nature's own, stand as a metaphor *for* metaphor: a *contextio*, or "weaving together," of threads and tropes. Far from revealing an essential, universal truth, they seem instead to conceal that truth beneath multiple layers of representation. The appearance of the robes changes from moment to moment, even if the doctrine that they reveal is supposed to be insistent and permanent. Moreover, the status of the robes as representation is emphasized at least as much as the message of unity they signify: they tell tales [*fabulae*] in pictures [*picturae*]; those pictures are actually a book [*libro*]; and the book reveals its meaning by means of shaded outlines [*umbratiliter*]. As Burgwinkle observes, Genius's robes offer a dizzying *mise en abyme* of the *De planctu* as a whole, the embedding of a book within the book, a regression of texts "on a grand scale": "Within the art object before us, here a written text, we find the verbal representation of a dress and on that dress there is an image and within that image there is a book and that book contains within it other images."[121] For Burgwinkle, this accumulation of images ("six times removed from the Platonic or divine form") suggests Alan's awareness that "marriage is nothing more than a social construct like so many others, subject to degradation in the sublunary world: a faded human representation rather than an abjected divine model."[122] Ultimately, it is difficult to resist Burgwinkle's conclusion that "all is representation or rhetoric" here.[123]

Though Genius's anathema represents official, oral speech, it is equally tautological, improper, and perverse. Genius here addresses multiple sins against nature in addition to sexual ones: gluttony, drunkenness, avarice, arrogance, envy, and flattery. Speaking with "the authority of the super-essential [Ousia] and his eternal Idea, with assent of the heavenly army, with the combined aid and help of nature and the other recognized virtues" (220), he commands that these sinners "be separated from the kiss of heavenly love as his ingratitude deserves and merits," that they "be demoted from Nature's favour," and that they "be set apart from the harmonious council of the things of Nature" (220). He then suggests specific, logical *contrapassi* for each sin: the glutton will suffer impoverishment; the drunkard will thirst; the miser will want; the arrogant man will suffer humiliation; the envious man will discover that he is his own worst enemy; and the flatterer will be "cheated by a reward of deceptive worth" (221). On the face of it, there is nothing unusual about this system of crimes and punishments. And yet as Scanlon observes, the theology of the anathema is rather blatantly "inaccurate": "Of the various categories of sinners it names, only the sexual sinner might actually have been subject to excommunication, and even that wasn't true until after *De planctu* appeared."[124] Scanlon concludes that the excommunication should be taken as an example of the kind of poetic falsehoods Nature calls integumenta: it must be glossed in order to achieve any real validity.

When it comes to venereal sins, however, the theology is even more noticeably ambiguous: "Qui a regula Veneris exceptionem facit anomalam, Veneris priuetur sigillo" [Let him who makes an irregular exception to the rule of Venus be deprived of the seal of Venus] (18.150–51; 221). On one hand, the word "priuetur" suggests an orthodox notion of evil as privation: the sinner, by dint of the nothingness of his sin, will himself be divested of being. Evil must be separated from nature in order to preserve the necessary link between being and goodness, metaphysics and ethics. The result is that evil must be understood as privation and the evildoer as unmanned and therefore tending toward nothingness. On the other hand, there are serious problems with Genius's performative enactment of the nonexistence of unnatural sinners. As Burgwinkle argues, it is "already an exception to the rule of Venus" for "a male to receive passively the seal of Venus," since imprinting and inscribing are normative sexual roles for men.[125] The rule of Venus is, therefore, inextricably linked to the very crime it prohibits.

As we delve further into the passage, more ambiguities arise. The term *sigillum* (a diminutive of *signum*, or 'sign') could denote either the instrument used to imprint or the mark left by the imprinting. Moreover, the *regula Veneris* could signify either Venus's law or her punishing rod or ruler. Finally, the genitive *Veneris* is itself ambiguous, since it could refer to Venus herself or to things associated with Venus: love, sexuality, the genitals, procreation. As a result of these semantic slippages, the meaning of the edict verges on indeterminacy. Will the unnatural sinner be deprived of his signet? And if so, what does that deprivation mean? Will he be castrated because he has misused his "rod"? Will he be denied the opportunity to propagate and signify? Or will he instead be denied the pleasure of being imprinted *by* the signet, as Burgwinkle suggests? As for the *regula Veneris*, has the sinner deviated from a standard of conduct? Or has he instead misused the phallic instrument? Is this instrument the male genitalia? Or is it, rather, a monstrous female phallus? Since the name Venus is associated with both lawful sexual practices and horrific perversity, it seems reasonable to wonder whether this Venus is *caelestis* or *scelesta*—or indeed whether such a difference could ever be clearly established.

Far from resolving the problem of evil, then, Genius's anathema suggests that it is tainted by the very wickedness it condemns. Here, the repudiation of sexual deviance is itself a deviant form of pleasure. This is certainly Scanlon's conclusion: "Genius's final lesson, one he still has to teach," is that "sexual regulation is itself a species of desire."[126] Far from limiting the waywardness of the libido, Genius's disciplinary language instead allows the libido to invade and vitiate the tropes associated with morality and law. Just as the *De planctu* problematizes the idea of discovering truth in poetry or transcending the slippages of meaning in signs, it also points to the irresoluble nature of its own moral dilemmas. The goodness it associates with Nature is inextricable from the evil Nature proscribes; and even Genius, as the personification of the clergy, is incapable of articulating a pure moral language in which good and evil would remain fully distinct.

★   ★   ★

Though it may stretch the credibility of my argument, I will conclude by considering whether God himself is exempt from the corrupting effects of language or whether Peter Damian was right to fear that the language arts might yield apostasy and perverse "declensions." There are indeed a number of potentially destabilizing associations between the *vitium contra naturam* and the Creator who provides the foundation for Nature and her laws. According to the tradition of apophatic or negative theology to which Alan belongs, God is himself essentially unnamable, or can only properly be named through negation. Likewise, as Alan writes in his *Rhythmus de incarnatione Christi*, the Incarnation itself is not simply mysterious, but a deluding of reason and a deception of nature:

> Exceptivam actionem
> Verbum Patris excipit
> Dum deludit rationem
> Dum naturam decipit
> Casualum dictionem
> Substantivum recipit
> Actioque passionem
> In hoc verbo concipit
> In hac Verbi copula
> Stupet omni regula
> Verbum car factum est.

[The Word of the Father took to himself (or, with a more passive sense, *received*) a unique action when he violated reason and tricked nature. The noun received the use of cases, and the active voice of the verb contained the passive. In this copula of the verb, all the rules are stupefied. The Word was made flesh.][127]

As Leupin observes, the basis for Alan's argument is that the incarnate God is "the unnamable and inconceivable object of all knowledge" that "renders every science incapable of totalization."[128] Faith is not a hindrance to scientific knowledge and truth here but rather "the starting point for a rational effort."[129] For Alan, the "philosophy of mystery" [*philosophia caelestis*] is not incompatible with the "philosophy of creation" [*philosophia naturalis*]. Instead, he suggests an "innovative relation" between them, one that would not be attempted again until the Galilean revolution: the "incompleteness of 'natural' reason before the mysteries of theology" is the sign of "its fundamental accord with them."[130] Put another way, the mysterious unnaturalness of the Incarnation need not be incompatible with the laws of nature. Though God betrays reason and nature, his action is necessarily exceptional and unique. And if grammar cannot comprehend the fact that Christ "is both divine subject and complement of the human object," it does not lack validity as a discipline.[131] Nor does it necessarily imply that Christ, who plays both active and passive roles, is an unnatural sinner.

Still, the relationship between God (as the source of all law and goodness) and the sexual outlaw and miscreant is perhaps more than simply a common set of descriptors. In his discussion of Augustine and evil, Jonathan Dollimore writes that "perversion and deviation are concepts which facilitated the displacement of evil from God to man," most notably as Christianity moved away from monism toward a modified dualism.[132] At the same time, as we saw in chapter 1, "Perversion and deviation become lodged at the heart of those contradictions which were to haunt Christianity, and which ultimately sunder the faith itself, most notably the beliefs (1) that we are created wicked; (2) that God himself. . .bears 'the ultimate responsibility for the existence of evil'; (3) that evil is intrinsic to good."[133] Dollimore notes that a "happy consequence" of all of these three beliefs is that "God rather than Satan" is made into "the ultimate or original pervert."[134] Christian thinkers have been tireless in countering this conclusion, yet in spite of their efforts it returns consistently in Western thought. Indeed, Dollimore finds traces of it in two notable ironies in Augustine's *City of God*: first, that Augustine's meandering style is "inseparable" from that which he castigates most fervently, "deviation"; and second, that Augustine's famous proof of subjective being ("Si enim fallor sum," [For if I err, I am]) "founds his being upon erring movement, that which is the quintessence of the perverse and, as such, necessarily also a movement toward non-being" or evil.[135]

As we have seen, these same ironies can be found in Alan of Lille's own writings. As Zink argues, Alan believes that "verbal richness" is equivalent to "effeminate softness," that rhetorical ornamentation interferes with moral teaching, and that the pleasure of language may seduce the listener but fail to correct him.[136] And yet Alan also fails to conceive of a mode of expression that would be free of semantic deviations or moral pitfalls. As he attempts to lead his reader toward righteousness, he loses his way, wandering (like the *Venus scelesta*) from "the path of proper delineation" into the "byways of pseudography" (156). Scanlon argues that Alan is entirely conscious of the fact that orthography and pseudography arise from the same source, that the pen "must necessarily contain the capacity for *falsigraphia*, because its power to determine *orthographia* entails the power to distinguish between the two."[137] I agree. Alan's concern is not simply rhetoric and stylistics; he engineers an exceedingly complex, and ideologically potent, imbrication of proper and improper writing. If (as I argued in chapter 1) Augustine's definition of evil as an inner deviation prepares the ground for violent distinctions between good and evil, Alan's understanding of Nature as the betrayer of her own laws plays a similar role. Nature declares that sexual perverts are everywhere and that their sin converts virtue itself into vice: "This great multitude of men monsters are scattered hither and thither over the whole expanse of earth and from contact with their spell, chastity itself is bewitched" (136). Yet she acknowledges that to fight evil one must have some contact with it: "The knowledge of evil is advantageous as a preventive measure to punish the guilty, who are branded with the mark of shame, and to forearm the unaffected with the armour of precaution" (137).

If it becomes difficult to distinguish between chastity and perversion, good and evil, God and monsters, the consequences can be quite lethal. As French historian Jacques Chiffoleau argues, the *vitium contra naturam* was understood in the Middle Ages not just as an attack on Nature, but on the majesty of Church, state, and God himself.[138] By making the divinity itself vulnerable to unnatural sin and by blurring the boundaries between being and nothingness, good and evil, Alan of Lille enables the development of a deeply punitive moral and metaphysical system. The semantic ambiguities and sexual improprieties that pervade the *De planctu Naturae* are not simply a return of repressed desires or evidence of an unacknowledged continuum between the homoerotic and the homosocial. They are instead a ruse of power. By internalizing evil within the good and blurring the distinction between natural and unnatural, orthography and pseudography, God and pervert, Alan's poem points to a moral imperative: the endless labor of rooting out evil (which is always where it ought not to be, or *is* when it should not *be* at all) and excluding it through a formal rite or discourse, Genius's anathema. If the anathema involves itself in the very deviance it seeks to extirpate, its ideological power, which is fueled by an endless cycle of repudiation and contamination, remains undiminished.

As Chiffoleau demonstrates, notions of *contra naturam* and *nefandum* are used in the Middle Ages as means for constructing new forms of political sub jectivity in which culpability is generalized, internalized, and irremediable and in which the investigation and prosecution of crime participates in the very nature of the crime itself. The function of *inquisitio* is to extract confessions from the accused, using torture or the threat of torture if necessary. The goal of interrogation and prosecution is, of course, "to affirm the essential unity of Christendom" and "to ensure the pope's theocratic power."[139] However, that power is itself characterized by muteness: "not the deceptive silence that surrounds heresy and that which is impossible to say, but rather the essential and positive silence that always surrounds mysteries, the arcana of power."[140] Unspeakable evil is indeed "dangerously" close to another form of silence, "this one eminently respectable: the silence that always surrounds legitimate power and that is one of the clearest signs of majesty."[141] To investigate, prosecute, and punish unnatural or unspeakable sin is thus to reveal the scandalous proximity of law and transgression, righteous power and monstrous aberration, good and evil. In short, it is "to fight evil with evil, to oppose the secret to the occult, and to attempt to force the accused to speak the unspeakable in order to protect that zone of silence and mystery that surrounds legitimate power."[142]

An example of this paradoxical use of silence can be found in the omission of the word "sodomy," which is to be found nowhere in the *De planctu*. For Jordan, this omission begs the question of what category Nature will "put in its place."[143] Ultimately, he concludes that "Nature has no satisfactory substitute," and that Alan intends the reader to see Nature's "limits" as "a guide in morals."[144] She fails to "provide a compelling argument against a vice that directly affects what most concerns her, the reproduction of bodies. She is too various and variable to yield or to enact convincing regulations. Her representations tangle themselves or else are unraveled by the very conditions of their own making."[145] Like Whitman, Jordan concludes that "the *Plaint of Nature* is not only a complaint against sexual sins, it is a complaint against Nature's failure to speak satisfactorily about those sins."[146] Furthermore, he believes that Alan wishes his readers to discover "the exhaustion of a certain kind of moral representation" and to repudiate Nature and her web of Ovidian references as tools for moral rectification and spiritual restoration.[147] The only alternative is a return to "Christian scripture traditionally read," meaning specifically the story of Sodom and Gomorrah and Paul's condemnation of same-sex love in Romans.[148] Jordan here offers an apt illustration of Chiffoleau's argument: the sickness ("sodomy") and its cure (Scripture, "traditionally read") *both* remain unspoken in the *De planctu*, the one because it is a monstrous deviation, the other because it must withhold its truths from the uninitiated.

Without disagreeing with Jordan's conclusion, I would suggest that his argument could be pushed in a somewhat different direction. If, as I have argued above, the corrupt language of Nature and Ovidian myth *does* spill over into the realm of sacred eloquence and theological truth, and if the poem fails to distinguish monstrous, unspeakable acts from sublime, ineffable mysteries, then the text's ideological force lies precisely in its moral failures and in the threat those failures pose to majesty, whether the righteous power of the Church or the divine sovereignty from which that power derives. As the ethical and metaphysical system of the *De planctu* lapses into incoherence, we glimpse the text's greatest potential as an ideological weapon. Seducing the reader with the promise of moral recuperation, it taints him instead with the very crimes the text is meant to abolish. As with Original Sin, Alan's *vitium contra naturam* is so broadly generalized that it comes to inhabit, and subvert from within, the very discourses and institutions that seek out its remediation. If Alan insists in particular on the harm done to Nature and God, the reason is not that he wishes to compromise or undermine their moral authority. Instead, Alan, like Augustine before him, constructs a model of ethics and sexual ethics in which conformity is achieved through universal, irredeemable guilt, in which the good is pursued through the exclusion and annihilation of evil and in which evil is an indomitable internal enemy.

CHAPTER 4

AUTHORSHIP AND SEXUAL/ALLEGORICAL VIOLENCE IN JEAN DE MEUN'S *ROMAN DE LA ROSE*

It is fitting that the last text I consider in this book should be the *Roman de la rose*. Not only does the *Rose* represent a high point in the medieval allegorical tradition and a crucial influence on subsequent allegorical writings, but it also offers a provocative fusion of the genres, themes, and ideological worlds I considered in the two previous chapters: vernacular romance and the Latin poetry of the schools, the erotic quest and intellectual/spiritual longing, aristocratic circles and clerical or ecclesiastical ones. Guillaume de Lorris (author of the original *Rose*) was inspired by *trouvère* lyric and composed a courtly allegory devoted to the psychology of desire and in which "l'art d'amors est tote enclose" [the whole art of love is contained] (38; 31).[1] Jean de Meun (author of the continuation of the *Rose*) in turn inflected and critiqued his predecessor's work by incorporating into the romance a variety of alternative discourses and perspectives, including intellectual debates then current at the University of Paris. Ernest Langlois estimates that of Jean's 17,700 lines, a full 12,000 borrow directly from Latin sources.[2] The most important of these are Ovid's *Ars amatoria*, Boethius's *Consolation of Philosophy*, and Alan of Lille's *De planctu Naturae* and *Anticlaudianus*.

In this chapter, I will ask questions about how allegory operates ideologically in Jean's hybrid, encyclopedic, and polyphonic romance. More specifically, I will argue that the authorial signature in the *Roman de la rose* (one of the most famous, and famously ambiguous, moments of authorial self-presentation in the medieval canon) offers the modern reader access to some of the poem's subtler forms of rhetorical and ideological coerciveness. I will attempt to counter the position (advocated by a number of scholars over the past thirty years or so) that in thematizing and sexualizing the dissemination of allegorical meaning, Jean's poem also disrupts traditional gender order and codes of sexual morality.

To be sure, the *Rose* locates various forms of erotic and readerly pleasure in the disruption of signifiers of patriarchal authority and, more generally, in the pluralization of figural meaning beyond the constraints of authorial intent. As is well known, Jean retells the Ovidian myth of Jupiter and Saturn as an allegory of semiotic fertility, redeeming the castration of the symbolic father through a poetics of dispersal or dissemination. It is clear, moreover, that this act of castration is part of a larger project to release male subjectivity from certain of the inhibitions of courtly and ecclesiastical moralism, and to exempt vernacular poetry from euphemistic censorship and rigid rules of literary decorum and stylistic indirection.

And yet as we have seen in the preceding chapters, the internalization of disruptive meanings within allegory does *not* necessarily imply a subversion of the dominant ideology. It would be a mistake, in my view, to claim that in deconstructing patriarchal fictions the *Rose* actively critiques or subverts the assumptions of thirteenth-century clerical culture. Nor do I believe that the extraordinarily vehement and violent—but crucially ventriloquized—attacks on women in the *Rose* are neutralized by the poem's dialectical structure, its relativist, ironic critique of opinion, or its avoidance of an overarching, sovereign authorial voice. Instead, I will contend here that Jean de Meun's *Rose* works, often inconspicuously, to confirm the status of men as literary/sexual subjects and women as literary/sexual objects by allegorizing authorship and desire. If allegory works to disarticulate authorship and pluralize desire, this ultimately paves the way for an act of sexual aggression: the plucking (or "cueillette") of the beloved rose.

As is often the case with the allegorical mode, the figuration of authorship and desire in the *Rose* is antinomic and undecidable in nature. Nearly every strategy of representation or figuration is contravened by an opposing strategy, usually deliberately and self-consciously. Thus if Jean's poem analogizes the indeterminacy of allegorical meaning with the awakening of sexual desire, it also clearly betrays (to quote Daniel Poirion) "a certain nostalgia for plenitude,"[3] a longing for a Golden Age in which word and thing would have achieved real coherence. The *Rose* (like the *Eneas* and *De planctu Naturae*) works to encapsulate the unpredictable force of desire through abstract, essentialist tropes, even as it subjects those tropes to parodic, titillating, and comic repetition. Similarly, if Jean's poem subjects authorship to the effects of interpretation by incorporating the author into his own fiction as a signifier or signature, at the same time it suggests that the creation can never entirely be cut off from its creator, who looms throughout the work precisely because he cannot be definitively located *in* or *outside* it. Finally, if the plucking of the rose is coded as an act of *dis*semination (one that proliferates alternate meanings and resists deciphering), it is also a transparently phallic and violent act of *insemination*—an assault and conquest in which the object of desire remains utterly passive and mute even as it is being literally and metaphorically inflamed by desire.

Ultimately, then, by opening rhetoric to dialectic and allegory to irony, Jean's poem does not fully pluralize allegorical meaning or fully relativize opinions and values. Nor, in my view, does it celebrate, in the words of Jean-Charles Payen, "a sexual liberty founded on free consent."[4] Even as the *Rose* seeks to emancipate the sexual drives from certain kinds of moral restrictions, and erotic literature from certain forms of censorship, it replaces those constraints with others. In a brilliant new study of the Ovidian underpinnings of the *Rose*, Alastair Minnis asserts that Jean de Meun consistently rejects "traditional mythographic moralization" in favor of "phallocentric demythologization": "Stylistic equivocation and polite euphemism are stripped away to lay bare the insistent demands of male desire and men's preoccupation with their sexual potency."[5] Thus while Saturn's castration initially appears to illustrate a relinquishing of paternal or authorial control, the *Rose* immediately turns to another fiction of male mastery: a poetics of dissemination and ethics of procreation in which the phallus retains its privileged role as seminal agent. The conclusion of the romance turns the spotlight on the performance of masculinity: a "priapic posturing" and male "self-conceit" typical of writers who "worried about whether they had been emasculated. . .by their intellectual training and clerical status."[6] The humor attached to this posturing is not simply ironic, marginal, or subversive. Rather, it is evidence of a belief system that maintains patriarchy even as it subjects it to ridicule: "The laughter at issue here is that of those who fundamentally *believe*, who have no problem in accepting the tenets of the current culture but who nevertheless. . .are aware of its paradoxes, tensions, and apparent absurdities."[7]

The plucking of the rose itself, with its titillating proliferation of alternate meanings, is coded as a spectacular performance of male domination brought to fruition: a spilling and mixing of seed that causes the rose to "ellargir et estandre" [widen and lengthen] (21700; 352).[8] Jean's ribaldry rehearses, without ever fully ironizing, a metaphorical and metaphysical form of misogyny that, according to Gordon Teskey, is endemic to allegory: "the moment of *raptio*, or 'seizing,' in which Matter, perversely resisting the desire of the male, must be ravished by form before being converted and returned to the Father. To be ravished is what Matter secretly wants, so that it may bear in its substance the imprint of beautiful forms."[9] Though Teskey does not read the *cueillette* as a rape (nor is it clear that it is one), he does argue that the hylomorphism implicit in Jean's allegory can be linked to a standard narrative used to legitimate male sexual aggression under patriarchy: "the fantasy of the suppressed smile of the woman who only appears to resist what is happening to her."[10] Minnis in many ways confirms this view, describing the *cueillette* as a process of "masculation" whereby men become men through normative sexual performance and the subordination of women: "The spotlight must fall exclusively on Amant, and the more passive and objectified the woman, the better that effect may be achieved."[11] The rose is not raped, perhaps, but the allegorical assault is nonetheless a manifestation of "sexual violence" and "the depersonalization and objectification of woman."[12]

Taking Teskey and Minnis's analyses as a point of departure, I will argue that fictions of authorship and desire in Jean de Meun's *Rose* are symptomatic of, and work to sustain, the real system of power relations that Georges Duby famously (if reductively) termed "mâle Moyen Age": "The Middle Ages were resolutely male. All the opinions that reach and inform me were held by men, convinced of the superiority of their sex. I hear only them."[13] It should be said that Duby's views have at this point largely fallen from favor. Recent historical work has offered evidence to prove that women (especially aristocratic ones) could, and did, wield power throughout the Middle Ages, including influence over literary production and their own sexual destinies.[14] Still, many historians continue to believe that such liberties were granted only within the constraints imposed by a patriarchal super-structure. Judith Bennett has argued for a "patriarchal equilibrium" in the West, by which she means that advances for women in one area were typically met with a backlash in others.[15] Jo Ann McNamara sees less an equilibrium than a dramatic diminishment of the status and influence of women in public life beginning in the second millennium: "Women were disadvantaged by the development of more centralized states, a more hierarchical church, and an urban society based on the money economy."[16] She singles out the universities of the later medieval period as responsible for forming a new ruling class predicated on the total exclusion of women: the *clerici*.

Like Minnis, I believe that Jean de Meun's *Rose* is typical of the culture and ideology of this ruling class. Though the poem appears to celebrate unfettered, procreative desire and offers a formidable critique of celibacy, it is by no means clear that it consistently resists or subverts the masculinism and misogyny of thirteenth-century clerical culture. On the contrary, I will argue in this chapter that the *Rose* seeks a shelter for male power in the apparent disruption and demystification, but also the subtle affirmation and perpetuation, of a variety of patriarchal cultural codes. As Minnis puts it, if "much of [the *Rose*'s] wit remains uncontrolled, subversive," nonetheless it is "operative within certain definite limits, which are those of what may be identified as a medieval clerical sense of humour, the product of an exclusively male academic environment."[17]

I will begin my investigation of patriarchal and clerical ideologies in the *Rose* by examining Jean's authorial signature. I will read the signature as both a self-deconstructing game and an affirmation of the universality and authority of male subjectivity. I will then consider the relationship between allegory, ideology, and sexual violence in the *Rose*, looking in particular at questions of textual address in the *excusasion:* the passage in which the narrator apostrophizes his readers, both male and female, and denies responsibility for a misogyny he transmits without endorsing. I will conclude by considering Christine de Pizan's feminist critique of Jean de Meun in the context of the *Querelle de la Rose.* Throughout, my goal will be to demonstrate that even as the *Rose* marks male subjectivity, authorship, and authority as cultural fictions subject to repetition and difference, it simultaneously seeks to stabilize and naturalize an ideology of male authority and female subordination.

The Double Signature

As is well known, the *Roman de la rose* is the work of two different authors: Guillaume de Lorris, who began the text but apparently left it incomplete, and Jean de Meun, who wrote a lengthy continuation culminating in the highly equivocal, pornographic scene of the plucking of the rosebud from its branch. What is known of the authors themselves, however, is mostly speculative. Scholars have credibly argued that Jean de Meun was a deeply learned, high-ranking university scholar: a *maître ès arts* or (as Gontier Col believed) a *docteur en théologie.*[18] Indeed, it is clear, as Minnis explains, that Jean was, in his time, one of the great masters of the Scholastic art of *compilatio:* the encyclopedic accumulation and coordination of a variety of erudite *materiae* and *auctoritates.*[19] As is typical of the *compilator,* however, Jean's own intentions and desires are carefully obscured. According to medieval literary convention, the *compilator* must disavow any sort of *intentio auctoris* and must resist stating his own opinions. His goal is instead to collect, translate, and collate the opinions of "li preudome. . .qui les anciens livres firent" [the worthy men who wrote the old books] (15193–94; 259). Jean is thus careful to deny ownership of, or responsibility for, the content of his poem—though remarkably, he does this, too, in the voice of another. Addressing his audience, Jean de Meun's narrator (who, as we shall see, is actually named Guillaume de Lorris) offers an *apologia* for his work, what Minnis calls the "traditional protestation of the compiler":[20] "Je n'i faz riens fors reciter" [I do nothing but retell] (15204; 259). Jean is thus doubly dislocated from the work that bears his name. First, he submerges his own voice into an intricate polyphonic composition in which there apparently can be no single, authoritative discourses, only a melding of disparate voices. Second, he points to the polyphony of the poem by appropriating the voice of another, by ventriloquizing Guillaume the narrator, who speaks of the poem itself as the recitation of other voices. This ingenious verbal disappearing act has confounded generations of scholars invested in discovering the underlying intentions and designs of the second *Roman de la rose* or the historical and biographical truth about its author. As Sylvie Lefèvre aptly remarks, "Jean de Meun never stops playing tricks on serious, historicizing criticism."[21]

If Jean's identity is shadowy and enigmatic, Guillaume's is quite a bit murkier. Although the first *Roman de la rose* explicitly thematizes the erotic subjectivity of its narrator, the identity of the poet himself remains almost completely ambiguous, both at the level of narrative voice and at the level of authorial intention. The *Rose* is apparently Guillaume's only extant work, and all attempts to fill out his biography have proved fruitless.[22] Moreover, as is well known, Guillaume does not sign his own poem but is instead referred to in passing by his successor Jean de Meun—or rather by the god of love speaking about the dual authorship of the *Roman de la rose* to his assembled army. The little that can be said about Guillaume is that his poem is almost certainly addressed to an aristocratic audience and is inspired, as C.S. Lewis puts it, by "the muse of courtly love."[23] It is, in other words, an integral part of the tradition of romance love poetry that was inaugurated by the troubadours at the courts of Provence and that quickly spread to Northern France through the work of both *trouvères* and *romanciers*. Based on the subject matter of the first *Roman de la rose* and its professed goal, "vos cuers plus feire agueer" [to make your hearts rejoice] (32, 31), it is likely that Guillaume was a member of a northern French court who composed poetry for the pleasure of a noble patron and his entourage. If his name is any indication, Guillaume was in all likelihood a native of the Loiret, though as we shall see, his name, too, is a source of considerable confusion.

Before describing the naming of the two authors in the *Rose*, let me first offer a reminder of the basic narrative structure of the poem as a whole. Guillaume de Lorris opens the work by describing a supposedly prophetic dream, one that was actualized in reality after the fact of the dream itself and that forms the basis of a romance narrative recounted in the first person. As David F. Hult observes, there is "a layering of distinct and yet coalesced perceptual vantage points" within the narrative "I" in Guillaume's poem: the narrator ("the storytelling voice," which should be "distinguished from the author"), the dreamer (the "past self of the narrator who had the dream"), and Amant ("the persona *in* the dream who directly experienced the various events" of the dream).[24] The events are as follows: Amant [Lover, as he is called in manuscript rubrics] wanders through the garden of Deduit [Diversion] in spring, is struck by Amor's

[Love's] arrows, swears fealty to the god, and embarks on an erotic quest to pluck a beloved rosebud. Amant encounters Bel Acueil [Fair Welcoming], son of Courtoisie [Courtesy], who encourages him in his pursuit and even allows him to approach the rosebush. Eventually Bel Acueil is persuaded by Venus to allow Amant to kiss the rose. As soon as Amant takes his kiss, however, Jalousie [Jealousy] appears and excoriates Bel Acueil for his weakness. She commands that high walls be built around the rosebush, that Bel Acueil be locked up in a high tower within those walls, and that he be guarded day and night by Dangier [Resistance], Honte [Shame], Poor [Fear], and Male Bouche [Foul Mouth]. The poem is left in suspense at this point, since Guillaume apparently left off writing, either because he saw the love story as necessarily inconclusive or because (as Jean later surmises) death prevented him from completing his task. Amant is left despondent, longing for the company of Bel Acueil.

Jean de Meun, writing several decades after Guillaume, takes up the poem where his predecessor left off, turning from despair to hope and adding an additional 17,700 lines to the poem. Jean completes the erotic quest with a series of brief narrations and lengthy speeches, including the discourses of Reson [Reason], Ami [Friend], Faus Semblant [False Seeming], and La Vielle [the Old Woman], as well as the plaint of Nature and the sermon of Genius, which Jean borrows from Alan of Lille. The continuation culminates, of course, in the long-awaited scene of the plucking of the rose. Venus herself initiates the attack on the castle: aiming for "une petitete archiere" [a tiny aperture] (20762) set between two pillars, she lets fly a "brandon plein de feu ardant" [feathered brand, covered with burning fire] (21222; 347). The fortress is immediately engulfed in flames and is eventually razed to the ground. The only structure left standing is the sanctuary, which Amant now approaches "de queur devost et piteable" [with a devoted and pious heart] (21564; 351), consumed with "grant fain d'aourer" [a great hunger to wor-ship] (21562) before it. Amant lifts the curtain to reveal the relics inside the sanctuary and then uses his staff, "ou l'escharpe pendoit darriere" [with the sack hanging behind] (21576; 352), to penetrate and widen the aper-ture. After he struggles for some time to "assaillir" [assail or assault] (21587) the fortification of the aperture, he finally manages to force his whole staff inside. He then scatters seed from his sack onto the rosebud, mixing his own germ with the rose's. Cutting a little into the bark of the rosebush, he claims the rose from its branch "par grant joliveté" [with great delight] (21747; 354). The poem ends with the awakening of the dreamer, presumably as recounted from the point of view of the narrator: "Atant fu jorz, et je m'esveille" [Straightaway it was day, and I awoke] (21750; 354).

Now, the only intratextual indication of the authorship of the *Roman de la rose* arrives precisely at the midpoint of this narrative, in the portion of the romance that is attributed to Jean: lines 10,465–648 of a total 21,750 lines. What this means, of course, is that Guillaume never signed his own work. Indeed, he failed to attach any sort of proper name to the various narrative voices in the poem—the lover, the dreamer, and the narrator. Jean is more careful about owning his work, and yet remarkably he names himself and his predecessor, not in his own voice (which, as we have seen, is never entirely distinct anyway), but rather in the voice of Amor. Amor's revelation is, moreover, addressed not to the reader but to Amor's own army, which is assembled to receive its marching orders immediately prior to the initial assault on the castle. First, Amor introduces his assembled forces to Amant, presumably gesturing physically to the man who stands beside him: "Vez ci Guillaume de Lorriz" [Here is Guillaume de Lorris] (10496; 187). Though Guillaume is not particularly "sages" [wise] (10507; 187), he will be of considerable use to Amor in that he will begin "le romant / ou seront mis tuit mi conmant" [the romance in which all my commandments will be set down] (10519–20; 187). To reaffirm his fealty to Amor, Amant has in fact just repeated Amor's decalogue, which he first learned early on in the portion of the romance attributed to Guillaume. The commandments will be set down (or have been set down, since we are in the midst of reading them) not once but twice in the *Roman de la rose*, first in Guillaume's poem and then again in Jean's continuation. The naming of Amant is thus coupled with a signature, really a double signature, in which we understand two things: first, that Amant is Guillaume de Lorris, who will be (or was) the original author of the poem; second, that the poem will have (or had) a second author. The poem both *had* an author, since obviously it has been written, and *will have* an author, since Amor anticipates the fact that the fiction containing his commandments and in which he plays a role *will have been written*. The signature retrospectively describes the moment at which a prophecy of the text's authorship was first announced. Or, put another way, the *Roman de la rose* incorporates into the dream-narrative the written record of a prophecy of the writing down of that selfsame prophecy in the *Roman de la rose*.

This extraordinary complication of chronology and the scene of writing are rendered all the more intricate when Jean identifies himself as the author of the continuation of Guillaume's poem. Here, the text suggests a temporal paradox in which the act of signing the poem (that is, the writing of the fiction of Amor's naming of the poem's two authors) is described by Amor himself as lying chronologically somewhere between the death of the first author and the birth of the second. After introducing Amant/Guillaume to his army, Amor cites what will be the last few lines of Guillaume's poem—words that we have already read nearly 6,500 lines earlier. He then prophesies the death and entombment of Guillaume, who will leave his poem incomplete, and announces the birth, some forty years after the death of Guillaume, of a certain Jean Chopinel, a native of the village of Meun on the Loire River. Jean de Meun will love the romance so greatly that he will continue and eventually complete it, "se tens et leus l'en peut venir" [if time and place can be found] (10556; 187–88). Amor denies that he could lie in formulating this prophecy: "que je ne mante" [may I not lie] (10559; 188). And indeed from a certain perspective, the prophecy, in being read, is fulfilled *ipso facto* and therefore takes on at least a semblance of truth. Perhaps as further proof of the veracity of his statements, Amor announces what will be the opening lines of Jean's continuation—words that, again, we have already read: "Car quant Guillaumes cessera, / Jehans le continuera. . .et dira. . .'Et si l'ai je perdue, espoir, / a poi que ne m'en desespoir' " [For when Guillaume shall cease. . .Jean will continue it. . . . He will say, "And perhaps I have lost it. At least I do not despair of it"] (10557–66; 188). Jean will then add

> toutes les autres paroles
> quex qu'els soient, sages ou foles,
> jusqu'a tant qu'il avra coillie
> seur la branche vert et foillie
> la tres bele rose vermeille
> et qu'il soit jorz et qu'il s'esveille. (10567–72)

> [whatever they may be, wise or foolish, up to the time when he will have plucked the very beautiful red rose on its green, leafy branch, to the time when it is day and he awakes.] (188, modified)

Providing further evidence of his clear-sightedness, Amor describes the completion of the dream and anticipates almost exactly the way in which the narrator, writing in the first person, will describe the awakening of the dreamer: "Atant fu jorz, et je m'esveille."

Pronominal reference is indeed an altogether crucial aspect of the ontological, chronological, and narrative complexities of the authorial signature. Hult writes, "The peculiarity of this passage is underscored by the fact that no apparent narrative transformation has occurred such that the reader might expect an alteration in the fictional perspective of the 'I'–narrator, even though the change of authors is situated some 6000 lines previous to this point in the poem."[25] Throughout the dream-narrative, the identity of Amant ostensibly does not change, yet Jean has obviously "invested the narrative first-person pronoun with still another identity: his own."[26] As Hult suggests, Guillaume's poem had already split the "I" of the romance into a number of perspectives, in particular differentiating between "present Narrator and past Lover."[27] Jean ingeniously installs in the narrative "a 'new' narrator whose past 'self' becomes identified with the irresolvable existential difficulty of the courtly Guillaume. At once 'I am' refers to the author Jean de Meun and 'I was' continues to designate the poet Guillaume."[28] The "I" does not become, as a result, an "empty convention, a fraudulent use of a self-referential pronoun which now has no meaning."[29] Rather, "Jean meant to reveal his own identity, his exteriority, and simultaneously to maintain a personal identification with the narrative account."[30] The first-person pronoun is therefore "multireferential": "It has a personal *and* an impersonal identification: impersonal insofar as Guillaume-the-poet is a separate individual, but personal to the extent that Guillaume represents for the present narrator a type of creative urge which he perhaps shares but which he cannot simply repeat or imitate as if it were his own."[31]

Hult's argument could extend, however, to a discussion of the third-person singular pronoun as well, since the "il" appears to be similarly multireferential. The subject of the verbs "continuera" and "dira," for instance, is plainly Jean de Meun, and the citation of the lines we have already read allows us to locate the precise spot where Guillaume's poem ends and Jean's begins. Crucially, though, the referent for the third-person pronoun does not change when Amor refers to the plucking of the rose from its branch and the awakening of the dreamer. Indeed, the anticipation of the last line of the poem at its midpoint seems to suggest that the "il" of "il s'esveille" (Jean) could be confused with the "je" of "je m'esveille" (Guillaume). If Guillaume's poem merges narrator and lover, past and present, Jean goes a step further: he blurs the distinction between first author and second author using the very metafictional device that allows them to be distinguished in the first place. Is it Jean who will pluck the rose, rather than Amant/Guillaume? Is it Jean who will awaken, rather than Guillaume? Will Jean awaken *as* Guillaume, rousing himself as another self, entering into the consciousness of a person who died before Jean was born? Is Jean therefore the author of both portions of the romance, as one scholar has famously argued?[32] As with the metaphysical puzzles of a Nabokov or a Borges, we are left to wonder about the relationship between reality and fiction since the production of fiction in reality has itself been fictionalized—or rather, since the fiction is predicated on an infinite regression, a pure anteriority in which there seems to be no stable, real point of origin.

One might imagine that Jean's gloss on the dream-narrative might provide a solution to the puzzle. According to Amor, Jean "vodra si la chose espondre/que riens ne s'i porra reponde" [will want to explicate the affair in such a way that nothing can remain hidden] (10573–74; 188). And yet this anticipation of a final revelation does not clarify matters but only makes them more obscure. In fact, Jean does not provide any sort of explication, and the poem ends rather suddenly with the awakening of the narrator.

The omission of the gloss is all the more significant in that, as Amor states, both Guillaume and Jean would readily have offered their "conseill" [counsel] (10575; 188) at this point in the narrative—meaning, presumably, advice on how best to assault the castle, how to achieve textual closure, or how to produce the correct gloss. Obviously, though, neither is able to do so—the one (Guillaume) because he has not yet awoken from his dream and cannot understand its significance, the other (Jean) because he is not yet born and "n'est mie ci presanz" [is not here present] (10579; 188). Therefore, as soon as Jean will have left infancy behind, Amor will rush to his side, "por lire li vostre sentance" [to read your sentence to him] (10583; 188). Like the *compilator*, Jean does not create the meaning of the poem; rather, it is created by Amor and his army, and thus by the poem itself: "Endoctrinez de ma sciance" [indoctrinated with my knowledge], Jean "fleütera noz paroles / par carrefors et par escoles / selonc le langage de France" [will. . .flute our words through crossroads and through schools, in the language of France] (10610–13; 188). Jean's role will not be to write, but rather to read: "lira proprement" [he will read. . .fittingly] (10618; 188). Whereas Guillaume declares in the early moments of the *Rose* that Amor "prie et comande" [begs and commands] (33, 31) that he recount his dream in rhyme, Jean makes Amor and his army as much authors of the poem as Jean himself. Or as Hult puts it, "Amor's speech functions simultaneously as a poetic element interior to Jean de Meun's work *and* as an *exterior* agent of textual designation and delimitation."[33]

The Disseminated Text

Obviously, Jean is at pains both to exhibit and to obfuscate the scene of writing—if indeed it is possible to say that it is Jean who does so! Through his account of the romance's convoluted and virtually indeterminate genealogy, Amor manages to suggest that the mark of the external creator on the poem he has authored is, like the poem itself, a set of signifiers embedded within a cultural matrix and lacking stable, external referents. The name of the author does not contain or even approximate the truth of what it names, but instead points to an oscillation between various subject positions and temporal moments, all of which could be thought of as contingent fictional constructs.[34] Amor (himself obviously a fiction) tells us that the man who has authored the words he utters, and who identifies himself and his labor through those very words, "n'est mie ci presanz"—is not present/a presence in his own language. The authorial signature thus points to the contingent, fictional nature of authorship, subjectivity, and presence, and suggests that signs are incapable of preserving or reproducing a state of reality or consciousness. More to the point, the signature suggests that reality and consciousness are themselves discursive in nature and are therefore subject to difference and disruption in time. As Jean's narrator will put it just prior to the plucking of the rose, "diffinicion" [definition] in language and logic is not possible without "differance" (21548, 21550).

Many scholars have argued, on the basis of this reference to "differance," that Jean de Meun anticipates by some seven hundred years Jacques Derrida's familiar deconstruction of the metaphysics of Logos. R.A. Shoaf contends, for instance, that, "separated though they are by a chasm that cannot be crossed," "both men, Jean de Meun and Jacques Derrida, are concerned with what the latter encounters in. . .'difference as temporalization. . .the nonpresence of the other inscribed within the sense of the present. . .the relationship with death as the concrete structure of the living present.' "[35] Alexandre Leupin similarly believes that Jean de Meun is a Saussurian or even a Derridean *avant la lettre:* like Derrida, Jean understands that "in the world of the signifier there is no value that is not negative and differential with respect to all other signifiers."[36] The authorial signature, too, could be said to foreshadow Derrida's notion of iterability or citationality: "The unity of the signifying form is constituted only by its iterability, by the possibility of being repeated in the absence not only of its referent. . .but of a determined signified or current intention of signification."[37] Even a signature is subject to citation, in Derrida's view, and must therefore be recognized as "writing orphaned": writing that has been "separated at birth from the assistance of its father" and that points to the "disruption of presence in the mark" and the loss of the creator in the repetition of his own name.[38] The authorial signature in the *Rose* is indeed a kind of citation: Amor is clear that Jean will merely "recite," "flute," or "read" a poem in which his name figures quite prominently but in which his actual presence is explicitly called into question. The authorial name is thus not an index of authenticity, intention, or identity, but rather of absence, lack, and death. Amor's reference to Jean's future birth is analogous to what Derrida calls "a break in presence"—and that break implies not just "temporalization" but death, an inevitable, physical passing away.[39] Certainly Guillaume's fate awaits Jean as well, and the signature therefore stands as the trace of the alienation of the signatory, or even his elimination by his own signature. In short, the symbolic father is displaced or disseminated, one might even say castrated or murdered, by the sign that purports to identify him and situate him in speech.

For anyone familiar with patristic and medieval sign theory, especially the work of Augustine (see chapter 1), Jean's remarkable anticipation of the poststructuralist critique of logocentrism and the absolute ego should come as no real surprise. There are, to be sure, crucial differences between premodern and postmodern semiotics, especially in that medieval culture cannot possibly imagine a radical break with the metaphysics of Logos. Quite to the contrary, Augustine evinces the most basic foundation of medieval belief systems when he says that the divine Word has "no cessation or succession" but is "truly immortal and eternal."[40] And yet Augustine, like Derrida, does dismiss the idea that the Logos might exist as an actual presence in human language. Signs are not centered and stable, he argues, but are subject to temporality and difference: when compared to "your silent Word in eternity," human language, or "words sounding in time," is "something different, totally different."[41] Insofar as the Augustinian (and more generally medieval) subject is constituted discursively, consciousness is also necessarily an experience of self-alienation. A writer is always a secondary, deficient creator, in that he is himself a finite, kinetic creation, one with a beginning and an end but no moment of stasis or pure awareness in between. The autobiographical subject of Augustine's *Confessions*—a subject who attempts to write his past using a language that is itself constantly slipping into the past—is made up *of* time and utterly eviscerated *by* time: "I am my mind. . .yet here I am, unable to comprehend the nature of my memory, when I cannot even speak of myself without it."[42] Augustine confesses that he cannot understand time either, and then despairs at his inability to grasp the very cognitive process whereby he knows that he is saying he does not understand time *in* time: "Woe is me, for I do not even know what I do not know!"[43] In fact, Augustine believes that he will remain ignorant both of time and of the truth about himself until the moment, utterly beyond time and the self, at which his soul will have been returned to God: "What I know of myself I know only because you shed light on me, and what I do not know I shall remain ignorant about until my darkness becomes like bright noon before your face."[44] The confessional text is thus internally incoherent, in that the confessing subject can never entirely know his history, or even his mind: "No one knows what he himself is made of, except his own spirit within him, yet there is still some part of him which remains hidden even from his own spirit."[45] This theory of subjectivity leads Eugene Vance to conclude that the project of the *Confessions* is not at all analogous to modern autobiography, in which there is a presumption that the reader will subscribe "to a circular metaphysics of extroversion and presence-to-self."[46] Augustine, on the contrary, sees "the goal of self-knowledge implicit in his project" as "already insufficient—if not blameworthy, even, as a movement of pride."[47] Rather than seeking to achieve self-presence, Augustine hopes to transcend the narrative of his life and to move toward higher truths, however imperfect access to those truths may be. The soul, he writes, "is better when it forgets itself charitably in favor of an unchanging God, or else when it utterly condemns itself in comparison to him."[48]

Reading Jean de Meun's continuation of the *Roman de la rose* through the lens of Augustinian semiotics and psychology, we can easily see how the self-alienating signature is part of a larger project of subjecting the allegorical fiction to dissemination. Of course the *Rose* is concerned far less with charity and selflessness than with erotic subjectivity and desire—and even, as Minnis puts it, with "priapic posturing" and "self-conceit." Yet Augustine's reflections on the evasiveness of time, language, and the self are certainly germane to a discussion of the discursive and temporal alienation of the subject in the *Roman de la rose*, including the poem's attempts to deconstruct its own authorial origins. Inscribed at its precise physical center with the names of its authors, the *Rose* stands as a memorial for their creativity, but a memorial that evinces the loss of the creator in the creation that bears his name, the evacuation of the author from his own mark, and the transformation of the poet into a sign that signifies his absence. Time and place must have been found in order for Jean to continue the romance, and yet the romance foregrounds the loss of Jean himself both in place and in time, as a body occupying space and as a moment in history that has retreated into the past. In fact, time seems to have undone space, making a corporeal existence into little more than the fleeting of discourse into the past or an evanescence constantly disappearing on the horizon of futurity.

Based on the spectacular excesses of the double signature, however, it would seem that the *Rose* valorizes rather than simply regrets a theory of language as dismemberment and loss. Along with Reson's earlier recounting of the castration of Saturn, the signature may suggest that, for Jean de Meun, the dislocation of word and thing, author and text, creator and creation is the very condition of possibility for the production of meaning: in order to signify, signs must cast off concrete, identifiable intentions. The scattering of Amant's seed (like the tossing of Saturn's testicles into the sea) could thus be read not simply as a metaphorical ejaculation but as an ejaculation of metaphors, a celebration of an unfettered, erotically charged play of signifiers.[49] It is in fact quite a bit like Derridean dissemination in that the meaning of Amant's ejaculation "cannot be reduced by a *polysemia*" and refuses "a hermeneutic deciphering" or "the decoding of a meaning or truth."[50] From this perspective, the *cueillette* marks a repudiation of a realist conception of the sign and the opening of allegory to a play of differences. In keeping with the Augustinian notion of orgasm as a *summa voluptas* that escapes "conscious control,"[51] the metaphorical climax is so powerful that it appears to explode all constraints, subjecting the word to a refraction of intentions and disrupting the relationship between signs and meanings.

Rupture and Liberation

As I suggested above, a number of critics have pointed to this "will to rupture" in Jean's continuation as also a "will to liberation": a model for emancipating sexual desire and poetic meaning from the shackles of Guillaume's oppressive "courtly asceticism."[52] Writing in the early 1970s, Poirion sees Jean's continuation of the *Rose* as a correction of Guillaume's overly rigid code of decorum, "what we would today call censorship, or better, social repression."[53] Jean struggles bravely against such constraints and promotes a model of poetry and eroticism that is all encompassing, forward looking, and liberatory: "Seduction, liberation, conversion: everything is possible on the basis of this poetry."[54] In a similar vein, Payen proclaims in 1976, "Jean Chopinel, alias Jean de Meung, dreamed of a communitarian society. He preached sexual liberation. He anticipated a natural ethics comparable to that which Cook and Bougainville would discover in Polynesia in the eighteenth century."[55] Like Poirion, Payen sees Jean's vision of human liberty as *total*: "Jean de Meung denounces all forms of repression. He pleads for liberty, be it civil, moral, or metaphysical."[56] This vision of all-encompassing liberty, a "natural," unfettered sexual ethics, and a communitarian social order is indeed so radical and unprecedented that Payen believes its only counterpart is the "innocent" culture of Polynesia prior to colonization.

R. Howard Bloch in many ways echoes Poirion and Payen when, a decade later, he argues that Jean's poem strives to disrupt the "univocity of the true allegorical sign" (which Bloch associates with Guillaume de Lorris) and to effect a "radical problematizing of the nature of verbal signification."[57] The story of Saturn's castration in particular "entails a break in genealogical continuity, a disruption of lineage, that is indissociable from semiological dispersion, a break with the fixity of signs implying, in turn: (1) the breakdown of character and even logic . . .; (2) indiscriminate sexuality . . .; (3) indeterminate sexuality . . .; (4) and, finally, the allegorical poem itself."[58] By "problematizing" both "proper signification" and "proper genealogical succession," Jean's poem "ultimately transgresses its own familial or generic form."[59] This transgression allows Bloch to conclude that "the second half of the *Roman de la rose* is a directionless, never-ending, ever-supplemental, seemingly tumorous, multiform, 'hermaphroditic' text that, like Faux-Semblant, is difficult to pin down because it incarnates the very undefined principle of semiotic and sexual indeterminacy, free-floating desire, the abrogation of the rule of family and of poetic form."[60] Unlike Guillaume's univocal allegory of love, Jean's *Rose* is truly polyphonic and works to release desire from its moorings, including esthetic and social constraints.

Most recently, Simon Gaunt has claimed Jean de Meun as a "queer writer," a term he uses to refer not just to homoeroticism, but to a more general subversion of the sex/gender system of medieval patriarchy: "Jean's figurative language implicitly makes the repudiation of a 'proper' form of writing in favour of exuberant play and 'improper' allegory analogous to sexual drives. If the *Rose* exemplifies a form of writing that enacts a repudiation of the 'straight,' then it may not be anachronistic. . .to claim Jean de Meun as a queer writer."[61] Locating a "homoerotic seam" in the text (one that is, in my view, undeniably there), Gaunt goes on to argue that the apparent homophobia and misogyny in the *Rose* are parodic: they "flag an interpretive problem" in a text that repeatedly exposes the openness of its own meaning.[62] Gaunt does not make a claim for sexual or political liberation through exuberant play, but (citing Judith Butler) he does describe parody in the *Rose* as a form of subversive repetition: the *Rose* "challenges the repressive binary structure that subordinates non-heteronormative sexualities to a heterosexual matrix"—a structure that, according to Butler and others, sustains patriarchy generally.[63]

And yet Butler herself points to the potential pitfalls of a theory of political subversion that is grounded on Derridean citationality: "How to know what might qualify as an affirmative resignification—with all the weight and difficulty of that labor—and how to run the risk of reinstalling the abject at the site of its opposition?"[64] A similar question might be asked about citationality in the *Rose*: Does Jean's poem, with its spectacular celebration of authorial lack and internal difference, actually work to neutralize the political effects of the patriarchal, misogynistic, homophobic traditions it cites and perhaps also mocks?

A strict deconstructive feminism such as Bloch's might argue that it does. Bloch describes medieval misogyny as fundamentally discursive in nature: it is "a way of speaking about, as distinct from doing something to, women."[65] He then suggests that the most effective way to critique misogyny is to deconstruct defamatory speech—that is, to demonstrate the ways in which women are rendered as Woman through essentialist discourses that ultimately fail to locate the essences they describe. According to Bloch, deconstruction can expose the differences internal to misogynistic discourses and at the same time dispel their effects: "One must push antifeminist clichés to their limit in order to unmask their internal incoherences— to deconstruct, in short, whatever will not go away simply by exposure or by wishing that it were not so."[66] Certainly Bloch is right in arguing that deconstruction can be a useful tool for unmasking the ideological inflection of essential categories. Yet one might wonder in the case of a text like Jean de Meun's *Rose*—a text that deliberately exposes its own "internal incoherences"—whether we can make the leap Bloch has made from the "radical problematizing of the nature of verbal signification" to "sexual indeterminacy, free-floating desire, the abrogation of the rule of family and of poetic form." In her wonderfully incisive and politically savvy reading of Derrida's "The Double Session," Leslie Wahl Rabine argues that such a leap is a potentially dangerous one for feminism:

> The deconstructive gesture can be a courageous attempt to recognize, on the part of men, that their position of plenitude, mastery, and identity with respect to the phallus is indeed a fiction. It can be an attempt to recognize, as Jane Gallops says, that we are all in a position of lack. But a jump from this recognition to a facile assumption of textual bisexuality can prematurely close the question of sexual differentiation and sexual domination.[67]

In my view, scholars ought to reopen the question of Jean de Meun's sexual politics, not merely drawing attention to the various misogynistic and homophobic voices in the *Rose*, but focusing on the strategies by which the poem seeks to disavow ownership of and responsibility for its content. This is indeed the very same strategy that allows a whole tradition of criticism to view Jean as a sexual revolutionary: recitation, citation, polyphony, rupture. Is it possible that the poem's fascination with its own lack of unity, including its dislocation of the author from his signature, may actually serve to *privilege* antifeminist ideologies and shield them from attack, rather than exposing and unsettling the very foundations of medieval patriarchy? Does the *Rose* perhaps disrupt presence, self-presence, and intentionality in the authorial signature in order to prepare the ground for its indeterminate but also exuberant display of "priapic posturing and self-conceit"?

I would argue that we can locate in the signature both an apparent destabilization of male authorial power through temporalization and difference and a metaphysical puzzle whereby the author (or the ideology he stands for) is seemingly extracted from the shifting world of signs and transcends time and space. Though this illusion of transcendence is never any more than an effect of signifiers, it may nonetheless be endowed with considerable ideological weight. For what is at stake is not the biographical author and his actual opinions, but rather the historical, material, and ideological determinations that are indissociable from writing—especially so in a period when the clergy (a ruling class constituted in large part through the exclusion of women) was virtually the only literate segment of the population.

Time and Space

As I suggested above, Jean de Meun consistently allegorizes authorship and desire through antinomy or paradox. Thus the poem illustrates the fulfillment of sexual desire through an orgasmic explosion of metaphors that simultaneously marks the dislocation of the desiring subject and a self-assertive display of phallic prowess. Similarly, the double signature produces a distinctive mark of the poem's creators even as it dislocates the authorial voice through the act of reading itself. At this point in my argument, I would like to point to yet a third form of antinomy: the signature simultaneously enacts a temporalization of space and a spatialization of time. Since we cannot situate Jean, who is not yet born, *in* his poem, then the place of the poet is erased by a temporal game: he *is not yet* but always *will have been*. He is, therefore, always elsewhere than in signs. Similarly, time becomes a circle or even (as Leupin suggests) a Moebius strip: Jean authors Amor's prophecy of his authorship of Amor's prophecy, and so on.[68] Along with the dislocation of the author in time and space, then, the signature also implies his infinite temporal dilation and spatial distension.

Yet it is not simply that the signature allows Jean de Meun to encompass all time and space; it also implies (however ironically) that the author, like God, may transcend temporal and spatial realities. For if the poet will eventually be no more than a trace within his poem, a creation rather than a creator, he is still understood through the signature as the creator *of* the creation and therefore must be presumed at one point to have existed outside of, or prior to, the poem. Furthermore, if Jean is on one level unlocatable within the poem (where does he begin writing, and where does he end?), he could also be understood to be everywhere within it. Finally, if "Jean Chopinel," the mark of the author, stands for an infinite regression of fictions, then perhaps the text has no anteriority at all but is its own origin. Jean would therefore be *like* God in the medieval construction of divine Being as a metaphysical conundrum: a singularity beyond consciousness and representation that nonetheless shapes the system of relations in which being and meaning are produced.

The most obvious source for this kind of conundrum is Alan of Lille, whose fascination with paradoxes is legendary and whose influence on Jean de Meun can scarcely be overestimated. In the *Regulae Theologiae*, Alan offers two maxims on the existence of God that will be helpful here. The first is temporal: "Sola monas est alpha et omega sine alpha et omega."[69] God (who is known as the *monas* because of his utter simplicity and singularity, and because all reality derives from him) alone is both the alpha and the omega of all realities, and yet he utterly lacks alpha or omega. All things begin and end in God, but God himself has neither a beginning nor an end. The second maxim is spatial and indeed is cited in the *Rose* by Lady Nature as she attempts to describe the unimaginable immensity of God (19099–102): "Deus est spaera intelligibilis, cujus centrum ubique, circumferentia nusquam."[70] God is the "intelligible sphere" (that is, a power that contains in itself the very form of the world) of which the center is everywhere and the circumference nowhere. This is not a physical circle but a metaphysical one. The center is the creation, which is, with respect to the immensity of God, no more than a point, just as the finitude of time is nothing at all with respect to the eternity of God. Thus the circumference of the sphere is not just unlocatable but unimaginable: it is an immensity that organizes the creation and exerts force over it but that can never entirely be grasped by the mind or described in words.

I would contend that Jean's ironic double signature echoes Alan's maxims and the cultural logic that depicts God as a metaphysical puzzle. In effect, the signature renders Jean as a kind of singularity inaccessible within his own creation but nonetheless pervasive throughout it. Jean is both the alpha and the omega of the *Roman de la rose:* clearly he is the end of the creation, since he completes the poem that Guillaume began; but one could also make the argument that the end is simply another beginning. Through pronominal sleight of hand, Jean supplants Guillaume as the protagonist who will pluck the rose; as a result, he will awaken (or will have awakened) to Guillaume's reality in a moment chronologically prior to the composition of the first part of the romance. Jean will become his predecessor, who will die leaving his poem unfinished so that it can be completed by his successor, and so on. Or put another way, the future invents the past, and the past becomes what it will have been in the future.

On the basis of the circular logic of the authorial signature, two contradictory conclusions could be drawn. First, we might deduce that the authorship of the poem is an invention of the poem itself (since Amor prophesies that Jean will have written the poem in which Amor himself utters his prophecy) and does not depend upon Jean (who will merely act as a scribe transmitting the *sentance* dictated to him by Amor). Second, we might infer, on the basis of the very existence of the poem (which must have been written or it would not exist), that Jean has indeed authored the prophecy of his birth and authorship and therefore transcends his life and his poem. On one hand, Jean seems to be an invention of his text, his birth having been prophesied by Amor in a portion of the romance that Jean may appear to have authored but in which it is clearly stated that Jean himself "n'est mie ci presanz." On the other hand, Jean seems to have named Guillaume as the first author of the *Rose* in order eventually to call into question Guillaume's very existence by displacing him as the protagonist and author of the entire romance. Chronology in the *Rose* is therefore both linear and circular at the same time, and offers the illusion that Jean is both everywhere in the poem and nowhere. If Jean was at some point outside of or prior to his poem (since he *was* the author), he is also a construct of his poem (in which it is announced that he *will have been* its author). To make matters more complicated still, the poem renders Jean both as a perpetual imminence in his own work (he *always will have been* its author) and as an immanence everywhere and at all times (he is the creation of his creation and *is, was,* and *will have been* inside and outside of the poem simultaneously). We cannot locate the creator within his creation, since the creation dislocates him; nor can we find the limits of his creation, since the mark of the creator destabilizes the distinction between inside and outside, before and after, fiction and reality.

Oscillating between preterit and future perfect, "Jean de Meun" (the mark of the author) seems to be not simply a trace of a real person, now absent from the work and the world, but also an infinitely dilated presence that approximates eternity, a timeline that doubles back upon itself to encapsulate time itself. "Jean de Meun" thus bears an uncanny resemblance to Lady Nature's account of the Platonic Creator, a God "qui voit en sa presance / la trible temporalité / souz un momant d'eternité" [who in his presence sees the three aspects of temporality under a moment of eternity] (19044–46; 315). It also anticipates the description of the garden of the Good Shepherd in Genius's sermon, an earthly paradise in which infinite duration becomes place: "Il n'a futur ne preterit, / car se bien la verité sant, / tuit li troi tens i sunt presant" [It has neither future nor past, for, if I sense the truth well, all three times are present there] (19986–88; 329). Indeed, Jean's existence might be likened, however absurdly, to Christ's, since his coming can be retroactively discovered in a supposedly prophetic text that was supposedly written prior to his birth! Obviously, we are not meant to take this perverse *imitatio Christi* at face value. Still, the poem offers us the illusion, albeit fleeting and unconvincing, that the authorial signature might be a marker of pure subjectivity, suspended in time and limitlessly extended in space.

Ideology and Interpellation

Does this mean that we should reconsider Paul Zumthor's view that "the corpus of medieval poetry" is "almost entirely objectivized"—a form of representation in which "the subjectivity that formerly inhered in the text, deriving from the presentation of a living subject, has been lost to us"?[71] Working under the influence of Saussurean semiotics and Derridean deconstruction, Zumthor makes the claim that the author in medieval literature lacks any sort of extratextual determination: "All signs of an origin are wiped out; the individual voice is stifled in a composite, neutral text whose obliquity destroys personal identity. . . .The author has disappeared; what remains is the subject of the enunciation, a communicating psyche, integrated in the text and indissoluble from the way it functions."[72] Zumthor believes that this reification of the literary subject and neutralization of voice is not simply the result of historical loss, "the obscuring effects of time."[73] The opacity of medieval texts "may actually derive from some specific feature of the texts involved. It seems to be related to a sort of linguistic 'soft focus' [*une décentration du langage*] in the underlying poetic technique."[74] Authorial self-presentation in medieval literature should thus be understood as one of the "constituent parts of a system."[75] It is, however, never entirely dissociable from that system.

The double signature in the *Roman de la rose* plainly substantiates Zumthor's claim: the poetic subject becomes, through the very gesture of self-presentation, no more than a part of a depersonalized, "decentered" textual system. And yet in my reading, the signature also demonstrates that the "objectivization" of poetry can itself be translated into a totalization of the literary subject. An author who is "abolished" by time and space can also be removed from time and space altogether, constituting a fictional, contingent position of mastery, if not an actual, authentic self-presence.

This totalization is, moreover, far from "neutral" or "objective," at least from the standpoint of ideology. On the contrary, it reflects social norms, which in turn reflect the interests of those who wield power. Zumthor acknowledges the ideological inflection of cultural artifacts, arguing that the objectified subject position in medieval literature is inextricably linked to social and political determinations:

> The poet inserts himself in his language with the aid of techniques supplied by the social group, which controls the poem's motivations by means of the signs of which it is made up. The individual is rooted in his social situation and justifies his place in it by restructuring according to his own lights an imaginary universe, whose elements come to him preformed by his milieu.[76]

It is not possible to glimpse "authors' personalities" in medieval texts *except* "as members of social categories."[77]

Rather than an authentic presence in language or an extratextual origin, the authorial subject in the *Rose* might therefore be understood as an attempt to stabilize or naturalize a particular ideological order through the manipulation of rhetorical and fictional structures, an attempt to exempt the "dominant fiction" from discursive difference and historical change and to reduce a multiplicity of subjects to a fixed set of differences. That ideology is overdetermined from the outset, since, as Zumthor argues, the cultural imaginary is already fully constituted before the individual can be subjected to it. In short, the authorial signature in the *Rose* does not preserve the consciousness of the author, nor is it really an attempt to do so. Rather, it is concerned with legitimating and preserving a particular ideological world.

Or, as Minnis would have it, Jean's *Rose*, far from being "marginal" or subversive, actually works to legitimate "the cultural values which appertain in communities that are directed by comprehensive belief systems."[78] It seeks to safeguard the privileges of the clerical ruling class generally and, more specifically, to constitute male subjectivity through the seizure of a female object, through a performance of masculinity that requires the objectification of the feminine.

A critique of masculinism in the *Rose* should begin by examining the process whereby subjectivity is constructed and manipulated rhetorically— that is, the strategies by which the reader is addressed by the text and asked to assume a specific position within its fictional, symbolic, and ideological order. Zumthor, citing Gérard Genette, refers to such points of address (frequently using the first or second person) as "epiphrasis."[79] However, in the wake of Louis Althusser's tremendously influential *Lenin and Philosophy*, the term *interpellation* has achieved greater currency and is in many ways more useful. Kaja Silverman provides a lucid account of Althusserian interpellation in *The Subject of Semiotics:*

> Interpellation designates the conjunction of imaginary and symbolic transactions which results in the subject's insertion into an already existing discourse. The individual who is culturally 'hailed' or 'called' simultaneously identifies with the subject of the speech and takes his or her place in the syntax which defines that subjective position. The first of these operations is imaginary, the second symbolic.[80]

Althusser thus theorizes that the subject is a verbal and social construction and that the entry of the individual into the symbolic order as a subject marks the loss of imaginary plenitude and self-presence and the subordination of the self to a network of overdetermined ideological relationships.[81] In examining points of address in the *Roman de la rose*, we may therefore be able to discover how it uses rhetorical and fictional structures in order to ask its readers to accept a particular, ideologically weighted vision of love and desire, sex and gender.

The most extensive interpellation of the reader in the *Rose* is found in another major metatextual digression located nearly 5,000 lines after the authorial signature. This is the *apologia* or *excusasion* I referred to above: the moment at which the narrator (speaking as a *compilator*) denies ownership of and responsibility for the content of the poem. In my reading, the *excusasion* is a kind of ruse whereby the proliferation of alternate voices and the abolition of authorial agency serve to disguise strategies of rhetorical coercion. Even as the narrator/compilator offers an apology to women for the misogynistic content of his work, he interpellates his readers and imposes on them a long-established tradition of disparaging "les meurs femenins" [feminine ways] (15170; 258).

In the *excusasion*, the narrator first apostrophizes all "leal amant" [loyal lovers] (15105; 257)—presumably, that is, all those male readers who see themselves allegorized in Amant himself—and indicates that what he offers them in the poem being written is "d'amors. . .art souffisant" [an adequate art of love] (15114; 258). If these readers/lovers are troubled by any part of his text, they ought not to worry, as "g'esclarcirai ce qui vos trouble / quant le songe m'orrez espondre" [I will clarify what confuses you when you have heard me gloss the dream] (15116–17; 258, modified). The narrator then evokes the incredible temporal complications of the scene of writing in the poem, clearly marking a relationship between the authorial signature and the *excusasion* itself: "Et savrez lors par cel escrit / quant que j'avrai devant escrit / et quant que je bé a escrire" [And then, by this text, you will understand whatever I have written before and whatever I intend to write] (15121–23; 258). And yet before he will say more, the narrator wishes to pause for a moment "por moi de males genz deffandre, / non pas por vos fere muser, / mes por moi contre eus escuser" [to defend myself against wicked people, not so much to delay you as to excuse myself to them] (15126–28; 258). Indeed, he predicts that his text will provoke the indignation of certain ill-disposed readers and, as a result, will fall victim to malicious defamation:

> Si vos pri, seigneur amoreus,
> par les geus d'Amors savoreus,
> que se vos i trouvez paroles
> semblanz trop baudes ou trop foles,
> par quoi saillent li medisan
> qui de nos aillent medisant
> des choses a dire ou des dites,
> que courtaisemant les desdites. (15129–36)

> [Therefore I beg you, amorous lords, by the delicious games of love, if you find here any speeches that are too bawdy or silly and that might make slanderous critics who go around speaking ill of us rise up over things that I have said or will say, that you will courteously oppose them.] (258)

The logic of this particular act of interpellation is that just as the universal category subsumes particulars, so all "loyal lovers" and "amorous lords" must ally themselves with the narrator and rush to the defense of the text. Indeed, the almost imperceptible slippage from a first-person singular/second-person plural construction ("se vos pri") to a first-person plural ("de nos aillent medisant") slyly envelops male readers into the fiction, hailing them as a textual address but then containing them within the first-person narrative. If they are in fact who they believe themselves to be, their responsibility is to defend the poem—and themselves—against defamation.

The way they will know who they are is by listening for hidden meanings in the text:

> Or antandez, leal amant,
> que li dieu d'Amors vos amant
> et doint de voz amors joïr!
> En ce bois ci poez oïr
> les chiens glatir, s'ous m'antandez
> au connin prendre ou vos tandez,
> et le fuiret, qui sanz faillir
> le doit fere es raiseauz saillir. (15105–12)

[Listen now, loyal lovers, so that the God of Love may help you and grant that you may enjoy your loves! Here in this wood you may hear, if you listen to me, the dogs barking in chase of the rabbit that you are after and the ferret that must surely make him leap into the nets.] (257–58)

To be sure, attentive listeners of the period—and many inattentive ones as well—would have heard another meaning in the narrator's speech, one that belies his call for courtesy since it contains a rather blatant obscenity. As Maureen Quilligan has observed, the word *connin* "was much like the then current slang term for female sex organs, cognate to the now current English slang term [*sic*]. Thus, through the normal polysemous punning of allegory, Jean de Meun signals that his [male] readers' goal in reading the narrative of the 'love story' is salacious, mere cony-catching."[82] The obviousness of the pun (which Lavine's mother used in the *Roman d'Eneas*) suggests a corrosive irony: the injury to women lies not just in the vulgarity but also in the fact that the narrator feels no compunction about "carelessly" revealing his hypocrisy and disingenuousness. Through his interpellation of "leal amant," the narrator invents a community of implied male readers that finds solidarity in the pursuit of women as prey and a shibboleth in obscene glosses on allegorical love poetry. The shibboleth is, however, not at all a secret; and the real viciousness of the narrator's misogyny is to be found in his mock display of concern over the idea that he might one day be accused of defaming women.

If he should in fact be found out, the narrator asks that he be swiftly pardoned, since

> ce requeroit la matire
> qui ver tex paroles me tire

par les proprietés de sai;
et por ce tex paroles ai. (15143–46)

[my subject matter demanded these things; it draws me toward such things
by its own properties, and therefore I have such speeches.] (258)

He then justifies his claim by citing Sallust's *Catilina*, in which he finds confirmation that "les voiz" [words], which are "aus choses voisines" [neigh-
bors with things], must be "a leur fez cousines" [cousins to their deeds]
(15162–63; 258). If he wishes to describe what happened to Amant in deed
and "la verité descrivre" [to describe the truth] (15154; 258), then "li diz
doit le fet resambler" [the speech must resemble the deed] (15160). The
bawdiness or folly of the *Rose* ought to be defended on the grounds that in
order for the allegory to contain an element of "verité," words must seek
out harmony with the things and acts they claim to represent. Implicitly,
then, male lovers (the "seigneur amoreus" and "leal amant" apostrophized
by the narrator) must affirm their solidarity and like-mindedness with
Amant and Amor, and must seek to maintain stability within signs. Though
the *Rose* elsewhere deliberately dismantles realist theories of the sign, here
it seems to want to suture the gap between signs and meanings, to restore
plenitude in discourse that it has elaborately critiqued.

Predictably, the narrator proceeds quite differently when he addresses the
"vaillanz fames" [worthy women] (15165; 258) in his audience—readers
whose worth he has already impugned by metaphorically depicting them as
quarry and metonymically reducing them to their genitals. Since at this
point he can hardly enlist these women to assist him in his struggle against
defamers of the poem, he instead attempts to persuade them that he cannot
be held accountable for his poem's own defamation of women. His misogyny is not intentional but citational, and therefore belongs not to him but
to authoritative writings of the past:

Si vos pri toutes, vaillanz fames,
soiez damoiseles ou dames,
amoureuses ou sanz amis,
que se moz i trouvez ja mis
qui samblent mordant et chenins
ancontre les meurs femenins,
que ne m'an voilliez pas blamer
ne m'escriture diffamer,
qui toute est por anseignement;
c'onc n'i dis riens certainement
ne volanté n'é pas de dire,
ne par ivrece ne par ire,
par haïne ne par envie,

contre fame qui soit en vie;
car nus ne doit fame despire
s'il n'a queur des mauvés le pire.
Mes por ç'an escrit les meïsmes
que nous et vos de vos meïsmes
poïssons connoissance avoir
car il fet bon de tout savoir. (15165–84)

[And I pray all you worthy women, whether girls or ladies, in love or without
lovers, that if you ever find set down here any words that seem critical and
abusive of feminine ways, then please do not blame me for them nor abuse
my writing, which is all for our instruction. I certainly never said anything,
nor ever had the wish to say anything, either through drunkenness or anger,
in hate or envy, against any woman alive. For no one should despise a
woman unless he has the worst heart among all the wicked ones. But we
have set these things down in writing so that we may have knowledge of
you, and you of yourselves, for it is good to know everything.] (258–59,
modified)[83]

Remarkably, when the narrator speaks of women for the purpose of
"ansaignement," there suddenly appears to be a discrepancy between words
and deeds, universals and particulars: to speak ill of "les meurs femenins"
does not necessarily mean to despise women, nor does the defamation of
women necessarily target any individual "fame qui soit en vie." Whereas in
the previous passage the narrator sought to unify male readers by postulating
the existence of a real relationship between the text and its address, signifier
and signified, here he emphasizes discontinuity and difference, in particular
the gap between the text and its reception, between what it says and what it
should be understood to mean. The illogic of claiming that seemingly bit-
ing [mordant] and currish [chenins] words are not actually injurious is only
superficially resolved when the text offers a "feminist" moral: "Nus ne doit
fame despire." The sincerity of this moral is suspect at best, given, first, that the
narrator has already suggested that a text may not always mean what it says or
say what it means, and, second, that he has already metaphorically described
himself and other "leal amant" as curs stalking prey. If the narrator here
cleverly stresses that his words may *seem* to mean other than what they *do*
mean, we can only imagine that his lesson on avoiding discourteous speech
should also not be taken at face value. Nor, for that matter, can we be sure
what kinds of lessons the text hopes to teach. The narrator emphasizes that
if the poem discusses women at all, it does so in order that both men and
women can come to understand women better. Clearly, though, he hopes
to preclude the possibility of women understanding men or taking men as
epistemological objects: the "tout" of "tout savoir" exempts men, placing
them in a position of subjectivity without objectivity, whereas women

must play both roles. Men may wish to understand women, and women (with men's guidance) may seek to understand themselves. But women are not allowed to reverse the gaze, to learn about men, or to call into question men's teaching about women. The reason for this asymmetry becomes obvious when the narrator reveals that men's knowledge about women forms a single, continuous, and uninterrupted history:

> D'autre part, dames honorables,
> s'il vos samble que je di fables,
> pour manteür ne m'an tenez,
>   mes aus aucteurs vos an prenez
> qui an leur livres ont escrites
> les paroles que g'en ai dites,
> et ceus avec que g'en dirai;
> ne ja de riens n'an mentirai,
> se li preudome n'en mentirent
> qui les anciens livres firent.
> Et tuit a ma reson s'acordent
> quant les meurs femenins recordent,
> ne ne furent ne fos ne ivres
> quant il les mistrent en leur livres.
> Cist les meurs femenins savoient,
> car touz esprovez les avoient,
> et tex es fames les troverent
> que par divers tans esproverent;
> par quoi mieuz m'an devez quiter:
> je n'i faz riens fors reciter,
> se par mon geu, qui po vos coute,
> quelque parole n'i ajoute,
> si con font antr'eus li poete,
> quant chascuns la matire trete
> don il li plest a antremetre;
> car si con tesmoigne la letre,
> profiz et delectacion,
> c'est toute leur entencion. (15185–212)

[Besides, honorable ladies, if it seems to you that I tell fables, don't consider me a liar, but apply to the authors who in their works have written the things that I have said and will say. I shall never lie in anything as long as the worthy men who wrote the old books did not lie. And in my judgment they all agreed when they told about feminine ways; they were neither foolish nor drunk when they set down these customs in their books. They knew about the ways of women, for they had tested them all and had found such ways in women by testing at various times. For this reason you should the sooner absolve me; I do nothing but retell just what the poets have written between them, when each of them treats the subject matter that he is pleased to undertake, except that my treatment, which costs you little, may add a few speeches. For, as the text witnesses, the whole intent of the poets is profit and delight.] (259)

The narrator here establishes a genealogy leading from the great "aucteurs" of bygone days to the present moment of writing. He seeks to obviate dissent by allying himself with seemingly incontrovertible sources: "li preudome," whose worthiness is plainly indissociable from their gender. In fact, the wisdom of these men appears to transcend history altogether: even though they lived in "divers tans" (and presumably also diverse places), they nonetheless articulate the same consistent view of "les meurs femenins." Women readers may seek to incriminate the "aucteurs" or the narrator, who repeats their views; but together these men speak in a single voice: "Tuit a ma reson s'acordent." Again, the *excusasion* serves to form a collective body of men in which there is no dissent, only historical and textual continuity.

Following Bloch's lead, one might argue that the misogynistic force of this passage lies in its use of citational strategies: the repetition of the "anciens livres" obscures internal incoherences in the texts cited (and in the *Rose* itself) by representing the defamation of women as universal and transhistorical and therefore true. And yet it is crucial to note that the narrator has *already* subverted the notion of a singular authorial voice, and that the *excusasion* itself points to the disjunctions intrinsic to poetic or erotic subjectivity. Indeed, through the splitting of the narrative voice between "paroles dites" and "paroles dirai," between a past discourse (in which the author may not have been the same author) and a future one (whose meaning and status remain uncertain), the text manages to produce another temporal dilation. In this protracted moment of deferral—brought about by a game of ventriloquism—the text is able to propose its own truth-value: "ja de riens n'an mentirai."

Significantly, that truth-value relates to the univocity of allegory only insofar as allegorical poetry can preserve stability within patriarchy and continuity with an exclusively male literary heritage: "li preudome" and "les anciens livres." The *Rose* otherwise seeks ideological conformity precisely through the unsettling of a coherent or unified narrative voice. The fact that the author is alienated from his own text or that the text is aware of the poetic subject as fundamentally and internally split does not lead to an emancipation *of* or *in* the process of reading. On the contrary, the splitting of the subject would appear to be the condition of possibility for the exclusion or silencing of female readers and for the perpetuation of misogyny. Thus even though the *Roman de la rose* does not speak with a single voice, misogyny is nonetheless inherent in the poem's configuration of subjectivity as alienation and desire as lack. Beyond this dislocation of the subject, we find in Jean's poem a larger attempt to exclude women from public speech and to universalize a male subject, even if that subject is always already dislocated in language.

Whose "liberation" do we see, then, in Jean de Meun's continuation of the *Roman de la rose?* And whose "free-floating desire"? Unlike Bloch and others, I do *not* believe that the poem's unmasking of its "internal incoherences" leads to "textual hermaphroditism" or semiotic and sexual indeterminacy. Rather, like Minnis, I believe the *Rose* works to shore up men's sexual, social, and political power under patriarchy and to confirm women's status as mute, passive sexual objects, as the butt of a particularly vicious form of priapic humor. The self-deconstructing game of the double signature may initially lead us to believe that we are witnessing a far-reaching critique of discursive presence and male authorial power. Yet at the same time it affirms and strengthens patriarchy by situating "the author," or the patriarchal ideology he represents, beyond time and space. On one hand, the poem clearly understands itself as "writing orphaned, separated at birth from the assistance of its father"; on the other, the production and consumption of texts is depicted as an activity for men alone, one in which women and mothers play little or no role. Indeed, the genealogy by which authority is passed from one text to another through citation is clearly defined as a patrilineage—one that is not simply linear but circular. It refers to the passing of time and subjective loss *in* time, but it also allows time to double back on itself and to encapsulate the authorial and ideological subject within an infinite dilation: a presence in which past and future coincide. The dialectical, ironic, decentered nature of the romance—its coordination of multiple voices and repudiation of simple consensus or transparent meaning—does not therefore anticipate or lead to political emancipation and democratic or communitarian inclusiveness. On the contrary, the multivoicedness of the text is both centrifugal and centripetal: the fragmentation of point of view ends up binding difference to ideology even as it works to disarticulate its own representational system.

Rabine has suggested something similar in her essay on Derrida and feminism: deconstruction does not necessarily work to unsettle patriarchal privilege, she argues, but on the contrary works to bolster patriarchy against feminist critique at a particularly crucial moment in the history of Western philosophy—a moment that is witnessing a virtually unprecedented inter-rogation of the singular, male subject of philosophy. While "deconstructive writings customarily make a disclaimer of mastery over the system of knowledge and language employed," Rabine writes, it may well be that the deconstructor "plays at non-mastery in order to arrive at a different kind of mastery, not just of language and knowledge, but of a crumbling and rapidly changing phallocracy."[84] In Rabine's view, Derrida's attempts "to decenter the discourses of Western thought and representation" (discourses that, as we have seen here, may already be decentered) often involve the appropriation by "male theory" of the decentered position of "Woman," and thereby produce yet another essentialism and enact a double displacement of women. Feminism, she writes, "always has to do more than deconstruct. Even a deconstruction that does not universalize the male point of view can universalize the conceptual, theoretical levels of practice and exclude direct political action, which requires certain metaphysical practices."[85]

Of course, the phallocracy of Jean de Meun's time can hardly be said to be crumbling—though certainly one could argue (as Sarah Kay has) that the thirteenth century witnessed intellectual changes that placed medieval patriarchy in an unusually defensive position.[86] However, my goal is not simply to conflate the thirteenth century and the twentieth, Jean de Meun and Jacques Derrida; nor do I mean to suggest that the attempt to expose fault lines within traditional signifying codes is necessarily part of perpetuating a dominant ideology. Rather, I believe that contemporary feminist critiques of deconstruction can allow us to understand that the rupturing of representation and disintegration of the subject in texts like the *Roman de la rose* are not in and of themselves liberatory acts. In my view, the *Rose* offers convincing evidence that such self-inflicted wounds may be closely linked to a form of ideological coercion that works to confirm male mastery and female subordination. This coercion does not simply occur within the fictional space of romance, but, through acts of interpellation, extends into the world as well: words are, as it were, cousins to their deeds.

The most pertinent example, of course, is the plucking of the rose. Far from being a phantasmatic dream or parodic performance, the *cueillette* is symptomatic of a culture in which men *did* in fact signify masculinity through acts of sexual aggression and rape.[87] Ami's infamous incitement to rape is thus not an anomaly in the *Rose*, but merely the most extreme form of a misogyny that pervades Jean's poem and the clerical milieu in which it was produced:

Cuillez la rose tout a force
et moutrez que vos estes hon,
quant leus iert et tens et seson,
car riens ne leur porroit tant plere
con tel force, qui la set fere. (7656–64)

[When place and time and season occur, cut the rose by force and show that you are a man, for, as long as someone knows how to exercise it, nothing could please them so much as such force.] (144–45)

Is it merely a coincidence that Ami here echoes the authorial signature, the moment at which Amor informs his armies that Jean de Meun will complete the romance "se tens et leus l'en peut venire"? On the contrary, I would argue that Jean's romance is always teleologically oriented toward a ritualized act of "masculation" ("moutrez que vos estes hon") that celebrates and legitimates the violent seizing or capturing of women's bodies "tout a force."

Christine de Pizan and the Querelle du "Roman de la rose"

The claim that the *Rose* might actually inflict injury on women, including physical injury, has a long and illustrious history. Christine de Pizan in her letter to Pierre Col offers a version of that argument, though, as has often been noted, her position is significantly undermined by the tack she takes rhetorically. Christine recounts to Pierre a story she has heard from a mutual acquaintance about a particular "home marié" [married man] who believes in the *Roman de la rose* "comme a l'Euvangile" [as in the Gospel] (140; 136).[88] This man is "souverainnement jaloux" [supremely jealous] (140; 136), and in a fit of possessive rage beats his wife, reading choice passages from the *Rose* as he does so:

> Et a chascun mot qu'il treuve a son propos il fiert ung coup ou deux du pié ou de la paume; si m'est advis que quiconques s'en loe, telle povre fame le compere chier. (140)

> [And at every word he finds appropriate, he gives her a couple of kicks or slaps. Thus it seems clear to me that whatever other people think of this book, this poor woman pays too high a price for it.] (136)

What many critics have noticed about this passage is that it betrays a rather stark hypocrisy, that Christine emulates Jean's example even as she critiques it. Indeed, Christine does not report a personal experience, confirmed facts, or a story she knows firsthand; instead she relies on hearsay and rumor to prove her point. Similarly, though she cannot verify the anecdote herself (some argue that she may simply have invented it), still she has no qualms about passing it on for all to hear, claiming that there can be no distortion in retelling it: "Je te diray ung. . .exemple sans mentir" [I will give you (an) example without lying] (139; 136). More importantly, as Helen Solterer has cogently argued, even as Christine attacks Jean for slandering women, she puts herself in the position of a slanderer, paradoxically transgressing the very law she seeks to uphold.[89] In attacking Jean de Meun (who, for obvious reasons, can no longer defend himself), Christine confirms, in Solterer's words, "the time-honored stereotype of woman as defamer"—to say nothing of the equally pernicious stereotype of woman as scandalmonger and busybody.[90] Though she is not always so extreme, Christine at one point goes so far as to suggest that the *Roman de la rose* might deserve to be burned more than praised: "Je treuve. . .mieulx lui affiert ensevellissement de feu que couronne de lorier" [I consider it more fitting to bury it in fire than to crown it with laurel] (21, 55).[91]

Christine's rhetorical missteps have been attributed to a variety of factors, including irrationality, irritability, prudishness, and obtuseness.[92] Recent readings of the *Querelle* have tended to be more generous to Christine's intelligence, though her motives and methods are not held to be above reproach. Thus Hult claims that Christine's part in the *Querelle* constitutes a calculated attempt "to consolidate her position as a court author."[93] In defending herself against "charges of presumptuousness," Christine offers "a model of bad faith, in which the continued protestations of humility. . .simplicity. . .and a lack of design in engineering her fame. . .echo a humility topos which recurs throughout her letters and which serves rather as a method for consolidating and guaranteeing her fame."[94] Solterer takes for granted that Christine is genuinely concerned with women's welfare and argues that in spite of its excesses, her intervention in this very public debate has clear political benefits for women: she makes room within humanism for a female *clerc*; she theorizes the social function of literature and demonstrates that those who injure women can be held publicly accountable; and she defines the libeling of women as a threat to the common good. Yet as Solterer maintains, Christine herself will eventually realize that "a polemical mode cannot succeed in countering the public defamation of women."[95] In her subsequent works, especially the *Chemin de long estude*, she will turn to ethical reflection and prophetic vision, balancing her bitter denunciation of the great misogynists of the past with a forward-looking, affirmative advocacy of women.

I would tend to agree with Solterer's assessment and would add that more than anything, Christine's interventions in the *Querelle* tell us about the extraordinary challenges a text like the *Roman de la rose* poses to feminist criticism. If the *Rose* evacuates the author from his work and fragments the narrative voice beyond recognition, can the ideological underpinnings and social and political effects of the poem ever be identified? Indeed, how can feminists even begin to critique a text that calls into question the metaphysical foundations of discourse, subjectivity, and identity if (to quote Rabine) political action "requires certain metaphysical practices"?

As Solterer suggests, Christine's most clear-sighted response to these questions may not actually be found in the *Querelle*. The "sapiential writing" of the *Chemin* constitutes, in Solterer's view, an attempt "to counteract past symbolic violence" through a "commitment to the polis" and an ethical reorientation of writing toward "society's benefit."[96] The same certainly could be said of Christine's *La cité des dames*, a text that in many ways rewrites the *Roman de la rose*, rather than simply indicting its author or calling for the book to be burned. Collecting and coordinating narratives that affirm women's power and worth, Christine produces a *compilatio* that is also an impregnable, allegorical city: a castle in which women will forever be protected from calumny and assault. Almost literally taking a page from the master's own book, Christine reappropriates a strategy used to conceal misogyny in order to assemble a discursive structure that will protect women from misogyny.[97]

Yet in looking forward toward a utopian future, Christine does not lose sight of a political critique of the past. In the opening pages of the *Cité*, the narrator (who is named Christine) bemoans the fact that men's writing—which is, in effect, all she has in her library to read—is inclined to see so much evil in women. Christine (anticipating Duby) here plainly points to the exclusiveness of literacy in her time. Regardless of any problem of voice in their writings, male clerical authors (philosophers, poets, and moralists) typically speak with a single voice when it comes to women. More often than not, women are denied the opportunity to respond *in propria persona*—that is, without being ventriloquized by a man. Christine plainly understands this as not simply an intellectual problem but a material one as well. In fact, the mere sight of a book she has open on her table (the vicious antimatrimonial satire *Liber Lamentationum Matheoluli*) inspires in her a dread of the misogynistic tradition it represents:

> Mais la veue d'icelluy dit livre, tout soit il de nulle auttorité, ot engendré en moy nouvelle penssee qui fist naistre en mon couraige grant admiracion, penssant quelle puet estre la cause, ne dont ce puet venir, que tant de divers hommes, clercs et autres, ont esté, et sont, sy enclins a dire de bouche et en leur traittiez et escrips tant de diableries et de vituperes de femmes et de leurs condicions. Et nom mie seulement un ou deux ne cestuy Matheolus, qui entre les livres n'a aucune reputacion et qui traitte en maniere de trufferie, mais generaument aucques en tous traittiez philosophes, pouettes, tous orateurs desquelz les noms seroit longue chose, semble que tous parlent par une meismes bouche et tous accordent une semblable conclusion, determinant les meurs femenins enclins et plains de tous les vices.

> [Just the sight of this book, even though it was of no authority, made me wonder how it happened that so many different men—and learned men among them—have been and are so inclined to express both in speaking and in their treatises and writings so many devilish and wicked thoughts about women and their behavior. Not only one or two and not even just this Mathéolus (for this book had a bad name anyway and was intended as a satire) but, more generally, judging from the treatises of all philosophers and poets and from all the orators—it would take too long to mention their

names—it seems that they all speak from one and the same mouth. They all concur in one conclusion: that the behavior of women is inclined to and full of every vice.][98]

Christine is certainly aware of the dialectical nature of the tradition she is critiquing; indeed she deliberately plays on multivoicedness throughout the *Cité* and the rest of her corpus.[99] In this instance, however, she is interested in indicting a particular aspect of literate, clerical culture that seems to resist the splitting of voices—a tradition that is, as Duby suggests, "resolutely male." Boldly defying that tradition, she points to the specific material relationship between libraries and misogyny; between the privileged space set aside for the production, conservation, and interpretation of texts and the deliberate exclusion of women; between a form of social and political power predicated on literacy and the silencing of certain kinds of voices.

Crucially, Christine demonstrates that silence betrays an underlying violence—indeed, a specifically sexual violence that is realized on women's bodies. Speaking to Lady Rectitude, the narrator laments, "Si m'anuye et m'esgriesve de ce que hommes dient tant que femmes se veullent efforcier et qu'il ne leur desplait mie, quoyque elles escondissent de bouche, d'estre par hommes efforciees" [I am troubled and grieved when men argue that many women want to be raped (literally, "forced") and that it does not bother them at all to be raped ("forced") by men even when they verbally protest].[100] The plucking of the mute, nameless rose in Jean's romance, whether or not it is coded as a rape or merely a performance of phallic "force," certainly finds its counterpart in the reality Christine describes: sexual violence was a ubiquitous, if infrequently punished, crime, one that found considerable legitimacy in fictional and scientific accounts of women who resisted, but were ultimately conquered by their own desire. The speechlessness of the rose stands in stark contrast to the overt privileging of male speech and silently belies Payen's and others' claims that the *Roman de la rose* resists its own cultural context and offers up a manifesto for "a sexual liberty founded on free consent." Far from advocating free consent, Jean's poem, in particular the *cueillette*, marks the exaltation of phallic power through dissemination and insemination, through the proliferation of alternate voices and an assault on an utterly mute, inert object of desire. Scholars of the *Rose*—and of medieval misogyny generally—would do well, then, to concentrate their efforts not just on exposing internal incoherences within misogynistic speech, but also on discovering the ways those internally disrupted discourses have been used to perpetuate antifeminism, to inscribe a masculinist ideology onto silenced female bodies, and to demand that women pay the price for literary celebrations of male sexual aggression.

CONCLUSION

Ethics is the first victim of the struggle it instigated against ideology.

—Emmanuel Levinas, *Of God Who Comes to Mind*

Throughout this book, I have argued for a critique of medieval allegory and sexual ethics as cultural evidence pointing to concrete, historical situations of material domination. My overarching goal has been to draw attention to the relationship between literary, rhetorical, and ethical cultures in the High Middle Ages and their economic, political, and ideological foundations. That relationship is not as mechanical, causal, or predictable as some critics have supposed. But neither the unpredictability of allegorical meaning nor the apparent openness of the "hermeneutics of charity" should be construed as evidence of a fundamentally altruistic, pluralist, or liberatory culture. On the contrary, medieval allegory and sexual ethics operate as discursive regimes: they internalize difference, deviation, and dissent within figurations of truth, goodness, and belief, and then use the resulting crisis of meaning, knowledge, and belief to legitimate coercive, violent forms of discipline. They are exceedingly pernicious ideological fictions that draw attention to their own incoherence in order to motivate the consolidation of power within ruling classes and institutions, often through brutal forms of eliminationism.

If this argument is accepted as valid (and hopefully it will be), it still begs a number of tricky questions. Does the kind of critique I have offered here simply prove Nietzsche's claim that ethics is a "fabrication for purposes of gulling" or a means for translating "political superiority" into "superiority of soul"?[1] Does it discredit ethics as little more than a ruse of power, a cover for the machinations of politics and ideology? Or does it instead ask us to imagine a different kind of ethics, one that might shape our reading practices or strategies of critique as we strive to overcome the violent legacy of the historical past and to imagine a less violent, more tolerant future? Though the analysis I have offered in the preceding pages certainly owes a great deal to Nietzschean moral skepticism, I would like to conclude by interrogating the specifically ethical motivations behind ideology critique as a practice—motivations that have remained largely unspoken in this book, but can nonetheless be intuited throughout.

My reticence to articulate the ethics of my project is no doubt due in part to the generalized and enduring suspicion of ethics among literary scholars and critical theorists. Writing in 1981 and citing Marx, Fredric Jameson called for theory to transcend "the 'ethical' in the direction of the political and the collective."[2] Nearly twenty years later and citing Nietzsche, Judith Butler expressed her "ambivalence" about a recent "return to ethics," which she believes constitutes "an escape from politics" toward a "heightening of moralism."[3] And yet is it not possible to imagine an ethics of reading that would not revert to pious, apolitical moralism, one that would draw attention to the violent effects of ideology without resorting to sanctimonious pronouncements or meaningless self-flagellation?

A number of scholars have argued in recent years that this is indeed possible. In the field of literary criticism, Geoffrey Galt Harpham describes morality as merely "a particular moment" in ethics, a necessary but provisional delimitation of ethics' "august reticence" and "principled irresolution."[4] Harpham's ethics of reading "is definitely not a morality" or a means for solving problems, but rather a way of structuring problems without ever arriving at "a final interpretation."[5] In the field of political philosophy, Chantal Mouffe offers a similar account of ethics as a continuous, unfettered process of contestation and change that understands "agonistic confrontation," rather than rational consensus, as the "very condition of possibility" for democracy.[6] Mouffe calls this an "ethics of *dis-harmony*" in that it "does not dream of mastering or eliminating undecidability and of establishing transparency" and abandons altogether the idea of "a complete reabsorption of alterity into oneness and harmony."[7] Though it would constantly strive for a more just and democratic future, the ethics of "dis-harmony" would also recognize that the gap between lived realities and heuristic ideals requires an ongoing critique of justice, morality, and social order in the here and now; a political and ethical defense of the disenfranchised, socially alienated other; and a rigorous demystification of the mechanisms of ideological control, including the ideology of liberal democracy.

Butler would undoubtedly agree with Mouffe about the relationship between imagining the future and critiquing the ideologies of the present and past. She would, however, insist rigorously on the *politics* of futurity rather than its *ethics*. Summarizing an argument from Mouffe and Ernesto Laclau's *Hegemony and Socialist Strategy*, Butler writes,

> Every ideological formation is constituted through and against a constitutive antagonism and is, therefore, to be understood as an effort to cover over or

"suture" a set of contingent relations. Because this ideological suturing is never complete, that is, because it can never establish itself as a *necessary or comprehensive* set of connections, it is marked by a failure of complete determination, a constitutive contingency, that emerges within the ideological field as its permanent (and promising) stability.[8]

In an attempt to counter the effects of ideological suturing, Butler endorses Mouffe and Laclau's call for a "radical democracy": a "political futurity" imagined precisely by drawing attention to "the incompletion of every ideological formulation."[9] This kind of politicization requires unconstrained questioning of political order in order to imagine "a set of *future* possibilities for inclusion, what Mouffe refers to as part of the not-yet-assimilable *horizon* of community."[10]

Part of the problem with a politics predicated on the deconstruction of ideological fictions is that, as we have seen in this book, some of the most brutally repressive ideologies do *not* dream of "mastering or eliminating undecidability" and indeed continually unveil the contingency and instability at the heart of the "ideological field." Though critics have often assumed that medieval allegory (and medieval culture generally) is naively invested in discursive presence, philosophical realism, and ideal harmony, this is rarely the case. Typically, as we have seen, medieval allegory does not seek to suture its differences and contingencies but instead lays them bare. The self-deconstructing games of the *Roman d'Eneas*, the *De planctu Naturae*, and the *Roman de la rose* point repeatedly, even obsessively, to the internal fragmentation of subjectivity, discourse, morality, and culture. And yet in these texts, the debunking of the illusion of "oneness and harmony" does not lead to political liberation. Quite to the contrary, medieval allegories call for violent responses to symbolic or representational problems, for imposing consensus and conformity through physical brutality because it cannot be achieved through other means. The allegorical works I have discussed in this book allow us to understand that ideology critique must always do more than deconstruct, that we cannot begin to imagine a radical "political futurity" simply by pointing to "the incompletion of every ideological formulation."

Even more to the point, it is my firm conviction that ideology critique is most effective and valuable *politically* when it acknowledges its underlying ethical motivations, most notably the desire to expose social inequities and progress toward a more equitable, just, and compassionate future. Indeed, though Butler expresses concern over the potential pitfalls of moralization, at the same time she relies on a kind of moral idealism when she articulates the specifically political significance of performativity: "The ideal of a radical inclusivity is impossible, but this very impossibility nevertheless governs the political field as an idealization of the future that motivates the expansion, linking, and perpetual production of political subject-positions and signifiers."[11] An ideal future, one that is always elsewhere than where we are or that is separated from the present by a structural gap, would allow us to contest the injustice of the present and the past on both political *and* ethical grounds and to strive toward a goal of more expansive forms of social justice. John D. Caputo proposes that this notion of a "horizon of hope and expectation" is ethics' invitation to unbounded reflection: "Justice is always to come, and our aim is to expose the present to the white light of an absolute scrutiny which has zero tolerance for injustice, for injustice is all around us."[12] An ethics that acknowledges the burden of responsibility that the other places upon us may fail to be fully ethical—indeed, it necessarily does. But that does not mean that the project of ethics—and the project of ideology critique that it inspired—should be abandoned or sacrificed. As Emmanuel Levinas argues, we must not seek to escape the cynicism of Realpolitik by blindly embracing moral or spiritual idealism. We must instead strike a balance between ethical notions of responsibility and political imperatives, elaborating "a politics that's ethically necessary" (to quote Levinas) or a "politics as an ethics" (to quote Foucault).[13]

What an ethically necessary politics would look like is, by definition, a subject for vigorous, inexhaustible debate. I will not attempt to theorize it here but will simply propose that, as part of the project of imagining the future, we ought to turn to the past in order to challenge the oppressive, violent legacy of premodern ethics and sexual ethics. For in ways too numerous to mention (but painfully obvious to anyone attuned to the medieval origins of modern concepts of evil and perversion), that legacy continues to haunt the present. In articulating our critiques, we should not simply replace ethics with politics; nor should we contest the legacy of the past simply by *"working the weakness in the norm."*[14] We must also acknowledge that ethics calls for a political commitment to combating social alienation and victimization, and that politics in turn requires an ethical investment in imagining a radically inclusive, if never fully realizable, democracy.

NOTES

Introduction

1. Michel Foucault, *The History of Sexuality, Volume One: An Introduction*, trans. Robert Hurley (1978; repr. New York: Vintage, 1990), pp. 105–6.
2. See Louis Adrian Montrose, ' "Shaping Fantasies': Figurations of Gender and Power in Elizabethan Culture," *Representations* 2 (1983): 61–94; and David M. Halperin, "Is There a History of Sexuality?" in *The Lesbian and Gay Studies Reader*, ed. Henry Abelove, Michèle Aina Barale, and Halperin (New York: Routledge, 1993), pp. 416–31.
3. Sheila Delany, *Medieval Literary Politics: Shapes of Ideology* (Manchester: Manchester University Press, 1990), pp. 42, 46.
4. Delany, *Medieval Literary Politics*, p. 48.
5. Delany, *Medieval Literary Politics*, pp. 52–53, 57.
6. Delany, *Medieval Literary Politics*, p. 57.
7. Peter Haidu, *The Subject Medieval/Modern: Text and Governance in the Middle Ages* (Stanford: Stanford University Press, 2004), p. 35.
8. See, for instance, John Fiske, "Culture, Ideology, Interpellation," in *Literary Theory: An Anthology*, ed. Julie Rivkin and Michael Ryan (Oxford: Blackwell, 1998), pp. 305–11.
9. Friedrich Nietzsche, *On the Genealogy of Morals and Ecce Homo*, trans. Walter Kaufmann and R.J. Hollingdale (New York: Vintage, 1989), pp. 25–26.
10. Nietzsche, *Genealogy of Morals*, p. 31.
11. Geoffrey Galt Harpham, *Shadows of Ethics: Criticism and the Just Society* (Durham: Duke University Press, 1999), pp. 19–20, citing Nietzsche, *Genealogy of Morals*, p. 20.
12. See Marcia L. Colish, *The Mirror of Language: A Study in the Medieval Theory of Knowledge*, rev. ed. (Lincoln: University of Nebraska Press, 1983), pp. 176–77.
13. Cor. 13.12. Colish emphasizes the vital importance of this passage for medieval intellectuals, who held that signs "would always be limited in their cognitive function, both in the degree to which they could represent the transcendent God at all and in the degree to which they could convey the knowledge of God to the subject in the first instance. They always distinguished the reflection of God in the mirror of faith from God himself. They never confused signification with an identity between sign and object" (*Mirror of Language*, p. ix).

14. See Jon Whitman, *Allegory: The Dynamics of an Ancient and Medieval Technique* (Cambridge, MA: Harvard University Press, 1987), pp. 263–68, esp. p. 266.
15. Gordon Teskey, *Allegory and Violence* (Ithaca: Cornell University Press, 1996), p. 6.
16. I am by no means ruling out the existence of dissent in medieval culture. On the relationship between institutional and oppositional tendencies in the Middle Ages, see Rita Copeland, ed., *Criticism and Dissent in the Middle Ages* (Cambridge, UK: Cambridge University Press, 1996).
17. Erich Auerbach, *Mimesis: The Representation of Reality in Western Literature*, trans. Willard R. Trask (Princeton: Princeton University Press, 1953), p. 136.
18. Auerbach, *Mimesis*, pp. 136–37.
19. See the essays collected in *The Cambridge Companion to Medieval Romance*, ed. Roberta L. Krueger (Cambridge, UK: Cambridge University Press, 2000).
20. Delany, *Medieval Literary Politics*, p. 50.
21. Haidu, *Subject Medieval/Modern*, p. 80.
22. As George D. Economou observes, in *The Goddess Natura in Medieval Literature* (Cambridge, MA: Harvard University Press, 1972), nature represents "an aggregate of ideas" for medieval thinkers: "The term nature could stand for the general order of all creation as a single, harmonious whole, whose study might lead to an understanding of the model on which this created world is formed. It could stand for the Platonic intermediary between the intelligible and material worlds; or for the divinely ordained power that presides over the continuity and preservation of whatever lives in the sublunary world; or for a creative principle directly subordinated to the mind and will of God" (p. 3).
23. Whitman, *Allegory*, p. 126.
24. Whitman, *Allegory*, p. 126.
25. Whitman, *Allegory*, p. 2.
26. Macrobius, *Commentary on the Dream of Scipio*, 1.2.3, 1.2.9, trans. William Harris Stahl (1952; New York: Columbia University Press, 1990), pp. 83, 85.
27. Macrobius, *Commentary*, 1.2.17, p. 86.
28. Macrobius, *Commentary*, 1.2.17, p. 85.
29. Macrobius, *Commentary*, 1.2.18, pp. 86–87, emphasis mine. A similar, and equally influential, statement on withholding intellectual truths from the hoi polloi is to be found in Boethius's *Quomodo substantiae*. On the importance of this text, see Hélène Merle's commentary in her edition and translation of Boethius, *Courts traités de théologie* (Paris: Cerf, 1995), pp. 85–110.
30. Haidu offers an analysis of medieval violence in *The Subject Medieval/Modern*, specifically arguing against recent attempts by historians to dispel the myth of a "violent Middle Ages." The medieval period was perhaps no more violent than other historical periods; certainly it was considerably *less* violent than our own time. However, the Middle Ages and modernity use violence in fundamentally similar ways: "In neither case is. . .violence simply illegal, anomalous, or 'opposed to legitimate rule.' In both, violence is deployed,

not outside the rule of law, but as a policy of those in power, those who claim legitimacy in the practices of governance. In the eleventh century as in the twentieth, law itself is violent. . . .Violence—Marc Bloch and Walter Benjamin got it right—inhered in law itself " (p. 25). See also Haidu, *The Subject of Violence: The "Song of Roland" and the Birth of the State* (Bloomington: Indiana University Press, 1993).

31. Alan of Lille, *De planctu Naturae*, 8.159, ed. Nikolaus M. Häring, in *Studi Medievali*, terza serie 19/2 (1978): 879.

32. Guillaume de Lorris and Jean de Meun, *The Romance of the Rose*, 3rd ed., trans. Charles Dahlberg (Princeton: Princeton University Press, 1995), p. 324.

33. Jody Enders, "Rhetoric, Coercion, and the Memory of Violence," in *Criticism and Dissent in the Middle Ages*, p. 28 [pp. 24–55]. See also *The Medieval Theater of Cruelty: Rhetoric, Memory, Violence* (Ithaca: Cornell University Press, 1999), in which Enders describes rhetoric as a "system of pain production" (p. 8).

34. Enders, "Rhetoric," in *Criticism and Dissent in the Middle Ages*, p. 29.

35. Enders, "Rhetoric," in *Criticism and Dissent in the Middle Ages*, p. 28.

36. Teskey, *Allegory and Violence*, p. 21. I discuss Teskey's theories of hylomorphism, allegory, and gender in greater detail in chapter 4.

37. Teskey, *Allegory and Violence*, p. 19.

38. Teskey, *Allegory and Violence*, p. 17.

39. Angus Fletcher, *Allegory: The Theory of a Symbolic Mode* (Ithaca: Cornell University Press, 1964), p. 368, cited in Teskey, *Allegory and Violence*, p. 132.

40. Teskey, *Allegory and Violence*, p. 132.

41. Teskey, *Allegory and Violence*, p. 19.

42. Teskey, *Allegory and Violence*, p. 18.

Chapter 1 Rhetoric, Evil, and Privation: From Augustine to the "Persecuting Society"

1. The classic studies are Marie-Dominique Chenu, *Nature, Man, and Society in the Twelfth Century: Essays on New Theological Perspectives in the Latin West*, ed. and trans. Jerome Taylor and Lester K. Little (Chicago: University of Chicago Press, 1968); and Winthrop Wetherbee, *Platonism and Poetry in the Twelfth Century: The Literary Influence of the School of Chartres* (Princeton: Princeton University Press, 1972).

2. Hugh of St. Victor, *The Didascalicon*, 6.5, trans. Jerome Taylor (New York: Columbia University Press, 1961), p. 145.

3. Chenu, *Nature, Man, and Society*, p. 103.

4. Chenu, *Nature, Man, and Society*, p. 100.

5. Chenu, *Nature, Man, and Society*, p. 112.

6. Wetherbee, *Platonism and Poetry*, p. 220.

7. Wetherbee, *Platonism and Poetry*, p. 220.

8. Edgar de Bruyne, *Etudes d'esthétique médiévale*, 2nd ed., 2 vols. (Paris: Albin Michel, 1998), vol. 1, p. 704.

9. All cited in Chenu, *Nature, Man, and Society*, p. 117. See also Ernst Robert Curtius, *European Literature and the Latin Middle Ages*, trans. Willard R. Trask (Princeton: Princeton University Press, 1953), pp. 319–26.

10. Hugh of St. Victor, *Didascalicon*, 5.3, p. 122.

11. For a discussion of medieval sign theory, including Augustine and Aquinas, see Marcia Colish, *The Mirror of Language: A Study in the Medieval Theory of Knowledge*, rev. ed. (Lincoln: University of Nebraska Press, 1983).

12. Thomas Aquinas, *Expositio super Librum Boethii de Trinitate*, ps3qu6ar2ra1, in *Selected Philosophical Writings*, trans. Timothy McDermott (Oxford: Oxford University Press, 1993), p. 42.

13. Thomas Aquinas, *Expositio*, ps3qu6ar2ra1, in *Selected Philosophical Writings*, p. 42.

14. Thomas Aquinas, *Expositio*, ps3qu6ar3co5, in *Selected Philosophical Writings*, p. 46.

15. Augustine, *The City of God against the Pagans*, 8.16, trans. R.W. Dyson (Cambridge, UK: Cambridge University Press, 1998), p. 557.

16. Augustine, *City of God*, 8.13, p. 555

17. Augustine, *City of God*, 8.20, p. 566.

18. Augustine, *On Christian Doctrine*, 3.5.9, trans. D.W. Robertson, Jr. (Upper Saddle River, NJ: Prentice Hall, 1958), pp. 83–84.

19. Augustine, *The Confessions*, 5.3.3, 5.3.5, trans. Maria Boulding (1997; repr. New York: Vintage, 1998), pp. 77, 78.

20. Augustine, *Christian Doctrine*, 3.5.9, p. 84, citing 2 Cor. 3.6.

21. Augustine, *Christian Doctrine*, 3.5.9, p. 84.

22. Augustine, *City of God*, 5.17, p. 217.

23. Augustine, *City of God*, 19.15, p. 944.

24. Augustine, *City of God*, 19.15, p. 943.

25. Augustine, *City of God*, 13.13, p. 944.

26. Augustine, *City of God*, 13.13, p. 555.

27. Augustine, *City of God*, 13.13, p. 555.

28. Colish, *Mirror of Language*, pp. 121–22.

29. Thomas Aquinas, *Summa Theologiae*, 1–2.91.2 (New York: McGraw Hill, 1964–81), vol. 28, p. 23.

30. Thomas Aquinas, *Summa Theologiae*, 2–2.10.12, vol. 32, pp. 76–77.

31. Colish, *Mirror of Language*, p. 1.

32. Colish, *Mirror of Language*, p. 1.

33. John Boswell, *Christianity, Social Tolerance, and Homosexuality: Gay People in Western Europe from the Beginning of the Christian Era to the Fourteenth Century* (Chicago: Chicago University Press, 1980), p. 330.

34. Boswell, *Christianity, Social Tolerance, and Homosexuality*, p. 330.

35. Thomas Aquinas, *Summa Theologiae*, 2–2.1.10, vol. 31, p. 55, citing 1 Cor. 1.10.

36. Thomas Aquinas, *Summa Theologiae*, 2–2, 11.3, vol. 32, p. 89.

37. Sarah Spence, *Rhetorics of Reason and Desire: Vergil, Augustine, and the Troubadours* (Ithaca: Cornell University Press, 1988), pp. 100–101.

38. Spence, *Rhetorics of Reason and Desire*, p. 100.

39. Spence, *Rhetorics of Reason and Desire*, p. 100.

40. Spence, *Rhetorics of Reason and Desire*, p. 101.

41. Spence, *Rhetorics of Reason and Desire*, p. 76.

42. Spence, *Rhetorics of Reason and Desire*, p. 101. Spence's reading of Augustine finds a measure of support in the recently rediscovered Divjak letters and Dolbeau sermons. As Peter Brown puts it in the epilogue to the new edition of his *Augustine of Hippo: A Biography* (1967; Berkeley: University of California Press, 2000), these texts reveal a "considerably less. . .authoritarian, stern figure" (p. 446) than we find in the formal theological works. Indeed, they suggest that Augustine the preacher and bishop was far less confident than Augustine the theologian in his intellectual and spiritual authority and in his ability to sway the opinions of congregants and imperial administrators. Augustine here demonstrates that he is capable of sustained "dialogues with the crowd," often allowing the exchange of ideas to remain open-ended and "inconclusive" (p. 446). It would be a mistake, however, to assume that the rhetorical and hermeneutical techniques of these texts pervade all of Augustine's writings. As Brown explains, this is not at all "the voice of Augustine the theologian or of Augustine the thinker. Rather, it is the living voice of Augustine the bishop, caught, in turns, at its most intimate and at its most routine" (p. 445). Above all, we should not imagine that this is the Augustine who influenced medieval posterity. Brown notes that the Venerable Bede read the masterpiece of the Dolbeau sermons around the year AD 700, and of its 1,543 lines, deemed only a hundred to be of any real interest.

43. Spence, *Rhetorics of Reason and Desire*, p. 101.

44. Spence, *Rhetorics of Reason and Desire*, p. 101.

45. Spence, *Rhetorics of Reason and Desire*, p. 120.

46. Spence, *Rhetorics of Reason and Desire*, p. 130.

47. Augustine, *Christian Doctrine*, 3.6.10, p. 84.

48. Augustine, *The Usefulness of Belief*, 3.9, in *Earlier Writings*, trans. John H.S. Burleigh (Philadelphia: Westminster Press, 1953), p. 298.

49. Jeremy Cohen, *Living Letters of the Law: Ideas of the Jew in Medieval Christianity* (Berkeley: University of California Press, 1999), p. 62.

50. Cohen, *Living Letters of the Law*, pp. 59–60.

51. Cohen, *Living Letters of the Law*, p. 37.

52. Augustine, *Enarratio in Psalmos*, 58.2.2–10, cited in Cohen, *Living Letters of the Law*, pp. 39–40.

53. Augustine, *The Literal Meaning of Genesis*, 11.30.39, trans. John Hammond Taylor, 2 vols. (New York: Newman Press, 1982), vol. 2, p. 162.

54. Jean A. Truax, "Augustine of Hippo: Defender of Women's Equality?" *Journal of Medieval History* 16 (1990): 279–99.

55. Augustine, Letter 147, cited in Truax, "Augustine of Hippo," 292.

56. Augustine, Sermon 232, cited in Truax, "Augustine of Hippo," 294.

57. Kim Power, *Veiled Desire: Augustine on Women* (New York: Continuum, 1996), pp. 32–36. Power cites Eric Osborn, *Ethical Patterns in Early Christian*

Thought (Cambridge, UK: Cambridge University Press, 1976), pp. 143–82. For a synoptic overview of scholarship on Augustine and women, see E. Ann Matter, "Christ, God, and Woman in the Thought of St. Augustine," in *Augustine and His Critics: Essays in Honour of Gerald Bonner*, ed. Robert Dodaro and George Lawless (New York: Routledge, 2000), pp. 164–75.

58. Power, *Veiled Desire*, p. 33.

59. Power, *Veiled Desire*, p. 76.

60. Gen. 1.27: "So God created humankind in his image, / in the image of God he created them; / male and female he created them"; 1 Cor. 11.7: "For a man ought not to have his head veiled, since he is the image of and reflection of God; but woman is the reflection of man."

61. As Power observes, Augustine not only insists on the difference between grammatical and conceptual gender here, but he also breaks with the imagery of the Hebrew tradition, in which "wisdom is not only feminine linguistically, but symbolized by the Feminine. In biblical symbols little distinction is made between the Feminine and the womanly" (*Veiled Desire*, p. 135).

62. Power, *Veiled Desire*, pp. 135, 142.

63. Power, *Veiled Desire*, p. 144.

64. Power, *Veiled Desire*, pp. 151, 154.

65. Power, *Veiled Desire*, p. 159.

66. Power, *Veiled Desire*, p. 160.

67. Augustine, *On the Sermon on the Mount*, 1.15.41, cited in Power, *Veiled Desire*, p. 160.

68. Alan of Lille, *Anticlaudianus, or The Good and Perfect Man*, trans. James J. Sheridan (Toronto: Pontifical Institute of Mediæval Studies, 1973), pp. 40–41.

69. Alan of Lille, *Anticlaudianus*, p. 41, citing Mat. 7.6.

70. Alan of Lille, *The Plaint of Nature*, trans. James J. Sheridan (Toronto: Pontifical Institute of Mediæval Studies, 1980), p. 116.

71. Alan of Lille, *The Plaint of Nature*, p. 120.

72. Alan of Lille, *The Plaint of Nature*, p. 119. I discuss this passage at greater length in chapter 3.

73. Alan of Lille, *De planctu Naturae*, 6.175–76, ed. Nikolaus Häring, *Studi Medievali* 19 (1978): 830; *Plaint of Nature*, p. 126.

74. Alexandre Leupin, *Barbarolexis: Medieval Writing and Sexuality*, trans. Kate M. Cooper (Cambridge, MA: Harvard University Press, 1989), p. 66.

75. Larry Scanlon, "Unspeakable Pleasures: Alain de Lille, Sexual Regulation and the Priesthood of Genius," *Romanic Review* 86/2 (1995): 219 [213–42].

76. Scott MacDonald, "Introduction: The Relation between Being and Goodness," in *Being and Goodness: The Concept of the Good in Metaphysics and Philosophical Theology*, ed. MacDonald (Ithaca: Cornell University Press, 1991), pp. 1–2 [1–28].

77. For background on Augustine's ethics and theodicy, see G.R. Evans, *Augustine on Evil* (Cambridge, UK: Cambridge University Press, 1982).

78. Lactantius, *The Wrath of God*, in *Lactantius: The Minor Works*, trans. Mary Francis McDonald (Washington: Catholic University of America Press, 1965), pp. 92–93.

79. Augustine, *Confessions*, 3.7.12, p. 45; *De Ordine*, 2.7.23, trans. Robert P. Russell, in *Divine Providence and the Problem of Evil: A Translation of St. Augustine's "De Ordine"* (New York: Cosmopolitan Science and Art Service, 1942), p. 115. Anselm refers to evil as a convention of speech ("secundum forman loquendi") rather than a form of being ("secundum rem"). See D.P. Henry, "Saint Anselm and Nothingness," *Philosophical Quarterly* 15 (1965): 243–46.

80. Augustine, *Confessions*, 7.13.19, p. 136.

81. Augustine, *City of God*, 14.13, p. 609.

82. See Frederick H. Russell, *The Just War in the Middle Ages* (Cambridge, UK: Cambridge University Press, 1975); Russell, "Love and Hate in Medieval Warfare: The Contribution of Saint Augustine," *Nottingham Medieval Studies* 31 (1987): 108–24; Jonathan Barnes, "The Just War," in *The Cambridge History of Later Medieval Philosophy*, ed. Norman Kretzmann, Anthony Kenny, and Jan Pinborg (Cambridge, UK: Cambridge University Press, 1982), pp. 771–84; R.A. Markus, "Saint Augustine's Views on the 'Just War,'" *Studies in Church History* 20 (1983): 1–13; and Robert L. Holmes, "St. Augustine and the Just War Theory," in *The Augustinian Tradition*, ed. Gareth B. Matthews (Berkeley: University of California Press, 1999), pp. 323–44.

83. Markus, "Saint Augustine's Views," 3.

84. Markus, "Saint Augustine's Views," 7.

85. Markus, "Saint Augustine's Views," 10, citing *City of God*, 22.22.4.

86. Markus, "Saint Augustine's Views," 11.

87. Markus, "Saint Augustine's Views," 12.

88. Markus, "Saint Augustine's Views," 12.

89. Holmes, "St. Augustine and Just War," in *The Augustinian Tradition*, p. 324.

90. Markus, "Saint Augustine's Views," 2.

91. Augustine, Sermon 302 ("On the Birthday of Saint Lawrence"), 10, 16, 21, trans. Edmund Hill, in *The Works of Saint Augustine: A Translation for the 21st Century*, ed. John E. Rotelle (Hyde Park, NY: New City Press, 1994), part 2, vol. 8, pp. 305, 308, 310.

92. Markus, "Saint Augustine's Views," 9.

93. Augustine, *Homilies on the First Epistle of John*, 7.8, cited in Holmes, "St. Augustine and Just War," in *The Augustinian Tradition*, p. 327.

94. Holmes, "St. Augustine and Just War," in *The Augustinian Tradition*, p. 328.

95. Holmes, "St. Augustine and Just War," in *The Augustinian Tradition*, p. 327.

96. Holmes, "St. Augustine and Just War," in *The Augustinian Tradition*, p. 329.

97. Holmes, "St. Augustine and Just War," in *The Augustinian Tradition*, p. 329.

98. Russell, *Just War*, p. 17.

99. Russell, *Just War*, p. 18.

100. Russell, *Just War*, p. 19.

101. Russell, *Just War*, p. 20.

102. Holmes, "St. Augustine and Just War," in *The Augustinian Tradition*, p. 344n62.

103. Holmes, "St. Augustine and Just War," in *The Augustinian Tradition*, p. 338.

104. Jonathan Dollimore, *Sexual Dissidence: Augustine to Wilde, Freud to Foucault* (Oxford: Oxford University Press, 1991), p. 140. Observers of the

nominally "secular" presidency of George W. Bush and of his campaigns against "evildoers" will find ample evidence to substantiate this claim!

105. Dollimore, *Sexual Dissidence*, pp. 134, 141.
106. Augustine, *The Enchiridion on Faith, Hope, and Love*, 13, trans. J.F. Shaw (Chicago: Regnery Gateway, 1961), pp. 13–14.
107. Dollimore, *Sexual Dissidence*, p. 135.
108. Dollimore, *Sexual Dissidence*, p. 135.
109. Dollimore, *Sexual Dissidence*, p. 136.
110. Dollimore, *Sexual Dissidence*, pp. 135–36.
111. Dollimore, *Sexual Dissidence*, p. 135.
112. Dollimore, *Sexual Dissidence*, p. 138.
113. Dollimore, *Sexual Dissidence*, p. 141.
114. Dollimore, *Sexual Dissidence*, p. 141.
115. Dollimore, *Sexual Dissidence*, p. 142.
116. Russell elaborates on the connections between Augustine's just war theory, his approach to the problem of evil, and his rhetorical approach to scriptural hermeneutics in "Love and Hate," esp. 108–11. All of these issues turn on a rejection of Manichean principles. In the case of just war theory, Augustine countered the position articulated by his Manichean opponent Faustus that "God's command that Moses wage wars was proof that God Himself was the author of evil" (111). Though Augustine remains ambivalent about violence throughout his career, he is forced to embrace the idea of righteous violence and to develop specific strategies of exegesis in order to "defend the normative integrity of both Testaments" (110).
117. Russell, "Love and Hate," 112.
118. Augustine, *City of God*, 16.2, p. 695, citing 1 Cor. 11.19.
119. Mark D. Jordan, *The Invention of Sodomy in Christian Theology* (Chicago: University of Chicago Press, 1997), p. 136.
120. Paul E. Sigmund, "Law and Politics," in *The Cambridge Companion to Aquinas*, ed. Norman Kretzmann and Eleonore Stump (Cambridge, UK: Cambridge University Press, 1993), p. 220 [217–31].
121. Aquinas, *Summa Contra Gentiles*, 3.81, and *Summa Theologiae*, 2–2.57.3, 1–2.94.5, and 2–2.104.5, cited in Sigmund, "Law and Politics," in *Companion to Aquinas*, p. 222.
122. See Thomas Aquinas, *Summa Theologiae*, 2–2.65.2, vol. 38, pp. 53–55.
123. Sigmund, "Law and Politics," in *Companion to Aquinas*, p. 222.
124. Thomas Aquinas, *Summa Theologiae*, 2–2.64.2, vol. 38, p. 23.
125. Thomas Aquinas, *Summa Theologiae*, 2–2.64.2, vol. 38, p. 25.
126. Thomas Aquinas, *Summa Theologiae*, 2–2.64.2, vol. 38, p. 25.
127. Boswell, *Christianity, Social Tolerance, and Homosexuality*, esp. pp. 267–332 ("The Rise of Intolerance"); R.I. Moore, *The Formation of a Persecuting Society: Power and Deviance in Western Europe, 950–1250* (Oxford: Blackwell, 1987).
128. See, for instance, James A. Brundage, *Law, Sex, and Christian Society in Medieval Europe* (Chicago: University of Chicago Press, 1987); Michael Goodich, *The Unmentionable Vice: Homosexuality in the Later Medieval Period* (Santa Barbara: Clio Books, 1979); Jeffrey Richards, *Sex, Dissidence, and*

Damnation: Minority Groups in the Middle Ages (New York: Routledge, 1991); and Goodich, ed., *Other Middle Ages: Witnesses at the Margins of Medieval Society* (Philadelphia: University of Pennsylvania Press, 1998).

129. Jacques Chiffoleau, "Dire l'indicible: Remarques sur la catégorie du *nefandum* du XIIe au XVe siècle," *Annales ESC* 45/2 (1990): 289–324; and "*Contra Naturam:* Pour une approche casuistique et procédurale de la nature médiévale," *Micrologus: Natura, scienze, e società medievali* 4 (1996): 265–312.

130. Helmut Puff, "Nature on Trial: Acts 'Against Nature' in the Law Courts of Early Modern German and Switzerland," in *The Moral Authority of Nature*, ed. Lorraine Daston and Fernando Vidal (Chicago: University of Chicago Press, 2004), pp. 232–53.

131. Marc Boone, "State Power and Illicit Sexuality: The Persecution of Sodomy in Late Medieval Bruges," *Journal of Medieval History* 22/2 (1996): 135–53.

132. Cited in Boone, "State Power and Illicit Sexuality," 138.

133. Boone, "State Power and Illicit Sexuality," 135.

134. Boone, "State Power and Illicit Sexuality," 139.

135. Boone, "State Power and Illicit Sexuality," 153.

136. Chiffoleau, "Dire l'indicible," 312.

137. Giorgio Agamben, *Homo Sacer: Sovereign Power and Bare Life*, trans. Daniel Heller-Roazen (Stanford: Stanford University Press, 1998), p. 1.

138. Agamben, *Homo Sacer*, p. 1.

139. Agamben, *Homo Sacer*, p. 8.

140. Agamben, *Homo Sacer*, p. 8.

Chapter 2 Sodomy, Courtly Love, and the Birth of Romance: *Le Roman d'Eneas*

1. Unless otherwise noted, citations of the *Eneas* will refer to line numbers in *Eneas: Roman du XIIe siècle*, ed. J.-J. Salverda de Grave, 2nd ed. (1964–68; rpt. Paris: Champion, 1982–85), in 2 vols.; and/or page numbers in *Eneas: A Twelfth-Century French Romance*, trans. John A. Yunck (New York: Columbia University Press, 1974).

2. Peter Haidu, *The Subject Medieval/Modern: Text and Governance in the Middle Ages* (Stanford: Stanford University Press, 2004), p. 80.

3. As Jerome Singerman argues, the *Eneas* was often collated with other texts to form a historical sequence culminating in Wace's *Brut*. A translation and paraphrase of Geoffrey of Monmouth's *Historia regum Britanniae*, *Brut* tells the story of Brutus's conquest of Great Britain and culminates in the disappearance of Arthur. See *Under Clouds of Poesy: Poetry and Truth in French and English Reworkings of the "Aeneid" 1160–1513* (New York: Garland, 1986), pp. 99–179.

4. These sources include Varro, Servius, Ovid, Tertullian, and especially Dares, whose *De excidio Troiae Historia* is the basis of Benoît de Sainte-Maure's

Roman de Troie. See Meyer Reinhold, "The Unhero Aeneas," *Classica et Mediaevalia* 27 (1968): 195–207.

5. Medieval readers often associated Virgil and Ovid with homosexuality and pederasty. A number of *Vitae Vergilii* circulated in the Middle Ages, including the so-called *Vita Suetonii*, which describes Virgil's love for a literate male slave named Alexander. Edmond Faral notes that Ovid, too, was often associated with the homosexual vice," especially given that the subject of the *Amores* was either a boy (*puer*) or a maiden (*puella*). See *Recherches sur les sources latines des contes et romans courtois du Moyen Age* (Paris: Champion, 1913), p. 132n1.

6. One passage in Virgil does perhaps offer a model: King Iarbas denounces Aeneas, his rival for Dido's love, as a perfumed and coiffed version of Paris, surrounded by "semiviro comitatu" [a band of half men]. See Virgil, *Aeneid*, 4.215–17, ed. and trans. H. Rushton Fairclough, 2 vols. (Cambridge, MA: Loeb Classical Library, Harvard University Press, 1934), vol. 2, p. 410; translation mine. Lavine's mother's accusation is, however, far more substantial and vicious than this somewhat minor insult.

7. See Francine Mora-Lebrun, *L'Enéide médiévale et la naissance du roman* (Paris: Presses Universitaires de France, 1994), pp. 187–208.

8. Simon Gaunt argues, in *Gender and Genre in Medieval French Literature* (Cambridge, UK: Cambridge University Press, 1995), that the homophobia of the *Eneas* is not simply "an attack on homosexuals" but "a means of regulating male homosocial bonds. . . .Every man will regulate carefully his homosocial bonds if he is concerned they may be perceived as homosexual, and thereby transgressional" (p. 81).

9. Lee Patterson, *Negotiating the Past: The Historical Understanding of Medieval Literature* (Madison: University of Wisconsin Press, 1987), pp. 180, 181.

10. Patterson, *Negotiating the Past*, p. 181.

11. Patterson, *Negotiating the Past*, p. 181.

12. Renate Blumenfeld-Kosinski, *Reading Myth: Classical Mythology and Its Interpretations in Medieval French Literature* (Stanford: Stanford University Press, 1997), p. 43.

13. Blumenfeld-Kosinski, *Reading Myth*, p. 34.

14. Jean-Charles Huchet, "*L'Enéas*: Un roman spéculaire," in *Relire le "Roman d'Enéas"* ed. Jean Dufournet (Geneva: Slatkine, 1985), p. 73 [63–81].

15. See Poirion, *Résurgences: Mythe et littérature à l'âge du symbole (XIIe siècle)* (Paris: Presses Universitaires de France, 1986), p. 74; and Huchet, "*L'Enéas*" in *Relire le "Roman d'Enéas,"* pp. 70–71.

16. On gender and subjectivity in the *Eneas* and romance generally, see Gaunt, *Gender and Genre*, pp. 71–121.

17. Huchet, "*L'Enéas*," in *Relire le "Roman d'Enéas,"* p. 73.

18. Huchet, "*L'Enéas*," in *Relire le "Roman d'Enéas,"* p. 76.

19. Huchet, "*L'Enéas*," in *Relire le "Roman d'Enéas,"* p. 75.

20. Huchet, *Le roman médiéval* (Paris: Presses Universitaires de France, 1984), p. 116.

21. Christopher Baswell, *Virgil in Medieval England: Figuring the "Aeneid" from the Twelfth Century to Chaucer* (Cambridge, UK: Cambridge University Press, 1995), pp. 199–200.

22. Baswell, *Virgil in Medieval England*, p. 200.

23. Huchet, *Roman médiéval*, p. 69.

24. Huchet, *Roman médiéval*, p. 70.

25. Baswell, *Virgil in Medieval England*, p. 199.

26. See Huchet, "L'*Enéas*," in *Relire le "Roman d'Enéas*," pp. 69–70. See also Singerman, *Under Clouds of Poesy*, pp. 56–59.

27. Virgil, *Aeneid*, 9.68–69, ed. Fairclough, vol. 2, p. 116.

28. The relevant passages from William of Malmesbury are cited in Yunck, *Eneas*, p. 183n113. The *De Regis* was a crucial historical source for legitimating Anglo-Norman empire and was widely read at the Angevin courts.

29. See *Le roman d'Enéas*, ed. and trans. Aimé Petit (Paris: Lettres Gothiques, Livre de Poche, 1997), p. 628n.

30. See Poirion, "De l'*Enéide* à l'*Eneas*: mythologie et moralisation," *Cahiers de civilisation médiévale* 19.3 (1976): 217–18 [213–29]; and Mora-Lebrun, *L'Enéide médiévale*, pp. 187–208.

31. Stephen G. Nichols, "Amorous Imitation: Bakhtin, Augustine, and *Le roman d'Enéas*," in *Romance: Generic Transformation from Chrétien de Troyes to Cervantes*, ed. Kevin Brownlee and Marina Scordilis Brownlee (Hanover, NH: University Press of New England, 1985), p. 72 [47–73].

32. Many thanks are due to my colleague Maria Manoliu for explaining the significance of this case inflection to me. Manoliu is currently completing a book on gender, voice, and aspect in romance that explains the shifting stylistic and cultural significance of the morpheme "–m."

33. See Faral, *Recherches sur les sources latines*, p. 144.

34. Michel Zink, "Héritage rhétorique et nouveauté littéraire dans le 'roman antique' en France au Moyen Age: Remarques sur l'expression de l'amour dans le *Roman d'Eneas*," *Romania* 105/2–3 (1984): 265–66 [248–69].

35. Gaunt, "From Epic to Romance: Gender and Sexuality in the *Roman d'Enéas*," *Romanic Review* 83/1 (January 1992): 18 [1–27].

36. Gaunt, "From Epic to Romance," 18.

37. Huchet, *Roman médiéval*, p. 136.

38. Baswell, *Virgil in Medieval England*, p. 171.

39. Gaunt, "From Epic to Romance," 25.

40. Erich Auerbach, *Literary Language and Its Public in Late Latin Antiquity and in the Middle Ages*, trans. Ralph Manheim (Princeton: Princeton University Press, 1965), p. 213, emphasis mine.

41. On Lavine's travesty, see Susan Crane, *Gender and Romance in Chaucer's "Canterbury Tales*," (Princeton: Princeton University Press, 1994), pp. 44–45.

42. Raymond J. Cormier, *One Heart One Mind: The Rebirth of Virgil's Hero in Medieval French Romance* (University, MS: Mississippi Romance Monographs, 1973), p. 286.

43. Blumenfeld-Kosinski, *Reading Myth*, p. 34; Patterson, *Negotiating the Past*, p. 181.

Chapter 3 Allegory and Perversion in Alan of Lille's *De Planctu Naturae*

I wish to express my gratitude to Emily Albu for her generous and expert assistance with Alan of Lille's notoriously difficult, abstruse Latin.

1. Unless otherwise noted, citations will refer to section and line numbers in Alan of Lille, *De planctu Naturae*, ed. Nikolaus M. Häring, in *Studi Medievali*, terza serie 19/2 (1978): 797–879; and/or page numbers in Alan of Lille, *The Plaint of Nature*, trans. James J. Sheridan (Toronto: Pontifical Institute of Mediæval Studies, 1980).

2. In the introduction to her translation of Alan of Lille's *Règles de théologie* (Paris: Cerf, 1995), Françoise Hudry reveals what she believes to be new evidence on Alan's early adulthood: a set personal letters found in BN, Lat. 13575. According to Hudry, these letters can be attributed to Alan. If this is the case, they suggest that after studying at the Abbey of Saint-Victor in Paris, Alan joined the household of the Archbishop of Canterbury and was assigned a variety of administrative and social tasks. While there, he was accused of an undisclosed crime and was consigned by an ecclesiastical tribunal to the Benedictine Abbey of Bec. It appears that while at Bec, Alan was accused of sodomy and was forced to take up residence at an even more remote abbey, Wearmouth. From there, he sent a letter to his spiritual advisor, possibly Richard of Saint-Victor, explaining that he was at work on a treatise, which Hudry believes to be the *De planctu Naturae*. According to the evidence in these letters, Hudry ascribes to the *De planctu* a tentative date (1168–70) and place of composition (Wearmouth). She also suggests that the moral zeal of the *De planctu* with regard to homosexuality may be a reaction to Alan's own castigation. See also Hudry, "Mais qui était donc Alain de Lille?" in *Alain de Lille, le Docteur Universel: Philosophie, théologie, et littérature au XIIe siècle*, ed. Jean-Luc Solère, Anca Vasiliu, and Alain Galonnier (Turnhout, Belgium: Brepols, 2005), pp. 107–24; and Hudry, ed., *Alain de Lille (?): Lettres familières (1167–1170)* (Paris: Vrin, 2003). Lena Wahlgren-Smith, in her review of the latter volume in *Speculum* 81/2 (2006): 536–37, expresses reservations about Hudry's ascription of the letters to Alan of Lille.

3. See Edmond Faral, *Recherches sur les sources latines des contes et romans courtois* (Paris: Champion, 1913); Reto R. Bezzola, *Les origines et la formation de la littérature courtoise en occident* (Paris: Champion, 1944–63), 3 vols. See also Winthrop Wetherbee, *Platonism and Poetry in the Twelfth Century: The Literary Influence of the School of Chartres* (Princeton: Princeton University Press, 1972), pp. 220–41.

4. "Postquam Genius huius anathematis exterminio finem orationi concessit"
   [After Genius concluded his speech with the devastation of this anathema]
   (18.159).

5. Larry Scanlon, "Unspeakable Pleasures: Alain de Lille, Sexual Regulation
   and the Priesthood of Genius," *Romanic Review* 86/2 (1995): 241 [213–42].
   Scanlon refers his readers to Elisabeth Vodola's *Excommunication in the
   Middle Ages* (Berkeley: University of California Press, 1986).

6. PL 210:622.

7. See especially Winthrop Wetherbee, "The Function of Poetry in the *De
   planctu Naturae* of Alain de Lille," *Traditio* 25 (1969): 87–125.

8. Scanlon, "Unspeakable Pleasures," 219.

9. Scanlon, "Unspeakable Pleasures," 222, 219.

10. Scanlon, "Unspeakable Pleasures," 220. For a reading along similar lines,
    see Elizabeth Pittenger, "Explicit Ink," in *Premodern Sexualities*, ed. Louise
    Fradenburg and Carla Freccero (New York: Routledge, 1997), pp. 223–42.

11. Alan of Lille, *The Art of Preaching*, trans. Gillian R. Evans (Kalamazoo:
    Cistercian Publications, 1981), p. 3.

12. Boethius, *The Consolation of Philosophy*, 4.3.47–48, 67–69, trans. S.J. Tester,
    in *The Theological Tractates and the Consolation of Philosophy*, 2nd ed., ed. and
    trans. H.F. Stewart, E.K. Rand, and S.J. Tester (Cambridge, MA: The Loeb
    Classical Library, Harvard University Press, 1973), pp. 334–35. Alan was
    also familiar with privative evil from the writings of the fifth-century
    philosopher and theologian known as Pseudo-Dionysius the Areopagite.
    See Andreas Niederberger, "Les écrits dionysiens et le néoplatonisme
    d'Alain de Lille," in *Alain de Lille, le Docteur Universel*, pp. 3–18.

13. On the manuscript tradition of the *De planctu*, see Jeanne Krochalis's
    Harvard dissertation, *Alain de Lille, De planctu Nature: Studies towards an
    Edition* (1973); and Häring, "Manuscripts of the *De planctu Naturae* of
    Master Alan of Lille," *Cîteaux* 29/1–2 (1978): 93–115.

14. Robert Holcot, *Super libros sapientiae*, 10.128.A (1494; repr. Frankfurt:
    Minerva G.M.B.H., 1974), n.p.

15. Cited in Krochalis, *Alain de Lille*, p. 557.

16. Maurice Gandillac, "La nature chez Alain de Lille," in *Alain de Lille, Gautier
    de Châtillon, Jakemart Giélée et leur temps*, ed. H. Roussel and F. Suard (Lille:
    Presses Universitaires de Lille, 1980), p. 62 [61–75].

17. Jan Ziolkowski, *Alan of Lille's Grammar of Sex: The Meaning of Grammar to a
    Twelfth-Century Intellectual* (Cambridge, MA: The Medieval Academy of
    America, 1985), p. 95. See also Jeffrey T. Schnapp, "Dante's Sexual
    Solecisms: Gender and Genre in the *Commedia*," in *The New Medievalism*,
    ed. Marina S. Brownlee, Kevin Brownlee, and Stephen G. Nichols
    (Baltimore: Johns Hopkins University Press, 1991), pp. 201–25.

18. Cited in Ziolkowski, *Alan of Lille's Grammar of Sex*, p. 116.

19. Alan of Lille, *Anticlaudianus, or The Good and Perfect Man*, trans. James J. Sheridan
    (Toronto: Pontifical Institute of Mediæval Studies, 1973), p. 85.

20. PL 210:578.
21. G.R. Evans, *Alan of Lille: The Frontiers of Theology in the Later Twelfth Century* (Cambridge, UK: Cambridge University Press, 1983), p. 51. See also Alexandre Leupin, *Fiction and Incarnation: Rhetoric, Theology, and Literature in the Middle Ages*, trans. David Laatsch (Minneapolis: University of Minnesota Press, 2003), pp. 130–45.
22. PL 210:333.
23. PL 210:621, trans. in Ziolkowski, *Alan of Lille's Grammar of Sex*, p. 106.
24. Alan of Lille, *Anticlaudianus*, p. 90.
25. Marie-Dominique Chenu, *Nature, Man, and Society in the Twelfth Century: Essays on New Theological Perspectives in the Latin West*, ed. and trans. Jerome Taylor and Lester K. Little (Chicago: University of Chicago Press, 1968), p. 280.
26. Chenu, *Nature, Man, and Society*, p. 281.
27. PL 210:621.
28. Chenu, *Nature, Nature, and Society*, p. 290.
29. Alan of Lille, *Anticlaudianus*, p. 91.
30. Alan of Lille, *Anticlaudianus*, p. 91.
31. Alan of Lille, *Anticlaudianus*, pp. 91, 94, 160.
32. Alan of Lille, *Anticlaudianus*, p. 92.
33. Alan of Lille, *Anticlaudianus*, p. 96.
34. Alan of Lille, *Anticlaudianus*, pp. 91–92.
35. Alan of Lille, *Anticlaudianus*, pp. 96–97.
36. Alan of Lille, *Art of Preaching*, p. 17.
37. Alan of Lille, *Art of Preaching*, p. 18.
38. Michel Zink, "La rhétorique honteuse et la convention du sermon 'ad status' à travers la *Summa de arte praedicatoria* d'Alain de Lille," in *Alain de Lille, Gautier de Châtillon*, p. 180 [171–85].
39. Zink, "Rhétorique honteuse," in *Alain de Lille, Gautier de Châtillon*, p. 180.
40. Zink, "Rhétorique honteuse," in *Alain de Lille, Gautier de Châtillon*, p. 180.
41. PL 210:983, trans. in Ziolkowski, *Alan of Lille's Grammar of Sex*, p. 103.
42. PL 210:1000, trans. in Ziolkowski, *Alan of Lille's Grammar of Sex*, p. 102.
43. Alan of Lille, *Art of Preaching*, p. 117.
44. Kathryn L. Lynch, *The High Medieval Dream Vision: Poetry, Philosophy, and Literary Form* (Stanford: Stanford University Press, 1988), pp. 79–80.
45. Leupin, *Fiction and Incarnation*, pp. 139, 240n15.
46. I have somewhat altered Häring and Sheridan here, following suggestions made by Danuta R. Shanzer in "Parturition through the Nostrils? Thirty-three Textual Problems in Alan of Lille's *De planctu Nature*," *Mittellateinisches Jahrbuch* 26 (1991): 140–49.
47. Pittenger, "Explicit Ink," in *Premodern Sexualities*, p. 224.
48. Pittenger, "Explicit Ink," in *Premodern Sexualities*, p. 233.
49. Again, I have altered Häring's text and Sheridan's translation following suggestions made by Shanzer in "Parturition through the Nostrils."

50. Jordan suggests that there may be a pun here on *predicare*, "to predicate," and *pedicare*, "to bugger." Alan would likely have known the latter term from Martial or Catullus. See *Invention of Sodomy*, p. 83n76.

51. See Alan of Lille, *Plaint of Nature*, trans. Sheridan, pp. 69n7, 161n22.

52. Elizabeth B. Keiser, *Courtly Desire and Medieval Homophobia: The Legitimation of Sexual Pleasure in "Cleanness" and Its Contexts* (New Haven: Yale University Press, 1997), p. 75.

53. Sheridan offers the following example: " 'All men are animals' by conversion becomes 'some animals are men,' " both of which are truthful statements. See Alan of Lille, *Plaint of Nature*, p. 161n22.

54. See Scanlon, "Unspeakable Pleasures," 221, and William Burgwinkle, *Sodomy, Masculinity, and Law in Medieval Literature: France and England, 1050–1230* (Cambridge, UK: Cambridge University Press, 2004), pp. 180–81.

55. Scanlon, "Unspeakable Pleasures," 221.

56. Scanlon, "Unspeakable Pleasures," 221.

57. See Alan of Lille, *Plaint of Nature*, trans. Sheridan, p. 69n8.

58. Keiser, *Courtly Desire*, p. 76.

59. Keiser, *Courtly Desire*, p. 76.

60. Jordan, *Invention of Sodomy*, p. 73.

61. Jordan, *Invention of Sodomy*, p. 73.

62. See Wetherbee, "Function of Poetry," passim; and *Platonism and Poetry*, pp. 187–219.

63. Augustine, *On Christian Doctrine*, 2.1, 1.2, trans. D.W. Robertson Jr. (Upper Saddle River, NJ: Prentice Hall, 1958), pp. 34, 8.

64. Augustine, *Christian Doctrine*, 1.3, p. 9.

65. Augustine, *Christian Doctrine*, 1.3, p. 9.

66. Augustine, *Christian Doctrine*, 1.4, p. 10.

67. Jon Whitman, "The Problem of Assertion and the *Complaint of Nature*," *Hebrew University Studies in Literature and the Arts* 15 (1987): 5 [5–26].

68. Whitman, "The Problem of Assertion," 6.

69. Whitman, "The Problem of Assertion," 13.

70. Hugh White, *Nature, Sex, and Goodness in a Medieval Literary Tradition* (Oxford: Oxford University Press, 2000), p. 9.

71. White, *Nature, Sex, and Goodness*, p. 13.

72. White, *Nature, Sex, and Goodness*, p. 44.

73. White, *Nature, Sex, and Goodness*, p. 95.

74. White, *Nature, Sex, and Goodness*, p. 95.

75. White, *Nature, Sex, and Goodness*, p. 95. See also Joan Cadden's illuminating new essay, "Trouble in Earthly Paradise: The Regime of Nature in Late Medieval Christian Culture," in *The Moral Authority of Nature*, ed. Lorraine Daston and Fernando Vidal (Chicago: University of Chicago Press, 2004), pp. 207–31.

76. See Mechthild Modersohn, *Natura als Göttin im Mittelalter: Ikonographische Studien zu Darstellungen der personifizierten Natur* (Berlin: Akademie Verlag, 1997).

77. Jordan, *Invention of Sodomy*, p. 71.

78. On the role of the *Timaeus* in Chartrian philosophy, see Wetherbee, *Platonism and Poetry*, esp. 28–36. On flesh and spirit, see Peter Brown, *The Body and Society: Men, Women, and Sexual Renunciation in Early Christianity* (New York: Columbia University Press, 1988).

79. Again, I have altered Häring's text and Sheridan's translation following suggestions made by Shanzer in "Parturition through the Nostrils," 143.

80. Alan of Lille, *Plaint of Nature*, trans. Sheridan, p. 121n13.

81. Scanlon, "Unspeakable Pleasures," 226.

82. See Isidore of Seville, *Etymologiarum sive originum*, 10.78–79, ed. W.M. Lindsay, 2 vols. (Oxford: Oxford Classical Texts, Oxford University Press, 1911), vol. 1, p. 399. Though Isidore's etymologies are often fanciful, this one is quite accurate.

83. Ovid, *Metamorphoses*, 10.79–85, trans. Mary M. Innes (London: Penguin, 1955), p. 227.

84. Susan Schibanoff, "Sodomy's Mark: Alan of Lille, Jean de Meun, and the Medieval Theory of Authorship," in *Queering the Middle Ages*, ed. Glenn Burger and Steven F. Kruger (Minneapolis: University of Minnesota Press, 2001), pp. 28–56. Schibanoff is specifically countering arguments made by Kevin Brownlee, in "Orpheus' Song Re-Sung: Jean de Meun's Reworking of *Metamorphoses X*," *Romance Philology* 36/2 (1982): 201–9; and by Michael A. Calabrese, in " 'Make a Mark That Shows': Orphean Song, Orphean Sexuality, and the Exile of Chaucer's Pardoner," *Viator* 24 (1993): 269–86.

85. Wetherbee, "Function of Poetry," 90.

86. Leupin, *Barbarolexis*, p. 74.

87. Leupin, *Barbarolexis*, pp. 65–66.

88. Burgwinkle, *Sodomy, Masculinity, and Law*, p. 198.

89. Pittenger, "Explicit Ink," in *Premodern Sexualities*, p. 227; Chenu, *Nature, Man, and Society*, p. 138.

90. This reading may seem a bit of a stretch. However, the word *suppositorium* was used in the Middle Ages to refer to medications inserted vaginally and anally, and the verb *supponere* was used to refer to the insertion of these preparations. By 1300, *supponi* was used in connection with homosexual intercourse, though presumably the usage was not new. My thanks to Joan Cadden for sharing her knowledge of these terms with me.

91. Wetherbee, "Function of Poetry," 107.

92. Wetherbee, "Function of Poetry," 107.

93. Wetherbee, "Function of Poetry," 107.

94. Wetherbee, "Function of Poetry," 103.

95. Scanlon, "Unspeakable Pleasures," 226.

96. Scanlon, "Unspeakable Pleasures," 226.

97. Macrobius, *Commentary on the Dream of Scipio*, 2.17, 2.11, trans. William Harris Stahl (1952; New York: Columbia University Press, 1990), pp. 86, 85.

98. Wetherbee, "Function of Poetry," 105.

99. Whitman, "Problem of Assertion," 19. Whitman is citing Isidore, *Etymologiarum*, 2.13.1.

100. Whitman, "Problem of Assertion," 19.
101. Lynch, *High Medieval Dream Vision*, p. 111.
102. Leupin, *Barbarolexis*, p. 77.
103. The text of the *De planctu* in PL 210 offers a different ending: a lapsing into sleep rather than an awakening. See Lynch, *High Medieval Dream Vision*, p. 218n19; and Jordan, *Invention of Sodomy*, pp. 76–77.
104. Leupin, *Barbarolexis*, p. 78.
105. Jordan, *Invention of Sodomy*, p. 77.
106. Jordan, *Invention of Sodomy*, p. 76n49.
107. Jordan, *Invention of Sodomy*, p. 76, citing *De planctu*, 4.143; *Plaint*, p. 140.
108. Burgwinkle, *Sodomy, Masculinity, and Law*, p. 174.
109. Guy Raynaud de Lage, *Alain de Lille: Poète du XIIe siècle* (Paris: Vrin, 1951), p. 92.
110. Lynch, *High Medieval Dream Vision*, pp. 81, 78.
111. Lynch, *High Medieval Dream Vision*, p. 111.
112. Lynch, *High Medieval Dream Vision*, p. 105.
113. Lynch, *High Medieval Dream Vision*, p. 106.
114. Schibanoff, "Sodomy's Mark," in *Queering the Middle Ages*, p. 37.
115. Schibanoff, "Sodomy's Mark," in *Queering the Middle Ages*, p. 29.
116. See Alan of Lille, *Plaint of Nature*, p. 206, especially Sheridan's notes 25 and 26.
117. Burgwinkle, *Sodomy, Masculinity, and Law*, p. 176.
118. Lynch, *High Medieval Dream Vision*, p. 106.
119. Lynch, *High Medieval Dream Vision*, p. 106.
120. Augustine, *The Excellence of Marriage*, 3, 6, 21, trans. Ray Kearney, in *The Works of Saint Augustine: A Translation for the 21st Century*, ed. John E. Rotelle (Hyde Park, NY: New City Press, 1994), part 1, vol. 9, pp. 34, 37, 49.
121. Burgwinkle, *Sodomy, Masculinity, and Law*, p. 178.
122. Burgwinkle, *Sodomy, Masculinity, and Law*, p. 178.
123. Burgwinkle, *Sodomy, Masculinity, and Law*, p. 178.
124. Scanlon, "Unspeakable Pleasures," 239.
125. Burgwinkle, *Sodomy, Masculinity, and Law*, pp. 191–92.
126. Scanlon, "Unspeakable Pleasures," 242.
127. Alan, *Rhythmus de Incarnatione Christi*, cited and translated in Leupin, *Fiction and Incarnation*, p. 131. I have modified the translation slightly.
128. Leupin, *Fiction and Incarnation*, p. 135.
129. Leupin, *Fiction and Incarnation*, p. 135.
130. Leupin, *Fiction and Incarnation*, p. 137.
131. Leupin, *Fiction and Incarnation*, p. 133.
132. Jonathan Dollimore, *Sexual Dissidence: From Augustine to Wilde, Freud to Foucault* (Oxford: Oxford University Press, 1991), p. 145.
133. Dollimore, *Sexual Dissidence*, p. 146.
134. Dollimore, *Sexual Dissidence*, p. 146.
135. Dollimore, *Sexual Dissidence*, pp. 146, 147.
136. Zink, "Rhétorique honteuse," in *Alain de Lille, Gautier de Châtillon*, pp. 176–77.
137. Scanlon, "Unspeakable Pleasures," 234.

138. Jacques Chiffoleau, "*Contra Naturam:* Pour une approche casuistique et procédurale de la nature médiévale," *Micrologus: Natura, scienze e società medievali* 4 (1996): 265–312. See also Chiffoleau's closely related essay, "Dire l'indicible: Remarques sur la catégorie du *nefandum* du XIIe au XVe siècle," *Annales ESC* 45 (1990): 289–324.

139. Chiffoleau, "*Contra Naturam,*" 301–2.

140. Chiffoleau, "*Contra Naturam,*" 309.

141. Chiffoleau, "*Contra Naturam,*" 294.

142. Chiffoleau, "*Contra Naturam,*" 302.

143. Jordan, *Invention of Sodomy,* p. 81.

144. Jordan, *Invention of Sodomy,* pp. 81, 87.

145. Jordan, *Invention of Sodomy,* p. 87.

146. Jordan, *Invention of Sodomy,* p. 87.

147. Jordan, *Invention of Sodomy,* p. 88.

148. Jordan, *Invention of Sodomy,* p. 87.

Chapter 4 Authorship and Sexual/Allegorical Violence in Jean de Meun's *Roman de la Rose*

1. Unless otherwise noted, parenthetical citations will refer to Guillaume de Lorris and Jean de Meun, *Le roman de la rose,* in 3 vols., ed. Félix Lecoy (Paris: Champion, 1965–70); and/or *The Romance of the Rose,* 3rd ed., trans. Charles Dahlberg (Princeton: Princeton University Press, 1995).

2. Ernest Langlois, *Origines et sources du "Roman de la rose"* (Paris: Ernest Thorin, 1891), pp. 119–27.

3. Daniel Poirion, "Les mots et les choses selon Jean de Meun," *L'information littéraire* 26 (1974): 9 [7–11].

4. Jean-Charles Payen, *La rose et l'utopie: Révolution sexuelle et communisme nostalgique chez Jean de Meung* (Paris: Hatier, 1976), pp. 9, 11.

5. Alastair Minnis, *Magister Amoris: The "Roman de la rose" and Vernacular Hermeneutics* (Oxford: Oxford University Press, 2001), p. 169.

6. Minnis, *Magister Amoris,* pp. 177, 192.

7. Minnis, *Magister Amoris,* p. 193.

8. Minnis argues that the "mingling of seeds" in this scene is evidence that the rose has been impregnated: "Conception was believed to take place when the male sperm or seed came together with the female seed (*Magister Amoris,* p. 177).

9. Gordon Teskey, *Allegory and Violence* (Ithaca: Cornell University Press, 1996), p. 18.

10. Teskey, *Allegory and Violence,* p. 21.

11. Minnis, *Magister Amoris,* pp. 201, 202.

12. Minnis, *Magister Amoris,* p. 197.

13. Georges Duby, *Love and Marriage in the Middle Ages,* trans. Jane Dunnett (Chicago: University of Chicago Press, 1994), p. vii.

14. For critiques of Duby, see the essays collected in Theodore Evergates, ed., *Aristocratic Women in Medieval France* (Philadelphia: University of Pennsylvania Press, 1999).

15. Judith M. Bennett, "Confronting Continuity," *Journal of Women's History* 9/3 (1997): 73–95.

16. Jo Ann McNamara, "Women and Power through the Family Revisited," in *Gendering the Master Narrative: Women and Power in the Middle Ages*, ed. Mary C. Erler and Maryanne Kowaleski (Ithaca: Cornell University Press, 2003), p. 22 [17–30].

17. Minnis, *Magister Amoris*, p. 178. In locating Jean within a misogynistic clerical culture, Minnis does not dismiss the fact that the *Rose* was read by, and at certain crucial moments addresses itself to, women. For medieval readers, the *Rose* was (in the words of Sylvia Huot) a "malleable text," one that could be read and copied selectively in order to emphasize or deemphasize particular content, including misogynistic material. Some readers clearly subscribed to the poem's misogyny, while others deliberately downplayed it or expurgated the text. See *The "Romance of the Rose" and Its Medieval Readers: Interpretation, Reception, Manuscript Transmission* (Cambridge, UK: Cambridge University Press, 1993), esp. pp. 34–40.

18. See Sylvie Lefèvre's entry on "Jean de Meun" in the *Dictionnaire des lettres françaises: Le Moyen Age*, ed. Robert Bossuat, Louis Pichard, and Guy Raynaud de Lage, rev. Geneviève Hasenohr and Michel Zink (Paris: Livre de Poche, 1992), pp. 817–19.

19. Minnis, *Medieval Theory of Authorship: Scholastic Literary Attitudes in the Later Middle Ages* (London: Scholar Press, 1984), pp. 197–98.

20. Minnis, *Medieval Theory of Authorship*, p. 198.

21. Lefèvre, "Jean de Meun," in *Dictionnaire des lettres françaises*, p. 818.

22. Scholars have argued that Guillaume de Lorris was perhaps either the Seigneur de Loury-aux-Bois or the son of Philippe Auguste's Sergeant. However, these claims have never been adequately substantiated. See Lefèvre's entry on Guillaume de Lorris in *Dictionnaire des lettres françaises*, pp. 629–30.

23. C.S. Lewis, *The Allegory of Love: A Study in Medieval Tradition* (1936; Oxford: Oxford University Press 1992), p. 116.

24. David F. Hult, *Self-Fulfilling Prophecies: Readership and Authority in the First "Roman de la rose"* (Cambridge, UK: Cambridge University Press, 1986), p. 110n9. See also Evelyn Birge Vitz, *Medieval Narrative and Modern Narratology: Subjects and Objects of Desire* (New York: New York University Press, 1989), pp. 38–63.

25. Hult, "Closed Quotations: The Speaking Voice in the *Roman de la rose*," *Yale French Studies* 67 (1984): 249–50 [248–69].

26. Hult, "Closed Quotations," 267.

27. Hult, "Closed Quotations," 267.

28. Hult, "Closed Quotations," 267.

29. Hult, "Closed Quotations," 267.

30. Hult, "Closed Quotations," 268.
31. Hult, "Closed Quotations," 268.
32. Roger Dragonetti argues in "Pygmalion ou les pièges de la fiction dans le *Roman de la rose*," in *Orbis Medievalis: Mélanges de langue et de littérature médiévale offerts à Reto Raduolf Bezzola à l'occasion de son quatre-vingtième anniversaire*, ed. Georges Güntert, Marc-René Jung, and Kurt Ringger (Bern: Editions Francke, 1978), that Guillaume de Lorris and Jean de Meun "are merely two fictions inserted into the project of a single, unique author, the writer of the *Roman* as a whole" (p. 90). He believes that this one author devised the fiction of "the work's bipartition" (p. 91) so that he might stage the "contestation at the heart of the work" of "any theory," "any view of things," or "any perspective that would tend to present its vision as truthful" (p. 94). Manuscript evidence has failed to corroborate Dragonetti's claim about the authorship of the poem: see Hult, *Self-Fulfilling Prophecies*, pp. 19–25.
33. Hult, *Self-Fulfilling Prophecies*, p. 100.
34. On the contingencies of discourse and subjectivity in the *Roman de la rose*, see Daniel Heller-Roazen, *Fortune's Faces: The "Roman de la rose" and the Poetics of Contingency* (Baltimore: Johns Hopkins University Press, 2003), esp. pp. 29–62.
35. R.A. Shoaf, "Medieval Studies after Derrida after Heidegger," in *Sign, Sentence, Discourse: Language in Medieval Thought and Literature*, ed. Julian N. Wasserman and Lois Roney (Syracuse: Syracuse University Press, 1988), p. 22 [9–30]. Shoaf is citing Jacques Derrida, *Of Grammatology*, trans. Gayatri Chakravorty Spivak (Baltimore: Johns Hopkins University Press, 1977), p. 103.
36. Alexandre Leupin, "Le temps dans le *Roman de la rose*," in *Il tempo, i tempi: Omaggio a Lorenzo Renzi*, ed. Rosanna Brusegan and Michele A. Cortelazzo (Padua: Esedra, 1999), p. 144 [141–52].
37. Jacques Derrida, "Signature Event Context," in *A Derrida Reader: Between the Blinds*, ed. Peggy Kamuf (New York: Columbia University Press, 1991), p. 94 [80–111].
38. Derrida, "Signature Event Context," in *Derrida Reader*, pp. 92, 106.
39. Derrida, "Signature Event Context," in *Derrida Reader*, p. 91.
40. Augustine, *The Confessions*, 11.7.9, trans. Boulding (1997; repr. New York: Vintage, 1998), p. 252.
41. Augustine, *Confessions*, 11.6.8, p. 251.
42. Augustine, *Confessions*, 10.16.25, pp. 212–13.
43. Augustine, *Confessions*, 11.25.32, p. 266.
44. Augustine, *Confessions*, 10.5.7, p. 201.
45. Augustine, *Confessions*, 10.5.7, p. 201.
46. Eugene Vance, *Mervelous Signals: Poetics and Sign Theory in the Middle Ages* (Lincoln: University of Nebraska Press, 1986), pp. 1–2.
47. Vance, *Mervelous Signals*, p. 4.
48. Augustine, *De libero arbitrio*, 3.25.77, cited in Vance, *Mervelous Signals*, p. 4.
49. This point is made eloquently by Simon Gaunt in "Bel Acueil and the Improper Allegory of the *Romance of the Rose*," *New Medieval Literatures* 2 (1997): 86 [65–93].

50. Derrida, "Signature Event Context," in *Derrida Reader*, p. 108.

51. See Peter Brown, *The Body and Society: Men, Women, and Sexual Renunciation in Early Christianity* (New York: Columbia University Press, 1988), p. 417.

52. Poirion, "Les mots et les choses selon Jean de Meun," 8.

53. Poirion, *Le roman de la rose* (Paris: Hatier, 1973), p. 207.

54. Poirion, *Roman de la rose*, p. 207.

55. Payen, *La rose et l'utopie*, p. 7.

56. Payen, *La rose et l'utopie*, p. 9.

57. R. Howard Bloch, *Etymologies and Genealogies: A Literary Anthropology of the French Middle Ages* (Chicago: University of Chicago Press, 1983), p. 140.

58. Bloch, *Etymologies and Genealogies*, p. 140.

59. Bloch, *Etymologies and Genealogies*, pp. 140–41.

60. Bloch, *Etymologies and Genealogies*, p. 141.

61. Gaunt, "Bel Acueil," 93.

62. Gaunt, "Bel Acueil," 90. Unlike Minnis, I find Gaunt's argument on homoeroticism in Jean de Meun's *Rose* utterly convincing. Citing Eve Kosofsky Sedgwick, Minnis claims that there may be a "homosocial bond" between Amant and Ami or between Amant and Bel Acueil, but not a specifically homoerotic one: Amant's sexuality is "utterly conventional," and "the poem's master discourse of heteronormativity strives to keep any suggestion of sexual deviance in check" (*Magister Amoris*, pp. 207, 205). Unfortunately, Minnis seriously misconstrues Sedgwick's account of the relationship between homosociality and homoeroticism. In *Between Men: English Literature and Male Homosocial Desire* (New York: Columbia University Press, 1985), Sedgwick seeks above all to "draw the 'homosocial' back into the orbit of 'desire,' of the potentially erotic" and to "hypothesize the potential unbrokenness of a continuum between homosocial and homosexual" (p. 1), even if that continuum is not visible, or is actively disavowed. I would argue, along with Gaunt, that homosociality in the *Rose* is potentially, perhaps even constitutively, erotic and homoerotic. I disagree, however, with Gaunt's claim that the poem's homoeroticism works to challenge the "repressive binary structures" of medieval patriarchy. On the contrary, I believe that both homoerotic and homosocial desire in the *Rose* work to stabilize a clerical ideology predicated on male solidarity and the exclusion and subordination of women.

63. Gaunt, "Bel Acueil," 92.

64. Judith Butler, *Bodies That Matter: On the Discursive Limits of "Sex"* (New York: Routledge, 1993), p. 240.

65. Bloch, *Medieval Misogyny and the Invention of Western Romantic Love* (Chicago: University of Chicago Press, 1991), p. 3.

66. Bloch, *Medieval Misogyny*, p. 3.

67. Leslie Wahl Rabine, "The Unhappy Hymen between Feminism and Deconstruction," in *The Other Perspective in Gender and Culture: Rewriting Women and the Symbolic*, ed. Juliet Flower MacCannell (New York: Columbia University Press, 1990), p. 36 [20–38]. Rabine's focus is on Derrida, "The Double Session," in *Dissemination*, trans. Barbara Johnson (Chicago: University

of Chicago Press, 1983), pp. 187–316. Rabine is part of a larger tradition of feminists who have critiqued the phallocentrism of deconstruction, including Alice Jardine, Gayatri Spivak, Teresa de Lauretis, and Nancy K. Miller.

68. Leupin, "Le temps dans le *Roman de la rose*," in *Il tempo, i tempi*, p. 152.

69. PL 210:625.

70. PL 210:627.

71. Paul Zumthor, *Toward a Medieval Poetics*, trans. Philip Bennett (Minneapolis: University of Minnesota Press, 1992), p. 40.

72. Zumthor, *Toward a Medieval Poetics*, p. 44.

73. Zumthor, *Toward a Medieval Poetics*, p. 40.

74. Zumthor, *Toward a Medieval Poetics*, p. 40.

75. Zumthor, *Toward a Medieval Poetics*, p. 41.

76. Zumthor, *Toward a Medieval Poetics*, pp. 44–45.

77. Zumthor, *Toward a Medieval Poetics*, p. 67.

78. Minnis, *Magister Amoris*, p. 193.

79. Zumthor, *Toward a Medieval Poetics*, p. 42, citing Gérard Genette, *Figures II* (Paris: Seuil, 1969), p. 78.

80. Kaja Silverman, *The Subject of Semiotics* (Oxford: Oxford University Press, 1983), p. 219. Silverman is summarizing Louis Althusser's celebrated essay "Ideology and Ideological State Apparatuses," in *Lenin and Philosophy*, trans. Ben Brewster (London: Monthly Review Press, 1971), pp. 127–86.

81. In *Male Subjectivity at the Margins* (New York: Routledge, 1992), Silverman calls into question the idea that "primary identification" could ever stand outside "social determination" (p. 20). Citing Jane Gallop's work on Jacques Lacan's mirror stage, she argues that "secondary identification. . .in a sense precedes primary identification," and that primary identification is a retrospective invention (pp. 20–21).

82. Maureen Quilligan, *The Language of Allegory: Defining the Genre* (Ithaca: Cornell University Press, 1979), p. 243. Quilligan is wrong about the origins of the English word *cunt*, which does not derive from Old French but is related instead to *kunta* (from Norwegian and Swedish dialects) and *kunte* (from Middle Low German, Middle Dutch, and Danish).

83. The translation of the last sentence is my own, though it is confirmed by Armand Strubel, ed. and trans., *Le roman de la rose* (Paris: Lettres Gothiques, 1992): "C'est de nous permettre et de vous permettre de vous connaître vous-mêmes" (p. 887). Douglas Kelly discusses this sentence in *Internal Difference and Meanings in the "Roman de la rose"* (Madison: University of Wisconsin Press, 1995), p. 25.

84. Rabine, "Unhappy Hymen," in *Other Perspective*, p. 20.

85. Rabine, "Unhappy Hymen," in *Other Perspective*, p. 36.

86. Sarah Kay, "Women's Body of Knowledge: Epistemology and Misogyny in the *Romance of the Rose*," in *Framing Medieval Bodies*, ed. Kay and Miri Rubin (Manchester: Manchester University Press, 1994), pp. 211–35.

87. The literature on rape in the Middle Ages is dauntingly vast. The most recent reflection on the subject is an excellent collection of essays edited by

Elizabeth Robertson and Christine M. Rose, *Representing Rape in Medieval and Early Modern Literature* (New York: Palgrave Macmillan, 2001).

88. All references to the *Querelle* texts will refer to Eric Hicks, ed., *Le débat sur le "Roman de la rose"* (Paris: Slatkine, 1977); and Joseph L. Baird and John R. Kane, trans., *La querelle de la Rose: Letters and Documents* (Chapel Hill: North Carolina Studies in Romance Languages and Literatures, 1978).

89. Helen Solterer, *The Master and Minerva: Disputing Women in French Medieval Culture* (Berkeley: University of California Press, 1995), pp. 151–75.

90. Solterer, *Master and Minerva*, p. 153.

91. On the broader implications of this "verbal violence," see Solterer, "Flaming Words: Verbal Violence and Gender in Premodern Paris," *Romanic Review* 86/2 (1995): 355–79.

92. See especially D.W. Robertson, *A Preface to Chaucer: Studies in Medieval Perspectives* (Princeton: Princeton University Press, 1962), and John Fleming, *The "Roman de la Rose": A Study in Allegory and Iconography* (Princeton: Princeton University Press, 1969).

93. Hult, "Words and Deeds: Jean de Meun's *Romance of the Rose* and the Hermeneutics of Censorship," *New Literary History* 28/2 (1997): 354–55 [345–66].

94. Hult, "Words and Deeds," 354–55.

95. Solterer, *Master and Minerva*, p. 164. Christine is certainly not the only participant in the *Querelle* to get carried away with a polemical argument: see Minnis, *Magister Amoris*, pp. 209–56.

96. Solterer, *Master and Minerva*, p. 174.

97. The most crucial reference here is Quilligan, *The Allegory of Female Authority: Christine de Pizan's "Cité des dames"* (Ithaca: Cornell University Press, 1991). Quilligan gives careful consideration to Christine's own highly complex signature, her self-construction as both *compilator* and female *auctor*, and her responses to Jean de Meun's misogyny. Quilligan argues that Christine develops a kind of "hybrid" female authority in the *Cité* by appropriating the work of male *auctores* and revising that work according to her own experience as a biological female.

98. Christine de Pizan, *Le livre de la cité des dames*, ed. Maureen Curnow, PhD dissertation (Vanderbilt University, 1975), vol. 2, pp. 617–18; *The Book of the City of Ladies*, trans. Earl Jeffrey Richards (New York: Persea, 1982), p. 4.

99. See Minnis, *Magister Amoris*, pp. 219–34; and Kevin Brownlee, "Discourses of the Self: Christine de Pizan and the *Romance of the Rose*," in *Rethinking the "Romance of the Rose": Text, Image, Reception*, ed. Brownlee and Huot (Philadelphia: University of Pennsylvania Press, 1992), pp. 234–61.

100. Christine de Pizan, *Cité des dames*, vol. 2, p. 885; *City of Ladies*, pp. 160–61.

Conclusion

1. Friedrich Nietzsche, *On the Genealogy of Morals and Ecce Homo*, trans. Walter Kaufmann and R.J. Hollingdale (New York: Vintage, 1989), pp. 20, 31.

2. Fredric Jameson, *The Political Unconscious: Narrative as a Socially Symbolic Act* (Ithaca: Cornell University Press, 1981), p. 60.

3. Judith Butler, "Ethical Ambivalence," in *The Turn to Ethics*, ed. Marjorie Garber, Beatrice Hanssen, and Rebecca L. Walkowitz (New York: Routledge, 2000), p. 15 [15–28].

4. Geoffrey Galt Harpham, *Shadows of Ethics: Criticism and the Just Society* (Durham: Duke University Press, 1999), pp. 19–20.

5. Harpham, *Shadows of Ethics*, p. 29.

6. Chantal Mouffe, "Which Ethics for Democracy?" in *Turn to Ethics*, pp. 93, 92 [85–94].

7. Mouffe, "Which Ethics for Democracy," in *Turn to Ethics*, p. 94.

8. Butler, *Bodies That Matter: On the Discursive Limits of "Sex"* (New York: Routledge, 1993), p. 192, citing Ernesto Laclau and Mouffe, *Hegemony and Socialist Strategy* (New York: Verso, 1985).

9. Butler, *Bodies That Matter*, p. 193.

10. Butler, *Bodies That Matter*, p. 193. Butler is here referring to Mouffe, "Feminism, Citizenship, and Radical Democratic Politics," in *Feminists Theorize the Political*, ed. Butler and Joan W. Scott (New York: Routledge, 1992), pp. 369–84.

11. Butler, *Bodies That Matter*, p. 193.

12. John D. Caputo, "The End of Ethics," in *The Blackwell Guide to Ethical Theory*, ed. Hugh LaFollette (Oxford: Blackwell, 2000), p. 116 [111–28]. See also Caputo, *Against Ethics* (Bloomington: Indiana University Press, 1993).

13. Emmanuel Levinas, "Ethics and Politics," in *The Levinas Reader*, ed. Seán Hand (Oxford: Routledge, 1989), p. 292 [289–97]; Michel Foucault, "Politics and Ethics: An Interview," in *The Foucault Reader*, ed. Paul Rabinow (New York: Pantheon, 1984), p. 375 [373–80].

14. Butler, *Bodies That Matter*, p. 237.

BIBLIOGRAPHY

Primary Texts

Alan of Lille. *Anticlaudianus, or The Good and Perfect Man*, trans. James J. Sheridan. Toronto: Pontifical Institute of Mediæval Studies, 1973.

———. *The Art of Preaching*, trans. Gillian R. Evans. Kalamazoo: Cistercian Publications, 1981.

———. *The Complaint of Nature*, trans. Douglas M. Moffat. New York: Henry Holt, 1908.

———. *De planctu Naturae*, ed. Nikolaus Häring. *Studi Medievali* 19 (1978): 797–879.

———. *The Plaint of Nature*, trans. James J. Sheridan. Toronto: Pontifical Institute of Mediæval Studies, 1980.

———. *Règles de théologie*, trans. Françoise Hudry. Paris: Cerf, 1995.

———. *Textes inédits*, ed. Marie-Thérèse d'Alverny. Paris: Vrin, 1965.

Augustine of Hippo. *The City of God against the Pagans*, trans. R.W. Dyson. Cambridge, UK: Cambridge University Press, 1998.

———. *The Confessions*, trans. Maria Boulding, repr. New York: Vintage, 1998.

———. *Divine Providence and the Problem of Evil: A Translation of St. Augustine's "De Ordine,"* trans. Robert P. Russell. New York: Cosmopolitan Science and Art Service, 1942.

———. *Earlier Writings*, trans. John H.S. Burleigh. Philadelphia: Westminster Press, 1953.

———. *The Enchiridion on Faith, Hope, and Love*, trans. J.F. Shaw. Chicago: Regnery Gateway, 1961.

———. *The Literal Meaning of Genesis*, 2 vols., trans. John Hammond Taylor. New York: Newman Press, 1982.

———. *On Christian Doctrine*, trans. D.W. Robertson, Jr. Upper Saddle River, NJ: Prentice Hall, 1958.

———. *On Free Choice of the Will*, trans. Thomas Williams. Indianapolis: Hackett, 1993.

———. "On the Good of Marriage," in *On the Holy Trinity; Doctrinal Treatises; Moral Treatises*, trans. C.L. Cornish. Nicene and Post-Nicene Fathers, Augustine Series, vol. 3, repr. Grand Rapids: Eerdmans, 1988.

———. *Political Writings*, trans. E.M. Atkins and R.J. Dodaro. Cambridge, UK: Cambridge University Press, 2001.

Augustine of Hippo. *Ten Homilies on St. John* in *Sermon on the Mount; Harmony of the Gospels; Homilies*, trans. John Gibb and James Innes. Nicene and Post-Nicene Fathers, Augustine Series vol. 6, repr. Grand Rapids: Eerdmans, 1988.

Bernard Silvestris. *The Cosmographia*, trans. Winthrop Wetherbee. New York: Columbia University Press, 1973.

Boethius. *Courts traités de théologie*, ed. and trans. Hélène Merle. Paris: Cerf, 1995.

———. *The Theological Tractates and the Consolation of Philosophy*, ed. and trans. H.F. Stewart, E.K. Rand, and S.J. Tester, repr. Cambridge, MA: The Loeb Classical Library, Harvard University Press, 1973.

Christine de Pizan. *The Book of the City of Ladies*, trans. Earl Jeffrey Richards. New York: Persea, 1982.

———. *Le livre de la cité des dames*, ed. Maureen Curnow. PhD diss. Vanderbilt University, 1975.

Le Débat sur le "Roman de la rose," ed. Eric Hicks. Geneva: Slatkine, 1977.

Dionysius the Areopagite (Pseudo-Dionysius). *The Divine Names and Mystical Theology*, trans. John D. Jones. Milwaukee: Marquette University Press, 1980.

Eneas: A Twelfth-Century French Romance, trans. John A. Yunck. New York: Columbia University Press, 1974.

Eneas: Roman du XIIème siècle, ed. J.-J. Salverda de Grave, repr. Paris: Librairie Honoré Champion, 1982–85.

Guillaume de Lorris and Jean de Meun. *Le roman de la rose*, ed. Ernest Langlois. Paris: Firmin-Didot, 1914–24.

———. *Le roman de la rose*, ed. Félix Lecoy. Paris: Champion, 1965–70.

———. *Le roman de la rose*, ed. and trans. Armand Strubel. Paris: Lettres Gothiques, Livre de Poche, 1992.

———. *The Romance of the Rose*, 3rd ed., trans. Charles Dahlberg. Princeton: Princeton University Press, 1995.

Holcot, Robert. *Super libros sapientiae*, repr. Frankfurt: Minerva G.M.B.H., 1974.

Hugh of St. Victor. *The Didascalicon*, trans. Jerome Taylor. New York: Columbia University Press, 1961.

Isidore of Seville. *Etymologiarum sive originum*, 2 vols., ed. W.M. Lindsay. Oxford: Oxford Classical Texts, Oxford University Press, 1911.

Lactantius. *A Treatise on the Anger of God*, in *Fathers of the Third and Fourth Centuries: Lactantius, Venantius, Asterius, Victorinus, Dionysius, Apostolic Teaching and Constitutions, Homily, and Liturgies*, trans. A. Cleveland Coxe. Ante-Nicene Fathers, vol. 7, repr. Grand Rapids: Eerdmans, 1988.

Macrobius. *Commentary on the Dream of Scipio*, trans. William Harris Stahl, repr. New York: Columbia University Press, 1990.

Martianus Capella. *The Marriage of Philology and Mercury*, trans. William Harris Stahl and Richard Johnson. New York: Columbia University Press, 1977.

Ovid. *The Erotic Poems*, trans. Peter Green. London: Penguin, 1982.

———. *Heroides*, trans. Harold Isbell. London: Penguin, 1990.

———. *Metamorphoses*, trans. Mary M. Innes. London: Penguin, 1955.

———. *Metamorphoses*, 2 vols., ed. and trans. Frank Justus Miller, repr. Cambridge, MA: The Loeb Classical Library, Harvard University Press, 1984.

Peter Damian. *Book of Gomorrah: An Eleventh-Century Treatise against Clerical Homosexual Practices*, trans. Pierre J. Payer. Waterloo: Wilfrid Laurier University Press, 1982.

Plotinus. *The Enneads*, trans. Stephen MacKenna. Abridged edition. London: Penguin, 1991.

La Querelle de la Rose: Letters and Documents, trans. Joseph L. Baird and John R. Kane. Chapel Hill: North Carolina Studies in the Romance Languages and Literatures, 1978.

Le roman d'Eneas, ed. and trans. Aimé Petit. Paris: Lettres Gothiques, Livre de Poche, 1997.

Thomas Aquinas. *On Evil*, trans. Richard Regan. Oxford: Oxford University Press, 2003.

———. *Selected Philosophical Writings*, trans. Timothy McDermott. Oxford: Oxford University Press, 1993.

———. *Summa Theologiae*, trans. Fathers of the English Dominican Province, repr. New York: McGraw Hill, 1964–81.

Virgil. *Aeneid*, ed. and trans. H. Rushton Fairclough. Cambridge, MA: Loeb Classical Library, Harvard University Press, 1934.

Virgil. *Aeneid*, trans. Robert Fitzgerald. New York: Vintage Classics, 1990.

Secondary Texts

Abelove, Henry, Michèle Aina Barale, and David M. Halperin, eds. *The Lesbian and Gay Studies Reader*. New York: Routledge, 1993.

Adams, James Noel. *The Latin Sexual Vocabulary*. Baltimore: Johns Hopkins University Press, 1982.

Agamben, Giorgio. *Homo Sacer: Sovereign Power and Bare Life*, trans. Daniel Heller-Roazen. Stanford: Stanford University Press, 1998.

———. *Language and Death: The Place of Negativity*, trans. Karen E. Pinkus with Michael Hardt. Minneapolis: University of Minnesota Press, 1991.

———. *Stanzas: Word and Phantasm in Western Culture*, trans. Ronald L. Martinez. Minneapolis: University of Minnesota Press, 1993.

Allen, Peter. *The Art of Love: Amatory Fictions from Ovid to the "Romance of the Rose."* Philadelphia: University of Pennsylvania Press, 1992.

Althusser, Louis. *Lenin and Philosophy*, trans. Ben Brewster. London: Monthly Review Press, 1971.

Angeli, Giovanna. *"L'Eneas" e i primi romanzi volgari*. Milan: Riccardo Ricciardi, 1971.

Auerbach, Erich. *Literary Language and Its Public in Late Latin Antiquity and in the Middle Ages*, trans. Ralph Manheim. Princeton: Princeton University Press, 1965.

———. *Mimesis: The Representation of Reality in Western Literature*, trans. Willard R. Trask. Princeton: Princeton University Press, 1953.

Bailey, Derick Sherwin. *Homosexuality and the Western Christian Tradition*. London: Longmans, Green, 1955.

Baker, Denise N. "The Priesthood of Genius: A Study of the Medieval Tradition." *Speculum* 51 (1976): 277–91.

Baldwin, John. *The Language of Sex: Five Voices from Northern France Around 1200.* Chicago: University of Chicago Press, 1994.

Baswell, Christopher. *Virgil in Medieval England: Figuring the "Aeneid" from the Twelfth Century to Chaucer.* Cambridge, UK: Cambridge University Press, 1995.

Batany, Jean, ed. *Approches du "Roman de la rose."* Paris: Bordas, 1973.

Baumgartner, Emmanuèle, and Laurence Harf-Lancner, eds. *Entre fiction et histoire: Troie et Rome au Moyen Age.* Paris: Presses de la Sorbonne Nouvelle, 1997.

Bennett, Judith M. "Confronting Continuity." *Journal of Women's History* 9/3 (1997): 73–95.

Bezzola, Reto R. *Les origines et la formation de la littérature courtoise en occident,* 5 vols. Paris: Champion, 1944–63.

Bloch, Marc. *Feudal Society.* 2 vols., trans. L.A. Manyon. London: Routledge and Kegan Paul, 1961.

Bloch, R. Howard. *Etymologies and Genealogies: A Literary Anthropology of the French Middle Ages.* Chicago: University of Chicago Press, 1983.

———. *Medieval Misogyny and the Invention of Western Romantic Love.* Chicago: University of Chicago Press, 1991.

Blumenfeld-Kosinski, Renate. *Reading Myth: Classical Mythology and Its Interpretations in Medieval French Literature.* Stanford: Stanford University Press, 1997.

Boone, Marc. "State Power and Illicit Sexuality: The Persecution of Sodomy in Late Medieval Bruges." *Journal of Medieval History* 22/2 (1996): 135–53.

Bossuat, Robert, Louis Pichard, and Guy Raynaud de Lage, eds., *Dictionnaire des lettres françaises: Le Moyen Age,* rev. Geneviève Hasenohr and Michel Zink. Paris: Livre de Poche, 1992.

Boswell, John. *Christianity, Social Tolerance, and Homosexuality: Gay People in Western Europe from the Beginning of the Christian Era to the Fourteenth Century.* Chicago: Chicago University Press, 1980.

Brown, Peter. *Augustine of Hippo: A Biography,* rev. ed. Berkeley: University of California Press, 2000.

———. *The Body and Society: Men, Women, and Sexual Renunciation in Early Christianity.* New York: Columbia University Press, 1988.

Brownlee, Kevin. "Orpheus' Song Re-sung: Jean de Meun's Reworking of *Metamorphoses* X." *Romance Philology* 36/2 (1982): 201–9.

Brownlee, Kevin, and Marina Scordilis Brownlee, eds. *Romance: Generic Transformation from Chrétien de Troyes to Cervantes.* Hanover, NH: University Press of New England, 1985.

Brownlee, Kevin, and Sylvia Huot, eds. *Rethinking the "Romance of the Rose": Text, Image, Reception.* Philadelphia: University of Pennsylvania Press, 1992.

Brownlee, Marina Scordilis, Kevin Brownlee, and Stephen G. Nichols. *The New Medievalism.* Baltimore: Johns Hopkins University Press, 1991.

Bruckner, Matilda Tomaryn. *Shaping Romance: Interpretation, Truth, and Closure in Twelfth-Century French Fictions.* Philadelphia: University of Pennsylvania Press, 1993.

Brumble, H. David. "The Role of Genius in the *De planctu Naturae* of Alanus de Insulis." *Classica et Mediaevalia* 31/1–2 (1976): 306–23.

Brundage, James A. *Law, Sex, and Christian Society in Medieval Europe*. Chicago: University of Chicago Press, 1987.

Bullough, Vern L., and James A. Brundage, eds. *Handbook of Medieval Sexuality*. New York: Garland, 1996.

———, eds. *Sexual Practices and the Medieval Church*. Buffalo: Prometheus, 1982.

Burger, Glenn, and Steven F. Kruger, eds. *Queering the Middle Ages*. Minneapolis: University of Minnesota Press, 2001.

Burgwinkle, William. "Knighting the Classical Hero: Homo/Hetero Affectivity in *Eneas*." *Exemplaria* 5/1 (1993): 1–43.

———. *Sodomy, Masculinity, and Law in Medieval Literature: France and England, 1050–1230*. Cambridge, UK: Cambridge University Press, 2004.

Buschinger, Danielle, ed. *Le roman antique au Moyen Age* (Göppingen: Kümmerle, 1992).

Butler, Judith. *Bodies That Matter: On the Discursive Limits of "Sex."* New York: Routledge, 1993.

———. *Gender Trouble: Feminism and the Subversion of Identity*. New York: Routledge, 1990.

Cadden, Joan. *Meanings of Sex Difference in the Middle Ages: Medicine, Science, and Culture*. Cambridge, UK: Cambridge University Press, 1993.

Cahoon, Leslie. "Raping the Rose: Jean de Meun's Reading of Ovid's *Amores*." *Classical and Modern Literature* 6/4 (1986): 261–85.

Calabrese, Michael A. " 'Make a Mark That Shows': Orphean Song, Orphean Sexuality, and the Exile of Chaucer's Pardoner." *Viator* 24 (1993): 269–86.

Caputo, John D. *Against Ethics*. Bloomington: Indiana University Press, 1993.

———. "The End of Ethics," in *The Blackwell Guide to Ethical Theory*, ed. Hugh LaFollette. Oxford: Blackwell, 2000, pp. 111–28.

Chenu, Marie-Dominique. *Nature, Man, and Society in the Twelfth Century: Essays on New Theological Perspectives in the Latin West*, ed. and trans. Jerome Taylor and Lester K. Little. Chicago: University of Chicago Press, 1968.

Chiffoleau, Jacques. "*Contra Naturam*: Pour une approche casuistique et procédurale de la nature médiévale." *Micrologus: Natura, scienze, e società medievali* 4 (1996): 265–312.

———. "Dire l'indicible: Remarques sur la catégorie du *nefandum* du XIIe au XVe siècle." *Annales ESC* 45 (1990): 289–324.

Classen, Albrecht, ed. *Violence in Medieval Courtly Literature: A Casebook*. New York: Routledge, 2004.

Cohen, Jeremy. *Living Letters of the Law: Ideas of the Jew in Medieval Christianity*. Berkeley: University of California Press, 1999.

Colish, Marcia L. *The Mirror of Language: A Study in the Medieval Theory of Knowledge*, rev. ed. Lincoln: University of Nebraska Press, 1983.

Copeland, Rita, ed. *Criticism and Dissent in the Middle Ages*. Cambridge, UK: Cambridge University Press, 1996.

Copeland, Rita, and Stephen Melville. "Allegory and Allegoresis, Rhetoric and Hermeneutics." *Exemplaria* 3/1 (March 1991): 159–87.

Cormier, Raymond J. "The Mystic Bond of Ideal Friendship: Virgil's Nisus-Euryalus Story Rewritten in the 12th Century Affective Style." *Collegium Medievale* 4 (1991): 47–56.

———. *One Heart, One Mind: The Rebirth of Virgil's Hero in Medieval French Romance.* University, MS: Mississippi Romance Monographs, 1973.

———. "Une 'Pietà' précoce: La plainte pour le jeune prince arcadien Pallas dans le *Roman d'Eneas.*" *Australian Journal of French Studies* 31/2 (1994): 143–60.

———. "Taming the Warrior: Responding to the Charge of Sexual Deviance in Twelfth-Century Vernacular Romance," in *Literary Aspects of Courtly Culture,* ed. Donald Maddox and Sara Sturm-Maddox. Cambridge, UK: D.S. Brewer, 1994, pp. 153–60.

Cormier, Raymond J., and Harry J. Kuster. "Old Views and New Trends: Observations on the Problem of Homosexuality in the Middle Ages." *Studi Medievali* Third Series 25/2 (1984): 587–610.

Crane, Susan. *Gender and Romance in Chaucer's "Canterbury Tales."* Princeton: Princeton University Press, 1994.

Curtius, Ernst Robert. *European Literature and the Latin Middle Ages,* trans. Willard R. Trask. Princeton: Princeton University Press, 1953.

Daston, Lorraine, and Fernando Vidal, eds. *The Moral Authority of Nature.* Chicago: University of Chicago Press, 2004.

Davis, Colin. *Levinas: An Introduction.* Notre Dame: University of Notre Dame Press, 1996.

De Bruyne, Edgar. *Etudes d'esthétique médiévale,* 2 vols. repr. Paris: Albin Michel, 1998.

De Libera, Alain. *La querelle des universaux: De Platon à la fin du Moyen Age.* Paris: Seuil, 1996.

De Man, Paul. *Allegories of Reading: Figural Language in Rousseau, Nietzsche, Rilke, and Proust.* New Haven: Yale University Press, 1979.

———. *Blindness and Insight: Essays in the Rhetoric of Contemporary Criticism.* Minneapolis: University of Minnesota Press, 1983.

Delany, Sheila. *Medieval Literary Politics: Shapes of Ideology.* Manchester: Manchester University Press, 1990.

Derrida, Jacques. *A Derrida Reader: Between the Blinds,* ed. Peggy Kamuf. New York: Columbia University Press, 1991.

———. *Of Grammatology,* trans. Gayatri Chakravorty Spivak. Baltimore: Johns Hopkins University Press, 1976.

Desmond, Marilynn. *Reading Dido: Gender, Textuality, and the Medieval Aeneid.* Minneapolis: University of Minnesota Press, 1994.

Dodaro, Robert, and George Lawless. *Augustine and His Critics: Essays in Honour of Gerald Bonner.* New York: Routledge, 2000.

Dollimore, Jonathan. *Sexual Dissidence: Augustine to Wilde, Freud to Foucault.* Oxford: Oxford University Press, 1991.

Dragonetti, Roger. "Pygmalion ou les pièges de la fiction dans le *Roman de la rose*" in *Orbis Medievalis: Mélanges de langue et de littérature médiévale offerts à Reto Raduolf*

Bezzola à l'occasion de son quatre-vingtième anniversaire, ed. Georges Güntert, Marc-René Jung, and Kurt Ringger. Bern: Editions Francke, 1978, pp. 89–111.

Dronke, Peter, ed. *A History of Twelfth-Century Western Philosophy*. Cambridge, UK: Cambridge University Press, 1988.

Duby, Georges. *Love and Marriage in the Middle Ages*, trans. Jane Dunnett. Chicago: University of Chicago Press, 1994.

Dufournet, Jean, ed. *Etudes sur le "Roman de la rose" de Guillaume de Lorris*. Paris: Champion, 1984.

———, ed. *Relire le "Roman d'Enéas."* Geneva: Slatkine, 1985.

Eco, Umberto. *The Search for the Perfect Language*, trans. James Fentress. Oxford: Blackwell, 1995.

Economou, George D. *The Goddess Natura in Medieval Literature*. Cambridge, MA: Harvard University Press, 1972.

Eley, Penny. "The Myth of Trojan Descent and Perceptions of National Identity: The Case of the *Eneas* and the *Roman de Troie*." *Nottingham Medieval Studies* 35 (1991): 27–40.

Enders, Jody. *The Medieval Theater of Cruelty: Rhetoric, Memory, Violence*. Ithaca: Cornell University Press, 1999.

Erler, Mary C., and Maryanne Kowaleski, eds. *Gendering the Master Narrative: Women and Power in the Middle Ages*. Ithaca: Cornell University Press, 2003.

———, eds. *Women and Power in the Middle Ages*. Athens: University of Georgia Press, 1988.

Evans, G.R. *Alan of Lille: The Frontiers of Theology in the Later Twelfth Century*. Cambridge, UK: Cambridge University Press, 1983.

———. *Augustine on Evil*. Cambridge, UK: Cambridge University Press, 1982.

Evergates, Theodore, ed. *Aristocratic Women in Medieval France*. Philadelphia: University of Pennsylvania Press, 1999.

Faral, Edmond. *Recherches sur les sources latines des contes et romans courtois du Moyen Age*. Paris: Champion, 1913.

Ferrante, Joan. *Woman as Image in Medieval Literature*. New York: Columbia University Press, 1975.

Ferrante, Joan M., and George D. Economou, eds. *In Pursuit of Perfection: Courtly Love in Medieval Literature*. Port Washington: Kennikat, 1975.

Fitzgerald, Allan D., ed. *Augustine Through the Ages*. Grand Rapids, MI: William B. Eerdmans, 1999.

Fleming, John V. *Reason and the Lover*. Princeton: Princeton University Press, 1984.

———. *The "Roman de la rose": A Study in Allegory and Iconography*. Princeton: Princeton University Press, 1969.

Fletcher, Angus. *Allegory: The Theory of a Symbolic Mode*. Ithaca: Cornell University Press, 1964.

Foucault, Michel. *A Foucault Reader*, ed. Paul Rabinow. New York: Pantheon Press, 1984.

———. *The History of Sexuality, Volume One: An Introduction*, trans. Robert Hurley, repr. New York: Vintage, 1990.

———. *The History of Sexuality, Volume Two: The Use of Pleasure*, trans. Robert Hurley, repr. New York: Vintage, 1990.

Foucault, Michel. *The History of Sexuality, Volume Three: The Care of the Self*, trans. Robert Hurley, repr. New York: Vintage, 1988.

Fradenburg, Louise, and Carla Freccero, eds. *Premodern Sexualities*. New York: Routledge, 1996.

Frappier, Jean. *Amour Courtois et Table Ronde*. Geneva: Librairie Droz, 1973.

Garber, Marjorie, Beatrice Hanssen, and Rebecca L. Walkowitz, eds. *The Turn to Ethics*. New York: Routledge, 2000.

Gaunt, Simon. "Bel Acueil and the Improper Allegory of the *Romance of the Rose*." *New Medieval Literatures* 2 (1997): 65–93.

——. "From Epic to Romance: Gender and Sexuality in the *Roman d'Eneas*." *Romanic Review* 83/1 (January 1992): 1–27.

——. *Gender and Genre in Medieval French Literature*. Cambridge, UK: Cambridge University Press, 1995.

Girard, René. *The Scapegoat*, trans. Yvonne Freccero. Baltimore: Johns Hopkins University Press, 1986.

Goldberg, Jonathan, ed. *Queering the Renaissance*. Durham: Duke University Press, 1994.

——, ed. *Reclaiming Sodom*. New York: Routledge, 1994.

——. *Sodometries: Renaissance Texts, Modern Sexualities*. Stanford: Stanford University Press, 1992.

Goodich, Michael, ed. *Other Middle Ages: Witnesses at the Margins of Medieval Society*. Philadelphia: University of Pennsylvania Press, 1998.

——. *The Unmentionable Vice: Homosexuality in the Later Medieval Period*. Santa Barbara: Clio Books, 1979.

Gravdal, Kathryn. *Ravishing Maidens: Writing Rape in Medieval French Literature and Law*. Philadelphia: University of Pennsylvania Press, 1991.

Green, R.H. "Alan of Lille's *De planctu Naturae*." *Speculum* 31 (1956): 649–74.

Greenblatt, Stephen, ed. *Allegory and Representation*. Baltimore: Johns Hopkins University Press, 1981.

Guynn, Noah D. "Eternal Flame: State Formation, Deviant Architecture, and the Monumentality of Same-Sex Eroticism in the *Roman d'Eneas*." *GLQ* 6 (2000): 287–319.

——. "Historicizing Shame, Shaming History: Origination and Negativity in the *Eneas*." *L'esprit créateur* 34/4 (1999): 112–27.

Haidu, Peter. *The Subject Medieval/Modern: Text and Governance in the Middle Ages*. Stanford: Stanford University Press, 2004.

——. *The Subject of Violence: The "Song of Roland" and the Birth of the State*. Bloomington: Indiana University Press, 1993.

Häring, Nikolaus. "Manuscripts of the *De planctu Naturae* of Master Alan of Lille." *Cîteaux* 29/1–2 (1978): 93–115.

Harpham, Geoffrey Galt. *Shadows of Ethics: Criticism and the Just Society*. Durham: Duke University Press, 1999.

Heller-Roazen, Daniel. *Fortune's Faces: The "Roman de la rose" and the Poetics of Contingency*. Baltimore: Johns Hopkins University Press, 2003.

Henry, D.P. "Saint Anselm and Nothingness," *Philosophical Quarterly* 15 (1965): 243–46.

Herman, Gerald. "The 'Sin Against Nature' and its Echoes in Medieval French Literature." *Annuale Medievale* 17 (1976): 70–87.

Hick, John. *Evil and the God of Love*, 2nd ed. London: Macmillan, 1977.

Holsinger, Bruce, and David Townsend. "Ovidian Homoerotics in Twelfth-Century Paris." *GLQ* 8/3 (2002): 389–423.

Huchet, Jean-Charles, *Le roman médiéval*. Paris: Presses Universitaires de France, 1984.

Hult, David F. "The Allegorical Fountain: Narcissus in the *Roman de la rose*." *Romanic Review* 72 (1981): 125–48.

———. "Closed Quotations: The Speaking Voice in the *Roman de la rose*." *Yale French Studies* 67 (1984): 248–69.

———. *Self-Fulfilling Prophecies: Readership and Authority in the First "Roman de la rose."* Cambridge, UK: Cambridge University Press, 1986.

———. "Words and Deeds: Jean de Meun's *Romance of the Rose* and the Hermeneutics of Censorship." *New Literary History* 28/2 (1997): 345–66.

Huot, Sylvia. *The "Romance of the Rose" and Its Medieval Readers: Interpretation, Reception, Manuscript Transmission*. Cambridge, UK: Cambridge University Press, 1993.

Irigaray, Luce. "The Question of the Other." *Yale French Studies* 87 (Spring 1995): 7–19.

Jacquart, Danielle, and Claude Thomasset. *Sexualité et savoir médical au Moyen Age*. Paris: Presses Universitaires de France, 1985.

Jaeger, C. Stephen. *Ennobling Love: In Search of a Lost Sensibility*. Philadelphia: University of Pennsylvania Press, 1999.

Jager, Eric. *The Tempter's Voice: Language and the Fall in Medieval Literature*. Ithaca: Cornell University Press, 1993.

Jameson, Fredric. *The Political Unconscious: Narrative as a Socially Symbolic Act*. Ithaca: Cornell University Press, 1981.

Jauss, Hans Robert. "Allégorie, 'remythisation,' et nouveau mythe: Réflexions sur la captivité chrétienne de la mythologie au Moyen Age," in *Mélanges offerts à Charles Rostaing*. Liege: Association des Romanistes de l'Université de Liège, 1974, pp. 469–99.

———. "La transformation de la forme allégorique entre 1180 et 1240: d'Alain de Lille à Guillaume de Lorris," in *L'humanisme médiéval dans les literatures romanes du XIe au XIVe siècle*, ed. Anthime Fourrier. Paris: Klincksieck, 1964, pp. 107–46.

Jones, Rosemarie. *The Theme of Love in the Romans d'Antiquité*. London: The Modern Humanities Research Association, 1972.

Jordan, Mark D. *The Invention of Sodomy in Christian Theology*. Chicago: University of Chicago Press, 1997.

Jung, Marc-René. *Etudes sur le poème allégorique en France au Moyen Age*. Bern: Francke, 1971.

Kantorowicz, Ernst. *The King's Two Bodies: A Study in Mediaeval Political Theology*. Princeton: Princeton University Press, 1957.

Kay, Sarah. *The Romance of the Rose*. London: Grant and Cutler, 1995.

———. "Women's Body of Knowledge: Epistemology and Misogyny in the *Romance of the Rose*," in *Framing Medieval Bodies*, ed. Kay and Miri Rubin. Manchester: Manchester University Press, 1994, pp. 211–35.

Keiser, Elizabeth B. *Courtly Desire and Medieval Homophobia: The Legitimation of Sexual Pleasure in "Cleanness" and Its Contexts*. New Haven: Yale University Press, 1997.

Kelly, Douglas, *Internal Difference and Meanings in the "Roman de la rose."* Madison: University of Wisconsin Press, 1995.

Klosowska, Anna. *Queer Love in the Middle Ages.* New York: Palgrave Macmillan, 2005.

Kretzmann, Norman, and Eleonore Stump, eds. *The Cambridge Companion to Aquinas.* Cambridge, UK: Cambridge University Press, 1993.

Kretzmann, Norman, Anthony Kenny, and Jan Pinborg, eds. *The Cambridge History of Later Medieval Philosophy.* Cambridge, UK: Cambridge University Press, 1982.

Krochalis, Jeanne Elizabeth. *Alain de Lille, "De planctu Nature": Studies towards an Edition.* PhD diss. Harvard University, 1973.

Krueger, Roberta L., *Women Readers and the Ideology of Gender in Old French Verse Romance.* Cambridge, UK: Cambridge University Press, 1993.

————, ed. *The Cambridge Companion to Medieval Romance.* Cambridge, UK: Cambridge University Press, 2000.

Langlois, Ernest. *Origines et sources du "Roman de la rose."* Paris: Ernest Thorin, 1891.

Lankewish, Vincent A. "Assault from Behind: Sodomy, Foreign Invasion, and Masculine Identity in the *Roman d'Eneas*," in *Text and Territory: Geographical Imagination in the European Middle Ages*, ed. Sylvia Tomasch and Sealy Gilles. Philadelphia: University of Pennsylvania Press, 1997, pp. 207–44.

Lees, Clare A., ed. *Medieval Masculinities: Regarding Men in the Middle Ages.* Minneapolis: University of Minnesota Press, 1994.

Leupin, Alexandre. *Barbarolexis: Medieval Writing and Sexuality*, trans. Kate M. Cooper. Cambridge, MA: Harvard University Press, 1989.

————. *Fiction and Incarnation: Rhetoric, Theology, and Literature in the Middle Ages*, trans. David Laatsch. Minneapolis: University of Minnesota Press, 2003.

————. "Le temps dans le *Roman de la rose*," in *Il tempo, i tempi: Omaggio a Lorenzo Renzi*, ed. Rosanna Brusegan and Michele A. Cortelazzo. Padua: Esedra, 1999, pp. 141–52.

Levinas, Emmanuel. *The Levinas Reader*, ed. Seán Hand. Oxford: Blackwell, 1989.

Levy, Raphael. "L'allusion à la sodomie dans *Eneas*." *Philological Quarterly* 27 (1948): 373–77.

Lewis, C.S. *The Allegory of Love: A Study in Medieval Tradition*, repr. Oxford: Oxford University Press, 1992.

Lynch, Kathryn L. *The High Medieval Dream Vision: Poetry, Philosophy, and Literary Form.* Stanford: Stanford University Press, 1988.

MacDonald, Scott, ed. *Being and Goodness: The Concept of the Good in Metaphysics and Philosophical Theology.* Ithaca: Cornell University Press, 1991.

MacDougall, Hugh A. *Racial Myth in English History: Trojans, Teutons, and Anglo-Saxons.* Hanover, NH: University Press of New England, 1982.

Marchello-Nizia, Christiane. "Amour courtois, société masculine, et figures de pouvoir." *Annales ESC* 36 (1981): 969–82.

————. "De l'*Enéide* à l'*Eneas*: les attributs du fondateur," in *Lectures médiévales de Virgile.* Rome: Ecole Française de Rome, 1985, pp. 251–66.

Markus, R.A. *Saeculum: History and Society in the Theology of St. Augustine.* Cambridge, UK: Cambridge University Press, 1970.

————. "Saint Augustine's Views on the 'Just War.' " *Studies in Church History* 20 (1983): 1–13.

Matthews, Gareth B., ed. *The Augustinian Tradition.* Berkeley: University of California Press, 1999.

McGrade, A.S. *The Cambridge Companion to Medieval Philosophy.* Cambridge, UK: Cambridge University Press, 2003.

Minnis, Alastair. *Magister Amoris: The "Roman de la rose" and Vernacular Hermeneutics.* Oxford: Oxford University Press, 2001.

———. *Medieval Theory of Authorship: Scholastic Literary Attitudes in the Later Middle Ages.* London: Scholar Press, 1984.

Modersohn, Mechthild. *Natura als Göttin im Mittelalter: Ikonographische Studien zu Darstellungen der personifizierten Nature.* Berlin: Akademie Verlag, 1997.

Montrose, Louis Adrian. " 'Shaping Fantasies': Figurations of Gender and Power in Elizabethan Culture." *Representations* 2 (1983): 61–94.

Moore, R.I. *The Formation of a Persecuting Society: Power and Deviance in Western Europe, 950–1250.* Oxford: Blackwell, 1987.

Mora-Lebrun, Francine. *L'Enéide médiévale et la naissance du roman.* Paris: Presses Universitaires de France, 1994.

Murphy, James J. *Rhetoric in the Middle Ages: A History of Rhetorical Theory from Saint Augustine to the Renaissance.* Berkeley: University of California Press, 1974.

Nietzsche, Friedrich. *On the Genealogy of Morals and Ecce Homo,* trans. Walter Kaufmann and R.J. Hollingdale, repr. New York: Vintage, 1989.

Nirenberg, David. *Communities of Violence: Persecution of Minorities in the Middle Ages.* Princeton: Princeton University Press, 1996.

Nolan, Barbara. "Ovid's *Heroides* Contextualized: Foolish Love and Legitimate Marriage in the *Roman d'Eneas.*" *Mediaevalia* 13 (1987): 157–87.

Noonan, John T. *Contraception: A History of Its Treatment by the Catholic Theologians and Canonists.* Cambridge, MA: Belknap Press of Harvard University Press, 1966.

Osborn, Eric. *Ethical Patterns in Early Christian Thought.* Cambridge, UK: Cambridge University Press, 1976.

Paré, Gérard. *Le "Roman de la rose" et la scolastique courtoise.* Ottawa: Publications de L'institut d'Etudes Médiévales d'Ottowa, 1941.

———. *Les idées et les lettres au XIIIe siècle: "Le roman de la rose."* Montreal: Presses de l'Université de Montréal, 1947.

Parker, Patricia A. *Inescapable Romance: Studies in the Poetics of a Mode.* Princeton: Princeton University Press, 1979.

Patterson, Lee. *Negotiating the Past: The Historical Understanding of Medieval Literature.* Madison: University of Wisconsin Press, 1987.

Payen, Jean-Charles. *La rose et l'utopie: Révolution sexuelle et communisme nostalgique chez Jean de Meung.* Paris: Hatier, 1976.

Payer, Pierre. *The Bridling of Desire: Views of Sex in the Later Middle Ages.* Toronto: University of Toronto Press, 1993.

———. *Sex and the Penitentials: The Development of a Sexual Code 550–1150.* Toronto: University of Toronto Press, 1984.

Pépin, Jean. *La tradition de l'allégorie: De Philon d'Alexandrie à Dante.* Paris: Etudes Augustiniennes, 1987.

Petit, Aimé. *Naissances du roman: les techniques littéraires dans les romans antiques du XIIè siècle,* 2 vols. PhD diss. Université de Paris III, 1985.

Piehler, Paul. *The Visionary Landscape.* London: Edward Arnold, 1971.

Poirion, Daniel. "De l'*Enéide* à l'*Eneas*: mythologie et moralisation." *Cahiers de civilisation médiévale* 19/3 (1976): 213–29.

———. *Ecriture poétique et composition romanesque.* Orléans: Paradigme, 1994.

———. "Les mots et les choses selon Jean de Meun." *L'information littéraire* 26 (1974): 7–11.

———. *Résurgences: Mythe et littérature à l'âge du symbole (XIIe siècle).* Paris: Presses Universitaires de France, 1986.

———. *Le roman de la rose.* Paris: Hatier, 1973.

Power, Kim. *Veiled Desire: Augustine on Women.* New York: Continuum, 1996.

Puff, Helmut. *Sodomy in Reformation Germany and Switzerland, 1400–1600.* Chicago: University of Chicago Press, 2003.

Quilligan, Maureen. "Allegory, Allegoresis, and the Deallegorization of Language: The *Roman de la rose,* the *De planctu Naturae,* and the *Parlement of Foules,*" in *Allegory, Myth, and Symbol,* ed. Morton W. Bloomfield. Cambridge, MA: Harvard University Press, 1981, pp. 163–86.

———. *The Allegory of Female Authority: Christine de Pizan's "Cité des dames."* Ithaca: Cornell University Press, 1991.

———. *The Language of Allegory: Defining the Genre.* Ithaca: Cornell University Press, 1979.

———. "Words and Sex: The Language of Allegory in the *De planctu Naturae,* the *Roman de la rose,* and Book III of the *Faerie Queen.*" *Allegorica* 2 (1977): 195–216.

Rabine, Leslie Wahl. "The Unhappy Hymen between Feminism and Deconstruction," in *The Other Perspective in Gender and Culture: Rewriting Women and the Symbolic,* ed. Juliet Flower MacCannell. New York: Columbia University Press, 1990, pp. 20–38.

Raynaud de Lage, Guy. *Alain de Lille: Poète du XIIe siècle.* Paris: Vrin, 1951.

Reinhold, Meyer. "The Unhero Aeneas." *Classica et Mediaevalia* 27 (1968): 195–207.

Richards, Jeffrey. *Sex, Dissidence, and Damnation: Minority Groups in the Middle Ages.* New York: Routledge, 1991.

Rivkin, Julie, and Michael Ryan. *Literary Theory: An Anthology* (Oxford: Blackwell, 1998).

Robertson, D.W. *A Preface to Chaucer: Studies in Medieval Perspectives.* Princeton: Princeton University Press, 1962.

Robertson, Elizabeth, and Christine M. Rose, eds. *Representing Rape in Medieval and Early Modern Literature.* New York: Palgrave Macmillan, 2001.

Rollinson, Philip. *Classical Theories of Allegory and Christian Culture.* Pittsburgh: Duquesne University Press, 1981.

Roussel, H., and F. Suard, eds. *Alain de Lille, Gautier de Châtillon, Jakemart Giélée, et leur temps.* Lille: Presses Universitaires de Lille, 1980.

Russell, Jeffrey Burton. *The Devil: Perceptions of Evil from Antiquity to Primitive Christianity.* Ithaca: Cornell University Press, 1977.

———. *Lucifer: The Devil in the Middle Ages.* Ithaca: Cornell University Press, 1984.

———. *Satan: The Early Christian Tradition.* Ithaca: Cornell University Press, 1981.

Russell, Frederick H. *The Just War in the Middle Ages.* Cambridge, UK: Cambridge University Press, 1975.

——. "Love and Hate in Medieval Warfare: The Contribution of Saint Augustine." *Nottingham Medieval Studies* 31 (1987): 108–24.

Scanlon, Larry. "Unspeakable Pleasures: Alain de Lille, Sexual Regulation and the Priesthood of Genius." *Romanic Review* 86/2 (1995): 213–42.

Sedgwick, Eve Kosofsky. *Between Men: English Literature and Male Homosocial Desire*. New York: Columbia University Press, 1985.

——. *Epistemology of the Closet*. Berkeley: University of California Press, 1990.

Shanzer, Danuta R. "Alan of Lille, Contemporary Annoyances, and Dante." *Classica et Mediaevalia* 40 (1989): 251–69.

——. "A New Prologue for the *De planctu Naturae*?" in *Arbor amoena comis*, ed. Ewald Könsgen and Dieter Schaller. Stuttgart: Franz Steiner, 1990, pp. 163–72.

——. "Parturition through the Nostrils? Thirty-three Textual Problems in Alan of Lille's *De planctu Nature*." *Mittellateinisches Jahrbuch* 26 (1991): 140–49.

Silverman, Kaja. *Male Subjectivity at the Margins*. New York: Routledge, 1992.

——. *The Subject of Semiotics*. Oxford: Oxford University Press, 1983.

Singerman, Jerome. *Under Clouds of Poesy: Poetry and Truth in French and English Reworkings of the "Aeneid," 1160–1513*. New York: Garland, 1986.

Solère, Jean-Luc, Anca Vasiliu, and Alain Galonnier, eds. *Alain de Lille, le Docteur Universel: Philosophie, théologie, et littérature*. Turnhout, Belgium: Brepols, 2005.

Solterer, Helen. "Flaming Words: Verbal Violence and Gender in Premodern Paris." *Romanic Review* 86/2 (1995): 355–79.

——. *The Master and Minerva: Disputing Women in French Medieval Culture*. Berkeley: University of California Press, 1995.

Spence, Sarah. *Rhetorics of Reason and Desire: Vergil, Augustine, and the Troubadours*. Ithaca: Cornell University Press, 1988.

Stock, Brian. *The Implications of Literacy: Written Language and Models of Interpretation in the Eleventh and Twelfth Centuries*. Princeton: Princeton University Press, 1983.

Strayer, Joseph R. *On the Medieval Origins of the Modern State*. Princeton: Princeton University Press, 1970.

Strubel, Armand. *"Grant senefiance a": Allégorie et littérature au Moyen Age*. Paris: Champion, 2002.

Stuard, Susan Mosher, ed. *Women in Medieval Society*. Philadelphia: University of Pennsylvania Press, 1976.

Stump, Eleonore, and Norman Kretzmann, eds. *The Cambridge Companion to Augustine*. Cambridge, UK: Cambridge University Press, 2001.

Taylor, Karen J., ed. *Gender Transgressions: Crossing the Normative Barrier in Old French Literature*. New York: Garland, 1998.

Teskey, Gordon. "Allegory," in *The Spenser Encyclopedia*, ed. A.C. Hamilton. Toronto: University of Toronto Press, 1990, pp. 16–22.

——. *Allegory and Violence*. Ithaca: Cornell University Press, 1996.

Truax, Jean A. "Augustine of Hippo: Defender of Women's Equality?" *Journal of Medieval History* 16 (1990): 279–99.

Vance, Eugene. *Mervelous Signals: Poetics and Sign Theory in the Middle Ages*. Lincoln: University of Nebraska Press, 1986.

Vitz, Evelyn Birge. *Medieval Narrative and Modern Narratology: Subjects and Objects of Desire*. New York: New York University Press, 1989.

Wasserman, Julian N., and Lois Roney, eds. *Sign, Sentence, Discourse: Language in Medieval Thought and Literature.* Syracuse: Syracuse University Press, 1988.

Wetherbee, Winthrop. "The Function of Poetry in the *De planctu Naturae* of Alain de Lille." *Traditio* 25 (1969): 87–125.

————. "The Literal and the Allegorical: Jean de Meun and the *De planctu Naturae.*" *Medieval Studies* 33 (1971): 264–91.

————. *Platonism and Poetry in the Twelfth Century: The Literary Influence of the School of Chartres.* Princeton: Princeton University Press, 1972.

————. "The *Romance of the Rose* and Medieval Allegory," in *European Writers,* ed. William T. H. Jackson. New York: Charles Scribner's Sons, 1983, vol. 1, pp. 309–35.

————. "Some Implications of Nature's Femininity in Medieval Poetry," in *Approaches to Nature in the Middle Ages,* ed. Lawrence D. Roberts. Binghamton: Medieval and Renaissance Texts and Studies, 1982, pp. 47–62.

White, Hugh. *Nature, Sex, and Goodness in a Medieval Literary Tradition.* Oxford: Oxford University Press, 2000.

Whitman, Jon. *Allegory: The Dynamics of an Ancient and Medieval Technique.* Cambridge, MA: Harvard University Press, 1987.

————. "The Problem of Assertion and the Complaint of Nature." *Hebrew University Studies in Literature and the Arts* 15 (1987): 5–26.

————, ed. *Interpretation and Allegory: Antiquity to the Modern Period.* Boston: Brill, 2003.

Zeikowitz, Richard E. *Homoeroticism and Chivalry: Discourses of Male Same-Sex Desire in the Fourteenth Century.* New York: Palgrave Macmillan, 2003.

Zink, Michel. "The Allegorical Poem as Interior Memoir." *Yale French Studies* 70 (1986).

————. "Héritage rhétorique et nouveauté littéraire dans le 'roman antique' en France au Moyen Age: Remarques sur l'expression de l'amour dans le *Roman d'Eneas.*" *Romania* 105/2–3 (1984): 248–69.

————. *La subjectivité littéraire autour du siècle de saint Louis.* Paris: Presses Universitaires de France, 1985.

Ziolkowski, Jan. *Alan of Lille's Grammar of Sex: The Meaning of Grammar to a Twelfth-Century Intellectual.* Cambridge, MA: The Medieval Academy of America, 1985.

Zumthor, Paul. "De Guillaume de Lorris à Jean de Meung." *Etudes de langue et de littérature du Moyen Age offertes à Félix Lecoy.* Paris: Champion, 1973, 609–20.

————. *Langue, Texte, Enigme.* Paris: Seuil, 1975.

————. *Toward a Medieval Poetics,* trans. Philip Bennett. Minneapolis: University of Minnesota Press, 1992.

INDEX

Note: Page numbers in *italics* indicate an endnote.